Praise for *Take Charge Now!*

D1124415

"Comprehensively covers many deadly aspects ~~ ~~er people, and external conditions. Shows its readers how to use Rational ___ ~~e-~~ havior Therapy (REBT) to reduce all aspects of blaming and does so in an exceptionally clear, readable, and charming manner."

—Albert Ellis, Ph.D., President,
Albert Ellis Institute for Rational Emotive Behavior Therapy

"Blaming is a pernicious habit. When we blame other and find fault with them, we tend to replace good feelings with resentment and pain. When we blame ourselves, we feel depressed and guilty. Dr. Knaus provides a clear path away from faultfinding and condemnation to a tolerant, assertive, and fulfilling modus vivendi. He provides a lucid prescription for achieving quality relationships. This is an important book and I heartily recommend it!"

—Arnold A. Lazarus, Ph.D., Distinguished Professor
Emeritus of Psychology, Rutgers University

"Brilliantly done. Dr. Knaus shows how to ditch blame and improve your life and relationships. Destined to be a classic."

—Susan Tapper, Professor, Health Education, San Francisco State University

"Bill Knaus's book—*Take Charge Now! Powerful Techniques for Breaking the Blame Habit*—is a real winner. Our culture has become filled with blamers. Thinking that all negative events are 'awful' and that we 'can't stand' them, we look for someone to blame. Of course, that doesn't really help us very much. Bill Knaus teaches us about the dimensions of blame and how to get out of the blame trap. Most importantly, he gives concrete and realistic suggestions to overcome blame, increase our skill to deal with adversity, and live a more fulfilling life. This easy-to-read book is filled with practical suggestions. Although I would not blame you if you don't read it, I strongly recommend this book."

—Howard Kassinove, Ph.D., Professor and Chairperson,
Department of Psychology, Hofstra University

"Once again, Dr. Bill Knaus accurately targets an often ignored, prevasively harmful human habit. This innovative book skillfully offers readers the tools for beating blame in their lives. I would not blame anyone for reading this timely self-help book!"

—Diane R. Richman, Ph.D., Psychologist

"How often do we buy a book for its alluring title, and it spends its life gathering dust on the office shelf? Now here is a book whose content is worthy of its title. Man was condemned with the curse of blame, as obviously someone has to be at fault! Dr. Knaus challenges that assumption by showing the origin, effect, and antidote to this destructive process. Use this book to put blame to rest, and maybe you will get some, too."

—John J. Shannon, Ed.D., ABPP

Also by William J. Knaus

Change Your Life Now: Powerful Techniques for Positive Change

Do It Now! Break the Procrastination Habit

Take Charge Now!

Powerful Techniques for Breaking the Blame Habit

Dr. William J. Knaus

John Wiley & Sons, Inc.
New York • Chichester • Weinheim • Brisbane • Singapore • Toronto

Published by John Wiley & Sons, Inc.
Published simultaneously in Canada

This publication is designed to provide accurate and authoritative information in regard to the subject matter covered. It is sold with the understanding that the publisher is not engaged in rendering professional services. If professional advice or other expert assistance is required, the services of a competent professional person should be sought.

Library of Congress Cataloging-in-Publication Data
Knaus, William J.
    Take charge now! : powerful techniques for breaking the blame habit / by William J. Knaus.
      p. cm.
    Includes bibliographical references.
    ISBN 0-471-32563-5 (paper)
    1. Interpersonal conflict. 2. Blame. I. Title.
  BF637.I48 K63 2000
  158.1—dc21   99-054874

Printed in the United States of America

10 9 8 7 6 5 4 3 2 1

Contents

Preface

You've picked the right book if you want to arm yourself to overcome the unnecessary miseries of blame. It amply provides many different ways for managing and getting beyond blame. In this book we'll look at ways to deal with self-blame, blaming others, "blamers," and, to some extent, blame conditions. We'll look carefully at common blame traps that cause more harm than good. Managing these areas effectively provides a realistic hope for good relationships.

Blame is the most common source of human tension. No one is exempt! Even when blame does not rise to a level of notable stress and strain, the blame process frequently but subtly will influence what we think and what we do. At the extreme, blame works at the core of negative human interactions. It ties together inhibitions, impulses, and negative emotional states, such as anxiety, depression, and hostility. Practically every dysfunctional family blames far more than their functional counterparts, who also frequently blame to excess. People commit suicide to avoid blame and shame. The beat goes on!

Take Charge Now! provides a powerful resource for understanding the legitimate forms of blame and how to get beyond the harmful types. I wrote this book to help my readers meet this challenge and to find blame-free zones in their lives where they can feel more satisfaction and accomplishment. To this end, this book can help readers overcome the stresses that relate to blame, adopt positive ways of asserting positions and interests without blame, and establish solid relationships based on understanding, trust, and tolerance.

To help achieve these objectives, I divided the book into three parts. In part I we'll examine information that can boost your awareness of the complexities of blame and of how to use this understanding to promote positive change. In part II we'll examine blame's role in primary relationships and ways to change the "blame script" when the results have a curdling effect. Finally, in part III we'll look at powerful change processes to permanently get beyond the stresses and strains of unnecessary blame.

Introduction

Blame, a highly contagious process, weaves through life like strands of hemp through a rope. We currently live in a *blame culture,* where finger-pointing, bickering, fault-finding, criticism, and condemnation commonly influence what we think, feel, and do. When something goes wrong, the first thing many of us hear is "Who is to blame?"

Blame is such a constant presence in our everyday life that we take it for granted. Indeed, within westernized cultures, blame is pervasive.

We may not have a "blame gene," but our species definitely has an aptitude for blame. After working with thousands of clients struggling to deal with critical life issues and talking to countless people from different walks of life, I found that practically everyone had highly unpleasant blame experiences to relate. Their blame stories came from such events as past recollections, current relationships, or conflicts with a boss or neighbor. Some seethed while recalling a badgering parent criticizing them. People complained about feeling surrounded by "blamers" with a fault-finding knack. Some highly critical people showed tunnel vision and went into denial over whether their blaming ways contributed to the conflicts that they confronted daily.

Practically anyone can learn and practice ways to stretch positive abilities, gain an appealing sense of self-confidence, and largely stay out of blame traps. If you choose this path, join me to look at conditions when blame is justified and when blame is wrong. You'll see ways to improve human relationships by understanding the views of others while standing up for your own rational beliefs. On this journey we'll explore positive substitutes for blame. We'll strive for truth and to build inner strength. By taking this journey, you may never see blame in the same way again.

PART ONE

Dimensions of Blame

Exiting the Blame Trap

> *The traps that truly bind us are those*
> *that exist within our minds.*

The specter of blame looms large in everyday life—perhaps larger than you think. Blame, like air, is everywhere. Let's look into this blame-filled world in order to find ways to liberate ourselves from the needless forms of blame that harm our relationships, degrade our self-confidence, and preoccupy our time. Through this journey you can substantially add to your understanding about what motivates unnecessary blame and how to take charge of your life by using powerful techniques to beat the blame game.

Blame has existed throughout the ages. Adam blamed Eve for getting them both thrown out of paradise. The ancient Greeks blamed fickle gods for pestilence and disaster. Priests in the Middle Ages blamed demons and devils for causing what we now know is mental illness.

The blame beat goes on. The child blames a broken pencil for a late school assignment. A friend blames a poor memory for not following through. The driver blames a pothole for a sideswiping accident. The rejected lover blames herself for everything. The meteorologist blames El Niño or La Niña for bad weather. The professor blames society for causing crime. The teacher tells the parent, "Your son is lazy and that is why he is failing." The basketball player looks at a spot on the floor to say symbolically that the floor caused his fall. We blame the coach for a losing season. We point the finger at fluorocarbons for global warming. We blame ourselves for the mistakes we make. We also hear blame disguised through harshly toned questions: "What are you trying to do?" "Why did you do it?"

We all engage in blaming, and sometimes with merit. Habitual blaming, however, can rise to the level of a syndrome, or a series of symptoms that characterize an undesirable condition. The blame syndrome includes various combinations of whining, complaining, criticizing, fault-finding, finger-pointing, accusing, reproving, insulting, demonizing, bickering, carping, backbiting, chiding, scolding, mocking, sneering, slurring, branding, and defensiveness that can occur without much forethought.

Of course blame has its place. Without social standards and controls, including measured forms of blame, we'd have chaos.

WELCOME TO THE WORLD OF BLAME

Let's start by defining "blame": To blame means to hold responsible and to censure for cause. When we blame, 1) we rely on standards and rules of conduct, 2) we evaluate behavior against those standards, and 3) based on the degree of verifiable accountability, we receive or dispense penalties for rule violations. The process of blame is part of a larger social process of "consequence."* A pragmatist rightly says that we need to follow reasonable codes of conduct and so we need sensible standards and guidelines to ensure that we live long and reasonably secure lives within our social world. We need rewards and penalties to ensure such an order. Blame is a part of this social-corrective process that includes negative consequences such as criticism, punishment, penalties, and censure. This pragmatic view asserts that blame serves both to assign fault and to encourage conformity to known and accepted rules. A well-placed, realistic and constructive criticism, for example, can help shape behavior.

Some people feel paralyzed by self-conscious fears of disapproval and blame. We counterbalance those fears of blame with compassion, empathy, forgiveness, tolerance, acceptance, charity, benevolence, sensitivity, fairness, and justice. We also tend to look at extenuating conditions when considering blame and consequences. The person who shows up late for a meeting blames a traffic jam. If this person is rarely late, the explanation probably is credible. Other exonerations are phony ploys. Wally batters his wife, June, and explains, "I was drunk at the time." Who chose to drink?

EXTENSIONS OF BLAME

Blame is necessary to maintain social order through holding people accountable for their actions. A person is culpable, for example, for causing an automobile accident by running a red light. If you habitually pay your bills late, you are responsible and you can suffer a penalty in the form of a lower credit rating.

If we each gave and accepted blame according to this more dispassionate view, blame would not be such an emotionally charged process. But as practically everyone knows, blame has extended meanings. Once we've established fault, when we

---

*Consequences can be positive and increase the frequency of the events they follow. If you scratched your head and got a $20 bill, you'd probably continue to scratch your head if followed by $20.

extend this blame by adding condemnations, character assassinations, and unwarranted criticism, we go beyond what is necessary. Understanding and defusing these extensions of blame is, perhaps, the most important thing people can do to increase their happiness, establish positive relationships, and reduce stress. Predictably, eliminating extensions of blame should promote fewer hassles, and people will lead happier, saner lives.

Extensions of blame add nothing constructive and detract from problem solving and positive human relationships. Alertness to extension-of-blame thinking opens opportunities for avoiding it. By the time you finish reading this book, you may be quick to recognize extension-of-blame thinking and defuse it with confidence.

The more dangerous blame extensions involve a blanket condemnation of people themselves rather than their mistakes and faults. When you totally condemn someone, you can justify retaliatory action against the person. At the extreme, we see these global retaliatory extensions of blame in Adolf Hitler's views toward Gypsies, Jews, and Slavs whom he blamed, depersonalized, condemned, and had murdered. Hitler's "big lie" asserted that these groups were unalterably and unambiguously evil. His extension-of-blame fiction becomes obvious when we ask: How can a complex person be only one way or another?

Sometimes we feel exasperated, and this feeling gains expression through direct *blame labeling*. Someone bumps into you and you think, "Clumsy oaf." Exasperation also may be expressed in *inferences of blame,* such as "It's *about time* that you *finally* got around to doing it," and in *subtle innuendoes,* such as "You really can't expect much from her," "He's out of date," or "They are just lazy."

False blame is an infuriating blame extension. To gain unfair advantage or evade responsibility, people wrongly blame others. This attack mentality occurs in many quarters from professionals who put down their colleagues to unfairly obtain clients to criminals who blame society for their problems.

Extensions of blame are clearly negative ways for us to communicate with others. Typically they are motivated by an anger that seeks to strip the targeted person of his or her individuality. (See chapter 17 for strategies to overcome blame-related anger.) Even an occasional excursion into the extensions-of-blame realm can disrupt relationships and create lingering ill will. But just as developing immunity to the various strains of the flu virus improves physical health, getting extensions of blame out of your thoughts and actions can do much to improve relationship health.

Extensions of Blame and Distortions

Blame can come about as a result of distortions that operate automatically to mask reality. These conditions of mind include exaggerating, overgeneralizing, thinking in circles, demanding what cannot be, and thinking dichotomously where we view life in black-and-white terms. Liz, for example, expected her dream date to take her to a romantic restaurant. When she discovered his idea of a romantic restaurant differed from hers, she ruined her evening by dwelling on his "bad taste" and blaming him for "insensitivity." "It's his fault," she thought, "for wrecking the date."

Liz was totally oblivious to how she spoiled a dream date with a man she previously found attractive by falling into an extension-of-blame, dichotomous-thinking blame trap. She thought there are only two kinds of restaurants: romantic and unromantic. She also believed that if her date took her to a romantic restaurant, he was worthy. Since her date took her to what she defined as an unromantic restaurant, he was blameworthy. She extended blame by taking this one step further by believing that her blameworthy date deserved damnation. Since most human activities exist on a continuum, where accountability can occur in disputable degrees, ascribing total blame under these conditions seems silly, especially when Liz's definitions are arbitrary and her date's responsibility is not clear to him.

Extensions of Blame and Violence

The American culture is a blame culture. When the blame process includes belittling, condemnation, disparagement, creating outcasts, or dehumanizing people, we've added needless extensions to the process of blame. Violence is one possible outcome of extension-of-blame thinking.

The psychology of violence is complicated. It involves a self-absorbed view and extension-of-blame thinking that fuels hostile emotions. This process frequently includes dehumanizing people, which justifies inflicting verbal or physical abuse or violence. Bob believes that Judy is not faithful enough to him. He has no factual basis for this conclusion. Nevertheless, he acts as if the belief were true. One day she arrives home late. Now he sees her as a "cheat" and her lateness as justifying his view. Viewing her as subhuman, he feels justified badgering her and berating her for being a "cheat."

Society would be a great deal safer without extension-of-blame thinking. Annoyances and frustrations would still exist. Certain events simply would not be tolerated, however. If blame extensions were reduced, there would be far fewer cases of abuse and violence.

Alternative Solutions to Violence

What are we to do to prevent violent extensions of blame? No perfect answer exists. However, we can reduce violence.

People who develop empathy for others are less likely to engage in extensions of blame and violent activities. Understanding and tolerance go a long way to defuse pernicious forms of blame. These conditions of mind are teachable, learnable, and transmittable.

Children who develop emotional problem-solving skills learn to build a solid self-concept, establish a sense of self-efficacy (the ability to organize, regulate, and direct efforts toward positive goals), establish the ability to interpose reason between impulse and action, build frustration tolerance, constructively assert their positive interests, communicate effectively, and challenge themselves to stretch their positive abilities. Such children are less likely to resort to extension-of-blame thinking habits and to resort to violence to solve their problems.

This book describes ways for adults to gain progressive mastery over extension-of-blame thinking and, by positive modeling, to pass this knowledge down to the next generation in the form of powerful alternatives to the extensions of blame. It also provides rational ways to view blameworthy actions and realistic ways to rid ourselves of the sort of extension-of-blame thinking that leads to harmful extremes.

BLAME TRAPS

A blame trap is a self-deceptive pattern in which we ensnare ourselves in a fruitless habit of blame and blame avoidance.

Blame traps come in different forms. Some of them are directed outward, as when we blame others for our own failings; others are directed inward, when instead of simply taking responsibility, we apply extension-of-blame thinking to ourselves or give flimsy excuses for our blameworthy actions. Some reflect a fear of blame. Others lead to paralysis and inaction. All involve a defensive deflection from personal accountability and responsibility for one's thoughts, feelings, and actions. (In chapter 3 we look closely at other ways that people attempt to exonerate themselves from blame.) Once you learn to recognize these traps, you are less likely to be fooled and ensnared by them. Here is a sampling:

➤ **The Perfectionist Trap.** Some people impose inflexible expectations, rules, roles, and requirements onto themselves or others. And when people invariably veer from these tight standards, the perfectionist is primed to blame. In this world, even the slightest mistake can rise to a calamity and the blame game follows. If you fall into this trap, start your exit by honestly evaluating whether your expectations are expectancies, opinions, or hypotheses. Chances are you'll find that you are expressing an opinion, and an opinion is not the same as a fact.

➤ **The Political Trap.** People who try to take the credit for all that is good and blame others for whatever goes wrong have fallen into the political blame trap. The goal of politicians is to look good. When events go sour, they will make others look bad to divert attention from themselves. If you're following this gambit, you'll find that you prioritize your image over your self-development. To stay out of the political blame trap, accept responsibility for your mistakes and use them as stepping-stones to self-improvement.

➤ **The Ego Trap.** Some people fall into the ego blame trap. If you're in this group, you probably follow Stephen Potter's one-upmanship gambit. By extending blame to others for their foibles and faults, you artificially boost your ego. However, this boost yields a false sense of security. Problems others exhibit do nothing to make your inner life blissful. To stay out of this trap, look for ways to praise others appropriately and to avoid degrading them.

➤ **The Projection Trap.** When you feel on top of the world, you may look around and see everybody as happy human beings. Envisioning others as thinking and feeling the same way that you do is a normal human tendency. A quick evaluation, however, can change this perspective. The same mechanism is at play when you fall into the projection blame trap. Here you attribute your undesirable motives to others. A con artist decides to cheat someone out of her money. Without a basis in fact, the con artist thinks that the person would do the same if given the chance. Now the victim is to blame for having similar motivations. This blame projection is a crutch to justify the unacceptable and to avoid blame. People stay out of this trap by recognizing and owning their own feelings and motivations.

➤ **The Rationalization Trap.** Rationalization trap people give credible-sounding but false reasons to excuse their behavior and to avoid blame: "I wasn't taught that"; "I thought that was permissible"; "It wouldn't have happened if the weather hadn't changed." This intellectual defense gives the individual a way to save face. However, time spent in blame-avoidance rationalizations often is better used to correct the reasons for the rationalizations. To stay out of the rationalization trap, act to fulfill responsibilities without excusing yourself. For example, if you forget to make a phone call, instead of blaming a colleague for distracting you, simply say "I forgot."

➤ **The Denial Trap.** Denial takes many forms. A Pollyanna-ish denial is to perceive the world in glowing terms. Another is to psychologically block painful realities, thoughts, or feelings. The more common denial, however, is to consciously disavow blameworthy actions. This form of denial is the first line of defense against blame among people in a blame culture. If you fall into the denial trap, when things go wrong you'll find yourself falsely claiming "I didn't do it"; "It's not my fault." This quick and easy escape technique diminishes opportunities for positive change. To stay out of this trap, put your efforts into addressing and solving problems rather than wasting time and energy on futile denials.

➤ **The Whiney Trap.** Whiney blame-trap people appear to feel overwhelmed, outgunned, and helpless to convincingly assert their preferences and interests. They whine and complain as a way of blaming. This is not a weak ploy but a highly manipulative blaming style. The trap has a big downside. The person frequently feels dependent and helpless. To stay out of the whiney blame trap, follow St. Thomas Aquinas's advice: "Let me change what I can, accept what I can't, and know the difference between the two."

➤ **The Depression Trap.** When you're in the depression blame trap, you falsely define yourself as helpless yet blame yourself for matters that, if you were truly helpless, you could not be expected to control. Scarcely aware of this self-blame–powerless paradox, people in this trap live life without hope. To stay out of the trap, recognize that you can practically always find an option and that the smallest step to execute that option is a signal of your ability to change.

➤ **The Terrible-Person Trap.** The terrible-person blame trap is among the most painful variety. You blame yourself and declare yourself a terrible person for being who you are. This blame belief boxes you into a self-defeating outlook. If you are a "terrible person," how can you correct who you are? Those who stay out of this trap convince themselves to make appropriate changes, including changing beliefs that lead to this type of faulty self-concept.

➤ **The Fear-of-Blame Trap.** The fear-of-blame trap places an artificial limit on ability. Many in this group refuse to take prudent risks unless they have a guarantee of success. Sadly, the person with an artistic vision pumps gas because he fears the words of critics. A fear-driven clerk with a cost-saving idea winces at the thought of her employer's scoffing at her idea. To stay out of this trap look for ways to accept rather than reject yourself.

Blame traps occur in different combinations. People in the rationalization trap often project and deny. A classic example is that of the alcoholic who believes everyone drinks heavily and who blames work, a flat tire, a "bad break," or an unhappy fourth-grade experience for his or her troubles. In this defensive state, the person denies the problem by pretending to be a victim and claims he or she drinks to "lift the spirit," to "forget," or to "reduce stress." These excuses are as valid as sitting in a garbage pit and saying it smells like roses.

THE TAR-BABY BLAME TRAP

In the world of blame we can find many people who, like the rabbit character in Joel Chandler Harris's classic story of Brer Rabbit, create blame conflicts and cause themselves harm. In the story, Brer Rabbit greeted a tar baby on a hot day. The tar baby, of course, couldn't respond. Demanding a response, an obviously frustrated Brer Rabbit blamed the inanimate figure for remaining silent, trounced it, and got stuck. The more the rabbit blamed and fussed, the deeper he dug himself into the tar baby.

People who fall into this tar-baby blame trap can scarcely contemplate an alternative reality, one where they settle their differences without extension-of-blame actions. By losing perspective and fighting false demons, such as Brer Rabbit fighting the tar baby, people in this state of mind spew blame with a scarce awareness of the consequences of this action. Like the classic "hillbilly" feud between the Hatfields and McCoys, whose long-standing hatred was based on long-forgotten grudges, we may not remember the point of origin for our conflicts but we still blame.

As with Brer Rabbit and the Hatfields and McCoys, not all consequences teach. Some repeat destructive patterns despite bad results. What is the explanation for smart people repeatedly falling into blame traps? Here are some common reasons:

1. Those with ego problems are primed to refuse to admit publicly to being wrong.
2. People practiced in the art of blame repeat this familiar pattern and get better at it.
3. Where people protect themselves from blame by blaming, this defensiveness stunts growth and positive change.
4. We sometimes escape consequences by shifting the blame onto others. This result can feel relieving or rewarding. That which is rewarded is likely to be repeated.
5. People who unrealistically see life through a highly personalized perspective and refuse to admit to any wrong discourage others from giving them honest feedback.

When you allow yourself and others latitude, reflect on your experiences, and accept responsibility for your thinking and actions, you are less likely to join Brer Rabbit in his tiring battle with the tar baby.

ESCAPE FROM THE TRAPS

A blame trap is where we ensnare ourselves in a fruitless pattern of blame. The best way to avoid blame traps is to keep blame at a descriptive level. At this level we objectively describe events, then dispassionately hold ourselves or others responsible. In a descriptive system, blameworthy actions are generally known. The penalties are flexibly fixed and measured against the person and situation. So, if you intentionally break a window in anger, you replace the glass and probably receive a reprimand as a result of your intent. If you are delirious and accidentally break a window, your level of accountability is lessened. If you break the window as a result of a slipping accident over which you have no control, you may be held blameless. In a nutshell, you keep "personalities" and extensions of blame out of the picture.

POSTSCRIPT

The American journalist P. J. O'Rourke once remarked, "One of the annoying things about believing in free will and individual responsibility is the difficulty of finding somebody to blame your problems on." To break free of blame thinking requires acting against the various extensions of blame, including condemnations. But that is only half of the story.

Regardless of the challenges you face, to move forward to enjoy life requires translating your clear-thinking abilities and positive motivations into sustained action. Doing so involves building a realistic awareness of your opportunities, challenges, and problem zones so that you can undertake constructive change. Learning to deal with blame, then, becomes a means to bring out both your active and your dormant potentials to put the best part of yourself forward. One of these prime potentials involves finding legitimate ways to engage people cooperatively when you also could choose contention and blame.

Tackling Stereotyped Blame

2

> *Mechanical thinking dilutes our reasoning.*

What do these phrases have in common?

"Cool."
"Nobody's perfect."
"Have a good day."
"Time flies when you're having fun."
"If everyone jumped off a bridge, would you?"

They're all clichés. Every day we convey meaning through these stereotyped phrases. Some are friendly ways to communicate, such as "How are things going?" Others convey blame. Some of these off-the-shelf blame phrases carry extension-of-blame messages. The angrily toned blame cliché "Can't you get anything right?" conveys the message that the subject is stupid.

Whether we are on the receiving end of blame clichés or whether we are the speaker, by recognizing and examining these clichés and other standardized blame expressions, we can prepare ourselves to ask the hard questions and come to truthful answers rather than rely on the lazy thinking these clichés encourage. In this chapter we'll probe these blame expressions and look at positive alternatives.

BLAME CLICHÉS

Blame clichés seamlessly blend into the way people think and express themselves. Practically everybody has used or has been the subject of these blame clichés. Some blame clichés boil down to a single word. A motorist drifts into your travel lane. You swerve to avoid the vehicle and mutter, "*jerk!*"

13

BLAME CLICHÉ INVENTORY

Instructions: The following thirty-six-item inventory samples common blame phrases. Check *Yes* if you've heard the phrase in any context. Check *True* for those items where someone directed the cliché toward you. In cases where you were the subject of the statement, list the emotion you felt under *Feeling*.

	Experienced		*Feeling*
1. How could you have been so stupid?	*Yes* ___	*True* ___	_____
2. How could you have done that?	*Yes* ___	*True* ___	_____
3. Can't you do anything right?	*Yes* ___	*True* ___	_____
4. Don't you know what you're doing?	*Yes* ___	*True* ___	_____
5. What's wrong with you?	*Yes* ___	*True* ___	_____
6. You had it coming.	*Yes* ___	*True* ___	_____
7. You're just like your mother (father).	*Yes* ___	*True* ___	_____
8. You're a disgrace.	*Yes* ___	*True* ___	_____
9. You'll be sorry after I'm gone.	*Yes* ___	*True* ___	_____
10. You're killing me.	*Yes* ___	*True* ___	_____
11. You should have listened to me.	*Yes* ___	*True* ___	_____
12. You are not supposed to do that.	*Yes* ___	*True* ___	_____
13. Don't you get it?	*Yes* ___	*True* ___	_____
14. Don't you know any better?	*Yes* ___	*True* ___	_____
15. You stupid fool (idiot, moron, loser, etc.).	*Yes* ___	*True* ___	_____
16. You shouldn't have done that.	*Yes* ___	*True* ___	_____
17. What in the world were you thinking?	*Yes* ___	*True* ___	_____
18. You're driving me crazy.	*Yes* ___	*True* ___	_____
19. I've had it with you.	*Yes* ___	*True* ___	_____
20. Shame on you.	*Yes* ___	*True* ___	_____
21. You're lucky I don't kick you out.	*Yes* ___	*True* ___	_____
22. If you had half a brain, you would not do that.	*Yes* ___	*True* ___	_____
23. I warned you.	*Yes* ___	*True* ___	_____
24. Don't you ever listen?	*Yes* ___	*True* ___	_____
25. Look what you've done.	*Yes* ___	*True* ___	_____

	Experienced	Feeling
26. Don't you know your place?	Yes ___ True ___	_____
27. I told you a long time ago not to do that.	Yes ___ True ___	_____
28. Who taught you that?	Yes ___ True ___	_____
29. Were you raised in a barn?	Yes ___ True ___	_____
30. I told you so.	Yes ___ True ___	_____
31. You're crazy.	Yes ___ True ___	_____
32. What goes around comes around.	Yes ___ True ___	_____
33. You don't know who you're dealing with.	Yes ___ True ___	_____
34. What do you think I am, chopped liver?	Yes ___ True ___	_____
35. You don't know what you are talking about.	Yes ___ True ___	_____
36. Why won't you listen to reason?	Yes ___ True ___	_____

The American culture froths with blame clichés with hidden extension-of-blame meanings. The blame cliché inventory above describes a sample of these bothersome statements. Although this is not a scientifically validated test, you can use this listing of stock blame phrases to boost your awareness of common blame formulas so you can better unravel their meaning and impact. These consciousness-raising questions, along with the other information in this book, can help you tally the role of blame in your life and to point to positive change opportunities.

You might smile or laugh over the incongruity between some of the blame phrases and good human relationships. When you're not directly affected by blame clichés, they can sound like jokes or part of a sitcom routine. However, some may touch a raw nerve or hit a hot-button. This suggests that you have a trouble zone that bears review to understand, bypass, or deal with when warranted.

Your interpretation of the significance of a hot-button blame cliché can tell you something about your associations and emotions toward the cliché. This awareness is useful for the following point-of-origin exercise.

Points of Origin

The first-century B.C. Roman orator Marcus Tullius Cicero passed on these words: "To not know what went on before you were born leaves you thinking as a child." We can say something similar about our own history. If we understand our personal history, we can better understand and change what we need to change in the present. You may have no reaction to blame clichés. But if you are like most others, some will evoke emotions that warrant understanding and change.

A *point-of-origin analysis* with regard to hot-button blame clichés can help you trace important blame patterns in your life. This analysis involves five parts: 1) identifying the basis for your current reaction; 2) determining the consequences of the reaction; 3) recalling your earliest recollection and reaction to a blame cliché(s); 4) deciding the significance of the point-of-origin experience; and 5) using that understanding to make positive changes in the present and future.

Let's suppose you had an emotional reaction to blame cliché inventory item 15, "You stupid fool." In part 1 of this analysis you find that you extend effort to avoid criticism because you fear you will be put down and blamed for mistakes. For part 2 you conclude that you have a strong tendency to avoid risks. In part 3 you recall that you had an uncle with a short temper who was prone to use that cliché with your cousins. You remember flinching in fear that your uncle would blame you next for a mistake. For point 4 you associate the blame cliché with irrationality, unpredictability, and mistake making. Even though you were not the subject of your uncle's tirade, you associated the cliché with your "self." At point 5 you decide that it is impractical to avoid all criticism by avoiding risk.

It is unusual that one traumatic blame cliché experience will have a long-term effect. If as a child you were barraged with blame clichés or their equivalent and if you uncritically applied them to yourself, you may be able to tie the clichés to self-consciousness, a sense of shame, or a proneness to guilt, anger, or other disruptive emotional state such as angst (a feeling of anxiety or apprehension often accompanied by depression). The following exercise can help you extend your ability to deal with your reaction for hot-button blame clichés.

Fighting Cliché Reactions

We can't resuscitate the past except in our minds. However, we can deal with the present moment. Here are a few general directions for dealing with present-moment reactions to blame clichés:

➤ Does the phrase affect your sense of personal dignity? Why? What can you concretely do to maintain dignity in the face of blame?

➤ If you rarely were the subject of a blame cliché yet fear making an error and getting blamed, what do you tell yourself to perpetuate this fear? Do you, for example, worry yourself by anticipating the worst thing that could happen to you? If so, consider the best that can happen and a range of alternatives that exist between the worst and best extremes. Once you see many alternatives, you can better prepare yourself to think in terms of probabilities. This makes it more difficult to magnify one possible outcome into a major worry.

➤ Some people develop a vicarious fear of blame by watching others being blamed. From this they develop an exaggerated fear of what they rarely experience. Although not personally affected, the idea of a blame cliché evokes fear. If you count yourself in this vicarious learning camp, intentionally separate out the vicarious dimension from your vision of the benefits of positive risk-taking.

➤ Assess the quality of judgment of the person employing a blame cliché. Assuming that the blamer is correct, you can simultaneously show yourself that it serves no useful purpose to transform everyday errors into extension-of-blame clichés. When feasible, correct the fault that evoked the cliché. When the cliché is false, and you find yourself anguishing over the "unfairness," the following analysis can help get you out of double trouble.

BLAME CLICHÉS AND DOUBLE TROUBLES

People can and do react and overreact when they are targets of blame clichés. First, it is normal to be annoyed and irritated when you are the subject of a false blame. Indeed, moderate levels of frustration, irritation, annoyance, and displeasure can propel constructive change. On the other hand, *double troubles* consist of making a situation more than it is. When you tell yourself you should not be the subject of blame, then anger yourself and dwell on your feelings of anger, you now have a double trouble: the original annoyance plus a lingering anger over having the annoyance. This lingering anger often results from telling yourself something such as "This should not have happened to me" and "I can't stand it."

Some double troubles lead to triple troubles where you blame yourself for blaming yourself. Let's suppose you were falsely accused. You first feel annoyed, then think, "It's my fault. I must have done something wrong." This is like layering a problem onto a problem. This layering takes you from dealing with the primary problem, false blame. Thus, in double troubles, the first reaction may be legitimate. You feel annoyed hearing what you don't like. The second phase of this process adds a layer of needless misery. At the third level we blame ourselves for blaming ourselves when we realize that this process is getting us nowhere. Each of these steps takes us farther from solving the original problem.

The advice "Know thyself," attributed both to Socrates and the Oracle of Delphi, suggests that you can do much to develop your ability to rid yourself of needless stress by getting rid of double and triple troubles. To deal with double troubles, accept your primary reaction. Debunk the secondary one by challenging its validity. To debunk triple troubles, refuse to blame yourself for blaming yourself!

BLAME CLICHÉ RESPONSES

What should you do if people direct blame clichés at you? Those using blame clichés are vulnerable to a legitimate challenge because the statements are overgeneralized, discriminatory, and represent sloppy thinking. Let's look at potential ways in which you might respond to extension-of-blame clichés.

How you deal with extension-of-blame clichés depends on the blamer. (You wouldn't want to get into an argument with a person pointing a pistol at you who has just blamed you and used a cliché.) However, you normally have choices, from making no response to a broad range of actions. If you choose to say something, the following provides a sample of techniques:

➤ *Direct clarification:* "Is it your intent to cause me to feel like a terrible person?" (If so, why? If not, why try?)
➤ *Refocusing:* "If we have a problem to solve, how does saying 'I have half a brain' help solve the problem?"
➤ *Emotional feedback:* You also can provide emotional feedback, such as "When I hear you call me stupid, I feel frustrated." (Note: Frustration is an example; other emotions are possible.)
➤ *Empathy-seeking response:* "If you were me, and someone called you stupid for making an error, how would you react?" (Absent a relaxed matter-of-fact tone, the risk with this question is that it can be taken as rhetorical and bitter.)
➤ *Direct assertion:* "I can't tell you what you should or should not say, but your comment causes me to _____." (You fill in the blank.)

The samples suggest ways to defuse a blanket assertion of blame. Nevertheless, all samples of how to respond to a cliché involve judgment and risk. In the area of human relations, even the most thoughtful responses can provoke unpredictable results. To use a few other clichés to clarify the matter, "You can't get through to some people," or "Trying to get through to some is like arguing with a stone." We've all met people, for example, who have a fixed position and are adept at filibustering.

Should you confront a blame cliché with a blame cliché? Doing so usually is not helpful. For example, saying "Is that how your mother taught you to talk to people?" can escalate conflict.

There are no pat formulas that fit all blame cliché situations. However, the more you know, the better you can prepare yourself to respond in a positive and self-affirming manner.

TONE, BEHAVIOR, AND BLAME

Most people would recoil upon hearing a harshly toned "You did that." The tone and phrase casts the person in an inferior, blameworthy position. Like clichés, a person's tone and physical expression can convey an unmistakable negative message.

Clichés uttered in anger add a severe sting to blame. Expressions like "Jeez" convey a muted but still unmistakable message of blame. We also hear the tone of blame echoing through the words of moralistic individuals with a practiced condescending tone.

Stereotyped blame messages frequently come through body language. Some people turn their shoulders, sneer, raise their eyebrows, roll their eyes, cross their arms, cast a disgusted look, shun, or engage in other juvenile expressions such as mocking by imitating and exaggerating a person's statements, voice, inflection, or facial expression.

Is there a benefit to calling someone's nonverbal blame behavior to his or her attention? "Dan, you turned your shoulder. Are you trying to make a point?" "Suzie, you wrinkled your forehead and raised your eyebrows. What are you trying to say?" In this scenario, you invite the person to define a problem. But when you call attention to people's nonverbal cues, some will get defensive.

Your response to nonverbal blame cues depends on your position of power, the quality of the relationship you enjoy with the other person, and your own psychological status. If you feel calm, nonflustered, and comfortable with yourself, and if you can respond diplomatically, your results are likely to differ from those of a person frothing with rage.

When you feel in charge of yourself and are prepared to respond constructively when you encounter a blaming person in an angered state of mind, don't count on reason prevailing. People obsessed with blaming often don't listen to reason. Nevertheless, you have options: You can say nothing. You can identify what you can agree with and what you cannot. Or you can make a statement that makes it clear that you disagree.

POSTSCRIPT

The thirty-third president of the United States, Harry S Truman, once said, "I never give them hell; I tell the truth and they think it is hell." The first-century A.D. Stoic philosopher-slave Epictetus said, "A person who seeks truth must be reckoned precious to any society." What Epictetus had in mind included self-discovery. Later, the twentieth-century existential philosopher Jean-Paul Sartre, in his study of "being," conveyed that honesty with oneself is among the most important existential values.

Those who go on an empirical search for truth will find little merit in extension-of-blame clichés.

3

Freedom from Exoneration Ploys

> *Deceptions dance like ghosts through the mind
> and enter the outside world in apparitional
> disguise to shift the eye from blame.*

A man came home a day early from a trip to find his wife in bed with another man. Outraged, he screamed, "How could you sleep with that man!" His wife responded, "What man?" The husband said, "That man." His wife said, "I don't see any man." Meanwhile, the lover dressed quickly and left through the window. The wife repeated, "Where is the man you speak of?" The husband stood in disbelief. Few people whose actions result in consequences step forward to take the blame when they have an option to do otherwise. Some go to ridiculous extremes to exonerate themselves from blame.

LOOKING FOR LOOPHOLES

How often have you heard the phrase "Who is to blame?" Even if you don't hear this phrase daily, you will find many examples of people denying a visible reality or defensively pointing their finger at others. Or you may notice those habits in yourself.

Few things in life operate flawlessly. Most of us have daily hassles and sometimes may think, "Why me?" We and others make mistakes. We misjudge. Memory is fallible. We get distracted. We have accidents. We can't know everything, so sometimes we will lack knowledge. Truly, there are many legitimate errors that we can justify, explain, excuse, and correct. However, people also will intentionally cause trouble, then use phony excuses or look for loopholes to get themselves off the hook.

If blame was not often painful, we'd have no good reason to find ways to explain away our less-than-stellar performances or blameworthy activities. However, blame can lead to pain and penalties. To avoid pain and penalties, people duck blame in many ways. We've already seen some blame-trap ploys in chapter 1 that serve a psychologically deceptive purpose. These blame-deflection efforts also include diverting criticism, shifting responsibility, casting blame, stonewalling, rationalizing, "passing the buck," denying, concocting excuses, minimizing significant problems, engaging in ad hominem arguments, parsing words, "spin control," and distorting reality in order to escape responsibility. *Exoneration theory* helps us understand the underlying reasons for people's oft-repeated efforts to duck blame.

The theory has these assumptions:

➤ We live in a blame culture where extension-of-blame thinking influences our judgment.
➤ Avoiding or escaping blame is a strong human social motivation.
➤ Given the choice of casting themselves in a favorable or an unfavorable light, most people will choose the former over the latter.
➤ Exoneration provides avenues for people to escape blame at least temporarily and to maintain a favorable impression.

Let's look at a few exoneration ploys and how we might interpret their meaning:

1. "It's not my fault."
2. "I didn't mean to do it."
3. "Nobody told me not to."
4. "I didn't do it."
5. "It wouldn't have happened if it weren't for _____."

What might these phrases mean?

1. "It's not my fault" is a blanket denial. Denial is a classic way in which people defend themselves against blame. These consciously contrived exoneration ploys often spring within a split second when exoneration is in the individual's interest.
2. "I didn't mean to do it" is a plea for tolerance based on a vague declaration of innocence for having no negative intention.
3. "Nobody told me not to" suggests that the person is playing dumb.
4. "I didn't do it" is a direct denial.
5. "It wouldn't have happened if it weren't for _____" is a way to negate accountability by externalizing responsibility.

Exoneration ploys yield specious rewards. You can feel rewarded by avoiding or delaying social consequences. Such reinforcement helps to make these ploys resist change. Often these exoneration efforts are partially or wholly successful; otherwise people would not use them. However, many times face-saving efforts lack credibility. "I would not have robbed the bank if I didn't grow up in a dysfunctional family" will fool only those who want to believe. Growing up in a dysfunctional family may be among the root causes for an action. However, since not everyone from a dysfunctional family becomes a bank robber, this excuse does not free a person from responsibility.

Despite the relief benefits that exoneration ploys sometimes offer, there can be external consequences. Most reasonable people normally treat conscious efforts at deception as more serious transgressions than inadvertent deceptions.

DUPLICITY PLOYS

To avoid risk of censure, most people in a blame culture will make a logical decision to deceive in order to avoid blame, especially when they *knowingly* engage in the censurable conduct. This is the principle of *blame duplicity,* and it illustrates another angle of blame.

When we knowingly engage in blameworthy activities, sometimes we give ourselves reasons for engaging in those activities that differ from the excuses we give to others. Sandra puts off doing her part of a group project because she tells herself she needs to get into the mood first. When the group confronts her about her delay, she tells them that she was ill.

When people seek to avoid blame, often they point to "shades of gray" or make intentional omissions of key information or outright lie to avoid criticism or retaliation. For example, not many procrastinators will say "I delayed the report because I don't like to do anything that is uncomfortable. I did not care if my delays caused others to fall behind. I was thinking primarily of how I felt at the time I put it off." Rather, they are more likely to say "I had a family crisis" or some other fabrication or exaggeration. The excuse can elicit sympathy. When this happens, procrastinators avoid a penalty and gain a perk. However, as the exoneration process becomes semiautomatic, it becomes less accessible to recognition and change. Automatic efforts to dodge justified blame are a subtle choice that limits other choices.

A common act of duplicity involves an appeal to a higher principle of "fairness." Following this ploy, people who engage in blameworthy actions attempt to avoid blame by appealing to "fairness." Since "fairness" (that which is just, proper, unbiased, and equitable) is often a matter of definition measured against fluctuating rules and interests, the appeal can sound plausible.

Duplicitous appeals to "fairness" characterize some adolescents' conflicts with their parents. Dan decided to drink at a party and then drove home under the influence. When he arrived home his parents smelled alcohol on his breath and told Dan he could no longer drive the family car. Dan jumped on the unfairness defense: "It's unfair that I lose my driving privilege. My sister did the same thing and nothing happened to her." The duplicity is that Dan defended a wrong act with a specious appeal to fairness.

Can deception be sensible? A child tells a parent that he was visiting a friend and so doesn't know how the family cat escaped from the house. Since a window was partially ajar, the parent can't tell for sure who or what is at fault. If the parent dispenses severe punishment for both small and major infractions, assuming the child opened the window, the child can decide to take his or her chances and deceive to avoid a harsh punishment.

What can we conclude about why people deceive and why they are truthful? There are no simple formulas for understanding why people do what they do. But ordinarily we can understand the choices people make when we understand their perceptions, thinking, and situations.

EUPHEMISMS AND BLAME

A "euphemism" is a mild word that leads us away from a harsher reality. Euphemisms are not always bad. Sometimes they can be used to eliminate blame where none is deserved; for example, most "politically correct" phrases are euphemisms that put a better spin on a bad situation and legitimately remove blame and stigmatization. At one time people who lived in shelters, cardboard cities, alleys, or abandoned automobiles were called bums. This is a *blame label* that does little other than to sanitize social neglect of this population. The term "homeless" or "residentially challenged" takes away the character description of the word "bum." Eliminating a blame label has merit in this sense: The "bum" label obscured the different reasons people live on the street. Some have psychoactive substance abuse problem habits. Others suffer from severe mental disorders. Some have mental retardation and little hope to obtain work. Some gradually lost their ambition for a better life and substituted a habit of surviving from day to day. Some were out of work because of an economic downturn.

Homelessness can be attributed to a long list of often interconnected reasons. However, the term "homeless" properly blunts the blame stigma associated with the "bum" label.

But soft words can mislead and deflect from legitimately blameworthy activities. Describe cocaine as a harmless recreational or casual drug, and you soft-peddle a harsh reality. Actually, cocaine can kill by interfering with the electrical impulses of the heart. Feeding the habit can prove costly. People do develop psychological dependencies on the drug. And cocaine can promote a craving by substituting itself for important neurotransmitters associated with feelings of well-being.

Euphemisms sanitize blameworthy actions in other ways. Hitler used the term "final solution" as a euphemism for murder. "Deal with extreme prejudice" or "take out" are euphemisms for murder. In business "spread the risk" is a euphemism for obscuring responsibility by putting a decision in the hands of a committee.

WHITE-GLOVE DEATHS
AND BLAME

People in positions of power have many ways to insulate themselves from blame, and that insulation serves as their exoneration. King Henry II of England exclaimed, "Who will free me from this turbulent priest?" Four of his knights then killed Thomas à Becket, the Archbishop of Canterbury. Henry could argue that he was blameless because he never gave a direct order to kill Becket.

Another Henry, King Henry VIII, conspired with Richard Rich to rid himself of a reformer, Sir Thomas More, by fabricating a case against him, then justifying More's execution based on the fabricated case. Such events served to give a noble pretense to murderous acts.

In contemporary times we blame systems—the political system, the economic system, the social system—but people who operate systems often insulate themselves from blame. Exoneration ploys of obfuscation and bureaucratic doublespeak commonly serve to deflect blame, as do traditional efforts to cover up or deny people access to information, or finger-pointing. However, in some cases the principle of duplicity prevails where the decision maker makes a conscious decision that puts people at risk of harm or death, then denies that the decision has any harmful effects. At the extreme, this is a white-glove death practice. Let's look at some extreme white-glove death examples where trickle-down policies and ideologies insulate decision makers from serious accusations.

White-glove deaths come about as a result of policy decisions made by top officials that trickle down through an organization in a way that causes harm, even death. The policy makers insulate themselves from the results of their decisions.

A quintessential example of white-glove death system practices involves the tobacco industry. When tobacco industry executives knowingly sell a product whose use correlates with shortening the lives of a significant number of its customers, this is a white-glove death choice. For decades tobacco industry executives defended themselves from assuming blame for their decisions on promoting and selling tobacco products by insisting that smoking represents a choice. By extension, those who die smoking-related deaths bear the responsibility for the "choice." This exoneration argument of "blaming the victim" for his or her own premature death has serious flaws. However, in 1997 the Liggett Group admitted that smoking cigarettes is addictive and can cause cancer. In October 1999, the Philip Morris Tobacco Company also admitted that smoking was dangerous to health, yet both companies continued their policy of selling a deadly substance.

The research on the correlation between smoking and disease has been replicated many times since at least the 1930s. The addictive data on smoking are compelling and probably have been known since the 1600s. Thus, it is increasingly difficult for tobacco company executives to define smoking as a pure choice, especially when they approve advertising campaigns that are designed to hook young people into smoking.

It can be demonstrated empirically that people get both psychologically and physically addicted to nicotine. These addictions exist on a continuum. Some people are more vulnerable to smoking-related disorders than are others. Approximately 400,000 U.S. smokers die prematurely each year due to smoking-related emphysema, coronary heart disease, lung cancer, and other cancers. What is insidious about smoking-related deaths is that often they are drawn out, painful, and costly. To the extent tobacco executives, subordinates, and paid legal professionals continue to profess that they have no evidence that smoking causes harm or proves addictive, they engage in white-glove death practices.

Chicago's Ravenswood Hospital illustrates a particularly sad case of medical officials insulating themselves from blame by hiding behind policy. The hospital refused to treat Christopher Sercye, a fifteen-year-old adolescent who lay dying of a gunshot wound within thirty-five feet of the hospital's door, allegedly on the grounds that such emergency treatment would violate hospital policy against admitting emergency patients. Christopher lay outside of the hospital until Chicago Police wheeled him in over the protests of hospital personnel. Unfortunately, by that time it was too late; the boy died. Months earlier hospital officials had refused treatment for a young girl who was hit by an automobile at the front of the hospital, also on the grounds of policy.

The hospital's medical director, Dr. Bruce McNutly, asserted that the hospital was waiting for an ambulance to transport the boy to another facility that had a trauma center. He noted that the ambulance was late and implicitly blamed the ambulance. The hospital president asserted, "Our staff is committed to helping everyone who needs our care, including those who are immediately adjacent to the hospital campus." The police noted that hospital workers were outside smoking while the boy lay dying. Dr. McNulty said that the staff was incredibly busy with heavy caseloads. However, President Bill Clinton, upon reviewing the facts in the case, threatened to withdraw $48 million in federal funds unless the hospital agreed never again to turn away a person who required emergency care.

Ravenswood's face-saving exoneration efforts appear unconvincing. The simple act of putting policy before common sense shows the poverty of the excuses. The result of the policy was a white-glove death—a situation where no one takes the blame and the loss of a human life is blamed on "policy."

POSTSCRIPT

The eighteenth-century German physicist and philosopher G. C. Lichtenberg asserted, "Before we blame we should first see whether we cannot excuse."

People have inventive and creative minds, so we can find ways to exonerate ourselves from the consequences of our behavior. However, when innocent, often we can legitimately deflect blame through fact, evidence, and logic. When we are truly blameworthy, we can accept the blame, but this can prove risky. If you betray a friend's confidence, facing up to the deception can ruin a friendship you want to preserve. To escape legitimate blame, some of us create smokescreens, offer vague or empty pretexts, make up fictitious arguments, change the subject, express half-truths, rationalize, double-talk, gloss over, or deny the obvious.

Exoneration efforts and ploys don't always work well, but the message in the attempt is clear enough: The person seeks to avoid disapproval, penalty, or punishment. In contrast to what we tell "little children"—"Tell the truth"—culture commonly includes a wide array of strategies to slant truth to avoid blame. Nevertheless, people normally prefer truth to falsehood.

The phrase "I was wrong" has great power. Most people can identify with people "messing up" because everyone will, from time to time, do something wrong. The courage to admit to being wrong increases personal credibility and creates opportunities for self-improvement.

Cause, Effect, and Blame

> *Consequences divorced from causes*
> *have no lesson to teach.*

It is the bottom of the ninth inning. The game is tied. There are two outs and the count is three balls and two strikes. The pitcher eyes the catcher, then the batter. He winds up and hurls a curveball. Crack! The ball streaks down center field lofting higher until caught by an eager fan in the stands. Home run. The game is over. We may guess at the pitcher's motivation for deciding to throw the curve, but the ball in flight is a fact. Blame follows when a fan of the losing team retorts that the pitcher should have thrown a fastball and then concludes, "Throw the bum off the team. He made us lose."

The question "Who's to blame?" bears on who or what caused an unwanted effect. Happenings have causes. Lightning strikes and shatters a tree in a forest. Some events have both human and natural causes. A gust of wind picks up an aluminum plate on a second-floor windowsill that lands near a cat who quickly startles. We could blame the wind for blowing the aluminum plate and startling the cat. We also could look elsewhere to assign fault. Who put the plate on the windowsill? To what extent do news reports on lawsuits, crises, scandals, disasters, crimes, or tragedies increase our sensitivity to blame? Do they encourage explanations for causes and consequences that saturate the mind with blameful thoughts?

The question of "Who is to blame?" is relevant to our examination of blame. Accurately assessing blame, even when the finger points back to us, is the first step in making a corrective action. On the other hand, when unwanted events occur, often we desperately seek something or someone to blame, and sometimes we seize on the most immediate or convenient scapegoat, which can prevent us from *ever* taking a truly corrective step.

WHO IS TO BLAME?

After years of development and testing, the time ship stood starkly sparkling on its launch pad with its eager crew of five ready to go. They heard the countdown: 10, 9, 8,

7, 6, 5, 4, 3, 2, 1—LAUNCH. Then the ship moved counterclockwise around Earth as the magnetic pull, like a giant sling, propelled the ship back toward the origins of time.

In a twinkle, the ship broke free of Earth's atmosphere. It was now two million years earlier. The crew peered transfixed. They did it! Captain Brown ordered, "Land!" After a few hours of examining the vegetation and electronically recording animal images, they captured a small dinosaur. Jane, the biologist, took its temperature. Yes, dinosaurs were warm-blooded creatures. Then she released it.

Mission accomplished, the crew returned to the ship. Jane hit the LOCK button and the titanium door slid into sealed position. With the crew members snuggled into their individual travel cocoons, Brown punched the REVERSE POLARITY button. The ship groaned, then slung faster and faster clockwise forward through time to where and when they started. Exiting their cocoons, the crew surveyed a barren world with scraggly trees, small yellow lizards, weird green birds, and giant red wormlike creatures. The worms herded some of the lizards into containers, while others of these small, scaly yellow creatures scampered and fled. Shocked, Brown exclaimed, "My God! We've erased our times."

In the time-space fantasy, we might conclude that when you mess with the past, you can change the future, perhaps dramatically and for the worse. Of course, you'd have to assume that all things are interconnected and that small, seemingly inconsequential actions can ripple through time and gather a momentum that leads to dramatic changes that can be known and understood only through their ultimate results. That fails as a generalization because billions of slight changes are taking place throughout the planet every second; if each of these changes had a dramatic long-term effect, we can only hope that a small change that could destroy the world would be countered by one that could save the world. Nevertheless, the "small changes" time-cause-effect chain may be valid in exceptional cases, as in the fourteenth century when fleas and rats from merchant ships carried the Black Death to Europe from Asia. This change killed between 25 and 50 percent of Europeans. In the arena of small changes, the challenge is to separate the relevant from the irrelevant and those with impact from those that are inconsequential.

Getting back to our fantasy, is it fair to heap blame on Brown, the crew, and whoever sent them on the trek? Despite Albert Einstein's theory of bending of time in space, time still moves forward and never backward. So, our time-travel story is a fictional example of cause-and-effect reasoning that differs little from the work of sophists who twist and distort reality to deceive the mind with paradoxes of unreality.

MENTAL GAMES AND BLAME

To blame, there must be a cause. But the cause need not be visible or real. As the philosopher Gilbert Ryle observed, many private events take place in the "theater of the mind." The following story depicts the art of creating a fictional theater-of-the-mind cause-effect-blame scenario.

While playing Frisbee, Leslie accidentally floated the disk over the neighbor's fence. As she walked toward the neighbor's door, she thought, "They will be mad at me if the Frisbee cut through their flowers." Then she thought, "It was an accident. They should understand." In carrying the debate further, she thought, "They have always been unreasonable people. How unfair of them to hassle me over the Frisbee." By the time she knocked on the door, she felt angry. Her neighbors opened the door and greeted her. Leslie snapped, "Why are you so mean?" Then she stormed off leaving her neighbors looking bewildered.

In this make-believe story, what caused Leslie's anger? Was it floating the Frisbee into the neighbor's yard? Why would she blame the neighbors for what was, in fact, an accidental event that *she* initiated? What caused her rapidly smoldering prediction of her neighbors' reaction? Predictably, the transactions that took place in the theater of her mind ballooned the Frisbee event into an angry sequence of blame in which anticipation of receiving unwarranted blame led her to project blame onto her perceived attackers. Ryle reminds us that this theater is an "I-land."

We need to alert ourselves to inventions of the mind that cause unwanted blame consequences. Words and imagination, for example, can turn small events into crises, minimize the seriousness of an event, pulverize reality, or create paradoxes that exist only in the mind. Ryle tells of the Greek Philosopher Zeno of Eleu who titillates us with a paradox. Zeno tells us that when you shoot an arrow, it travels half the distance to its target, then travels half the remaining distance, and then half the remaining distance, and so forth. Following this model, the arrow never hits the target.

Zeno's paradox introduces us to that mental part of the world of cause and effect where word games substitute for stark realities. For example, the cause of firing an arrow will have the effect of the arrow traveling until it hits a mark, usually within a matter of seconds. Would Zeno have stood in place of the target? Of course not. A well-directed arrow would have hit him, as he well knew. However, in the world of the mind, we can effortlessly create a surrealistic world that extends beyond the perimeter of reality. Because of the art of self-deception, mental chains of cause and effect prove challenging to figure out, especially in a psychological world where sorting truth from sophistry involves a clear perception and perspective about what is going on in the theater of the mind.

THE BRUNT OF BLAME

Have you ever been the brunt of blame where you were entirely innocent and couldn't do anything to change the outcome? Chances are that practically every reader can describe at least one such personal experience.

People make other people into scapegoats for their troubles and dispense blame for no good reason other than their targets are vulnerable to such blame. Amber's plight introduces us to this sometimes-murky private realm of cause, effect, and blame. Amber opened the door, put her school books at her desk, and walked to the kitchen where she saw her parents gulping their homemade beer. Upon seeing her, her stepfather arose, walked over to her, and smacked her. Stunned, Amber backed away. Her mom said, "We know you've done something rotten at school today. Let that be a lesson to you." Amber ran to her room crying. What could she possibly have done? Despite that she could not think of anything, she felt like a terrible person.

Blame can result for no apparent reason other than someone made something up in his or her head. Prior to this parental act of hostile sophistry, Amber actively sought to be good to avoid punishment. Her disturbed and inebriated parents acted irrationally toward her, and their condemnation of her reigned over reason. But, as a young adolescent, how was she to know that their reaction was irrational? Fortunately, a kindly neighbor took Amber under his wing and helped her see that the fault lay with her parents' refusal to stop getting drunk, that she had many fine traits and qualities that would be with her forever, and that moving in with her father was a better option than living in her current dysfunctional environment. Amber moved in with her dad and new stepmother and escaped the blame game.

Again, the point is that we need to see through to the underlying causes when we are blamed in order to assess whether we are worthy of blame or if we are merely being scapegoated. And when we find ourselves blaming others, as Amber's parents did, it's vital that we dig into ourselves to discover whether we are doing so accurately and justifiably, or whether we are misdirecting blame that should find its target elsewhere, possibly on ourselves.

CHOICE AND BLAME

Most reasonable people won't cast blame when factors are out of a person's control. They are more inclined to blame people who engage in premeditated actions that lead to negative results. A toddler staggers and knocks over a lamp. Most write this off as typical for a child learning to walk—since the child has not yet learned to control his or her movements or even mastered the concept that falling against a lamp causes it to fall. On the other hand, when the shoplifter tells the judge, "Your honor, I was destined to steal the shirt. It was written in the stars," the judge will probably respond, "Did the stars tell you that you would go to jail for the theft? Thirty days."

We are not born blank slates. We actively interact with our world from the moment of birth, and we influence what happens, sometimes more than we are influenced. Free will, or the ability to choose one direction when we could have chosen others, suggests that our sense of control lies within us and that we can definitely influence events around us. If so, we are responsible for our actions. We made the choice. We get the credit for blame or praise for the result. But, at times, our choices are contaminated: We lack information, act out of ignorance, suffer from some form of diminished capacity, operate under forced time pressures, get distracted by our emotional entanglements, shift attention, lose concentration, or fall victim to normal human foibles and faults including forgetfulness. Are we responsible for contaminated choices that turn out wrong? Sometimes, and especially when we anticipated the risk and could have taken reasonable steps to reduce it.

What Happens by Design?

Our biology, temperaments, learning, and cultural experiences contribute significantly and often seamlessly to how we think and what we do. Assuming this view has merit, at least part of our behavior is shaped by predisposing factors that are normally outside of conscious control. It is a magical leap, however, to declare ourselves the subjects of powerful and sometimes mysterious forces, and to say that these forces bear the blame for whatever goes wrong. Yet a sizable block of the U.S. population attributes significant chunks of their lives to conditions beyond their control, including "magical forces." To one degree or another, members of this externalizing group believe their destiny is predetermined. Some New Age group members may argue that their histories are charted for them through the positions of the stars at the moment of their birth. Radical behaviorists argue that our behavior is exclusively shaped by environmental rewards and penalties. A minister tells us that God has a master plan for us. Thus, when things go wrong, people with various determinist beliefs might pass off blame by saying "The devil made me do it." "It's not my fault." "It's in my genes." "I was a victim of bad conditioning." When events prove favorable, we might hear: "I was blessed." "I was lucky."

Many of us find these exotic external explanations intuitively appealing. When supported by complicated arguments or appeals to faith, purely external explanations can excite our imagination while conveying a false sense of certainty. But to what extent do they adequately explain reality?

Although it is tempting to "blame the fates" when things go wrong, people who believe in self-development will tend to take responsibility for their choices. They'll concentrate on finding ways to solve personal problems and to act to meet challenges head-on as a means to develop and grow. The alternative is to wait for a miracle or to declare that whatever bad happens comes about from something like bad karma—a phenomenal leap of cause-and-effect faith where you get punished for what you did from a past life until you reach nirvana, a state of bliss and liberation from rebirth.

Unconscious Motivation and Blame

"Are we aware of what causes or motivates our behavior? The founder of psychoanalysis, Sigmund Freud, proclaimed that human events do not happen by accident and that normally we are unconscious of what motivates our behavior and predisposes us to different conflicts throughout our lives. According to this theory, the events that explain our current conduct already have occurred deep in our past, sometimes before we learned to speak, and involve primitive sexual and aggressive impulses. The methods for getting at these "preordained truths," however, are controversial and unsupportable.

The analyst Otto Rank theorizes that our separation from our mothers at birth produces a trauma that predisposes us to separation anxiety. However, studies of the sensory process of infants suggest that they do not have the capacity to record the sensations of birth sufficiently well to recall them later. For this reason, credible professionals no longer accept birth trauma theory to explain anxiety.

If I am motivated by unconscious forces, does that mean if I walk outside and a branch hits me on the shoulder, it was meant to be? A psychoanalyst might say that I had an unconscious awareness of the weakness of the branch and getting hit was an act of self-punishment because the timing of this event happened by intent and not by accident. This argument is as silly as saying an arrow will never hit its target because its flight perpetually covers successive half distances or saying that there are angels dancing on heads of pins because we can't prove that they don't exist.

Do people who repeatedly get fired from their jobs operate with unconscious intent and repeat childhood battles with autocratic parents? Perhaps. But consider these alternatives. Some bosses act irrationally and their irrationality invites contention. Some members of this group may be incompetent in performing their key job functions, choose the wrong career direction, procrastinate excessively, worry and get distracted from attending to necessary details, display quirks that perturb coworkers, or abuse alcohol and drugs during the workweek. Although in some cases some people replay childhood conflict with authority figures, the outcome also could relate to a combination of "small" matters that add up to a major work-performance issue.

Despite the flaws in the analytic position, if you wish to avoid blame, psychoanalysis has an appealing feature. If you are the analysand, you might conclude that your parents bear the responsibility for your disturbance, and you probably can blame your mother for not being nurturing enough. Now that you've gotten yourself off the hook for your troubles, what do you do to improve the quality of your life?

Some self-defeating patterns do start early in life and come about partially because of environmental conditions. People do repeat early conflicts. Freud was right in this observation but was largely wrong in positing that infant childhood sexual and aggressive impulses are at the root of trauma and later disturbance. For example, George, a client, grew up in a blue-collar neighborhood. His parents emphasized getting a good education and strongly supported his academic efforts. George performed excellently in school and attended a quality college. However, following graduation, he obtained work far beneath his educational level and proven abilities. His problem was complicated and partly involved feelings of insecurity complicated by a low level of work aspiration that was out of sync with his demonstrated academic performance and academic confidence. Who or what is to blame for George's original plight?

George soon resolved the disparity when he came to realize that his self-image excluded conventional definitions of career success. He saw himself operating at a blue-collar level. As his self-view did, however, include challenging himself, he realigned his career objectives to coincide with his interest in challenging himself. He questioned the basis for his insecurity. Because of these developmental efforts, he's now progressing in a challenging career. The solution came from George discovering the reasons for his career frustration, followed by restructuring his thinking, feelings, and actions so that he felt confident about what he thought and did.

BREAKING A CAUSE-AND-EFFECT SELF-BLAME CHAIN

Some repetitive cause-effect-blame sequences are frustrating patterns. For example, you typically subordinate your rights to serve others' interests. You blame yourself by calling yourself a wimp. A cause-and-effect problem-solving approach can help put this psychological blame situation in perspective. We'll use Tom's case as an example.

Tom had an abnormal sensitivity to rejection. He routinely agreed to do favors and to help people out, even when he neither had the time nor the resources. Yet he thought he couldn't say no because he feared if he did, he would be rejected. The following eight-point framework shows how Tom overcame a frustrating, repetitive, cause-effect-blame pattern.

1. *What are the causes?* (e.g., People ask me to do them favors, such as serve on committees, drive them to the shopping mall, or engage in other time-consuming activities that benefit them at my expense.)
2. *What are the effects?* (e.g., I don't allow myself adequate time to complete my own personal projects. I do things I frequently dislike doing. I feel "imposed upon." I feel frustrated and inadequate. I frequently engage in activities that I dislike doing in order to act pleasing. I fear disapproval.)
3. *What are the examples of blame?* (e.g., My friend tells me that it's my fault that people walk all over me, that I'm a wimp for allowing this to happen, and that I treat my friend like a second-class citizen by doing favors for people who don't reciprocate. I dump on myself and resent myself for resenting myself. I whine and complain about this condition.)
4. *What are the consequences?* (e.g., Acquaintances don't contact me unless they want something from me. My friend has told me to stop whining and deal with my problem or find someone else to listen to my complaints.)
5. *What are the short-term benefits of taking no action to change?* (e.g., Short-term benefits include allowing myself to avoid the uncertainties and risks of refusing to comply with acquaintances' requests.)
6. *What are the long-term benefits for continuing the pattern?* (Other than repeat short-term benefits, there is no meaningful long-term benefit.)
7. *What changes hold promise for breaking this cause-effect-blame-consequence cycle?* (e.g., a) Practicing saying no to people who ask me to use my time on projects that favor their interests and that simultaneously distract from my interests. b) Becoming selective in choosing activities that promote personal advantage and that also allow me to make a contribution. c) Building sales resistance by asking for time to think so as to avoid making an impulsive decision for the wrong reasons. d) Testing diplomatic skills for turning people down to minimize bad feelings. e) Using an escalation approach that relies on increasingly stronger levels of refusal for those who won't take no for an answer. f) Exploring why I think I need approval to ac-

cept myself. g) Convincing myself that I still can accept myself even when others are disappointed. h) Refusing to put myself down by focusing on my strengths more than on my faults. i) Resisting complaining by shifting my focus to matters that are of mutual interest between me and my friend.)

8. *What are the advantages and benefits to testing the change solutions?* (e.g., Discovering and developing my strengths, learning my limitations, and effectively meeting the inevitable challenges of meeting people on a level playing field. Fewer unwanted obligatory activities. Increased self-confidence. Freedom from a very exasperating cause-effect-blame-consequence trap.)

This same process can help you get to the bottom of a cause-effect-blame pattern.

POSTSCRIPT

The founder of Individual Psychology, Alfred Adler, saw vanity at the heart of blame: "The vain one always knows how to shift the responsibility for any mistake to the shoulder of another. He is always right. The others are always wrong." From this radical perspective, causes are always external. Other people need to change. Self-improvement is not necessary because you can't improve on perfection. This form of vanity, and accompanying preferences toward blaming others, causes stagnation in personal growth and development.

In seeking relationships among cause, effect, and blame, we can approximate the truth and accept our best judgment with humility by recognizing the possibility that we could be wrong. Instead of assuming that the problem lies with others, or even in an unconscious part of ourselves, we continue to search for the actual causes of problems and work at resolving them. In accepting these truths, we set conditions to live with courage.

5

Foibles, Flaws, and Blame

> *Understanding human foibles and faults*
> *is wiser than denying them.*

Mark Twain wrote, "I've had many problems in my life, most of which didn't happen." Twain's humorous saying captures a very normal human tendency: At different times, practically all people fabricate fallacies and humble themselves before the demons they create. Fretting over invented problems is a notable human capability. Fortunately, we have many great abilities to countermand reality falsifications.

Human follies, flaws, frailties, foibles, and faults are pervasive and merit a volume of their own. For example, people blame themselves, or are blamed, for the results of forgetfulness, faulty assumptions, suggestibility, and superstitious thinking. Fortunately, we can reduce the instances of some of these "causes" that can lead to consequences and blame. But we can never be perfect!

FORGETFULNESS

Have you tried to recall a word that you once knew and later the word popped to mind? Psychologists call this the tip-of-the-tongue phenomenon. Have you ever driven on a highway, gotten absorbed in thought, and had amnesia for what happened the prior minute or so? Even though you are aware of your surroundings, you can blank out the memory of surroundings when distracted. Have you put down an umbrella at a restaurant and forgotten it, forgotten where you put your keys, failed to remember someone's name after you were just introduced, or had a great insight and then almost instantly forgot it? Forgetting umbrellas, keys, names, and ideas often results from your mind drifting or when something happens to disrupt short-term memory. Memory is normally vulnerable to interruption.

Memory, especially short-term memory, is fragile. Arbitrary information, such as a new phone number, vanishes from short-term memory unless rehearsed. Some people have trouble concentrating or remembering when they are in a situation with multiple stimuli to distract their attention. These stimuli can interfere with the retention of some of what is happening. For example, have you tried to concentrate on something, then been interrupted and forgotten what you were thinking? That is a classic condition for evoking frustration.

Most people will admit to forgetfulness. Nevertheless, people commonly blame others for misplaced papers, keys, files, or other items, when, in fact, it is their naturally faulty memories that are to blame. It is a paradox to admit to forgetting, then refuse to build the possibility of forgetfulness into an equation when something goes wrong and blame others for the losses while thinking "I couldn't have forgotten." As a good test for the fallibility of memory, recall all the multiple-choice tests you've ever taken that were based on information you read or heard. I'll bet you were not 100-percent accurate. If you were 100-percent accurate all through school, you are the rare exception.

Although we sometimes forget what we want to remember, we also can remember what we want to forget. The mind has the power to generate haunting memories. Remembrances pressed through hot emotions remain locked in the mind with greater impact than would a chapter from a boring text. Although hot emotional reactions are normally short-lived, we have the power to keep the representative events alive in the mind even when we want to stop thinking about them.

This ability to rekindle emotional intensity through the recollection of a hot event illustrates how thinking and beliefs can and often do evoke strong emotions. When engaged in hot extension-of-blame thinking, we risk clouding our problem-solving judgment with strong emotions such as hate. Finding ways to change this language of blame, in order to drop the extension, can change the quality of the emotion.

ASSUMPTIONS AND BLAME

An assumption is where we take something for granted without support or proof. Yet we live in a world where it is necessary to make assumptions. Many of these assumptions revolve around trust. You assume that the gallon of milk you bought was pasteurized. You assume your automobile will start. You assume the chair you are about to sit on won't collapse or the ceiling above your head won't fall down on you. You assume your best friend will stand by you in a crisis. These trust assumptions grow from empirical experience—what you directly observe. It's rare that repeated empirical experiences prove incorrect. However, when your car won't start, your assumption is wrong in that instance.

We develop assumptions to reduce uncertainty and to guide decisions. Some decisions we make on the run. You hear a used car salesperson's pitch about the quality of a four-year-old automobile driven carefully by a very finicky banker. You listen with skepticism as you observe that the wavy patterns on the driver's side door and rear quarter panel suggest that the automobile was sideswiped and repainted. The new gas and brake pedals and spark plug wires suggest that the vehicle had traveled more than the thirty thousand miles registered on the odometer. Based on these observations and assumptions, you conclude that the salesperson misrepresented the vehicle and you shop elsewhere. You could be wrong, but the evidence seems compelling.

Some assumptions deal with ego desires. Most of us prefer good affiliations, intimacy, respect, approval, accomplishment, being right, and maintaining a good image. We can interfere with these ego desires through smudging our wishes with assumptive blame.

Assumptive Blame

Assumptive blame is where you assume that someone did wrong and deserves retribution. The extrasensory perception (ESP) illusion shows one way that people can fall into this assumptive blame trap. ESP illusion people assume that their interests are universally valid and that other people "should" be able to read their minds and anticipate their wishes. Transfixed by the ESP illusion, people will leapfrog over reality and blame others for a lack of sensitivity. Since most people can't read minds, those who demand this of others will have many occasions to feel flustered, frustrated, and frazzled. Wanda's story describes how assumptive blame can come about.

Wanda felt angry with Lois. She believed that Lois *should* know enough to phone and ask how she, Wanda, was faring after her divorce became final. She assumed that a good friend would make this inquiry and that Lois *should* know of her grief. Wanda concluded that Lois was a selfish and insensitive friend. When Lois phoned Wanda to invite her to dinner, Lois heard a cool decline.

If you feel intensely about something, do your emotions validate your assumptions? Sometimes. For example, Wanda let her ego rule over her reason. She angrily believed she was right. She assumed her angry feelings supported her belief. What would change if Wanda assumed that Lois was preoccupied with a personal tragedy and might appreciate Wanda's efforts to reach out to her?

People who feel worthless define themselves as worthless. This *assumptive worthlessness* is a myth: A definition is not the same as a fact. Tony assumed he was a worthless wimp because he did not obtain an expected promotion to the head of his department. To examine this assumption, I encouraged him to consider that while a promotion may prove advantageous, how does losing an advantage equal worthlessness? Then Tony looked at the difference between disappointment and worthlessness. His disappointment was legitimate. Defining himself as worthless was folly.

Exasperating Expectations

A friend asked me to look at an antique truck. I walked out among a parking lot of vehicles and looked about for the truck. At first I couldn't find it. Hark—it was a pigmy-size truck no bigger than a low-lying motorized golf cart. I was looking for a standard-size vehicle. I expected—made a forward-looking judgment—an occurrence that wasn't true.

Few people go through life without expecting one thing and seeing another. These deviations are like looking for a large truck that isn't there.

Some expectations can lead to exasperation. For example, Tammy mentioned to Joe that she saw a great-looking necklace at the jewelry store. Later that day she sent him out for a loaf of bread. When he returned with the bread, she blamed him for not buying the necklace. As she explained, the jewelry store was next to the supermarket. Earlier she had given him a hint that she wanted the necklace. She assumed he knew the necklace was important to her, and she expected him to take the hint and "surprise" her with the necklace.

I asked Tammy why Joe should have known to buy the necklace. She responded, "Any sensitive husband would know enough to do this." When I asked her if she told him which necklace she wanted, she said, "No." I asked her how Joe was to know which among the store's necklaces she wanted. Tammy was stumped, then said, "He should have asked."

When we look forward to a desirable event, we have an *expectancy*. You hope your team will win. With that hopeful expectancy, you'll probably feel happy with a victory and disappointed with a defeat. On the other hand, when we demand, require, or insist on a result to satisfy our ego expectations, this demanding form of expectation leaves us with little room to move, such as when Tammy expected Joe to execute her wish without letting him know what she wanted.

Breaking Out of the Assumptive Blame Trap

Practically anyone willing to put time and rational thought to the task of thinking clearly can reduce needless blame and extension-of-blame thinking. Clear thinking is incompatible with assumptive forms of blame. You can boost your clear-thinking skill by following these four steps:

1. Recognize the cause-and-effect chain of emotional strain that starts with faulty assumptions and demanding expectations. You can do this by writing out your assumptions and expectations and then matching them against their results. The exercise is useful in exposing faulty thinking.

2. Reformulate assumptions by making them into probability statements, such as "I think it is likely that this will happen." The results will either support or not confirm your prediction.

3. Emphasize expectancies and deemphasize expectation-based thinking. Ask yourself, "Am I making a probability statement (expectancies), or am I engaging in a speculative expectation?

4. Use the phrase "I assume" when you present assumptions. This change shifts perspective from certainty thinking to probability thinking. By training yourself to tell yourself "I assume" before you announce a judgment, you are likely to get the facts in those ambiguous situations where it is important to have valid information. People who hear the phrase "I assume" have a legitimate opening to confirm or not confirm any assumptions that apply to them.

THE TRIPLE-S PATTERN

Suggestibility, sensitivity, and sentimentality contribute to empathy, social stability, and the development of friendships. This *triple-S pattern* can become a liability when each condition gets excessive.

Suggestion

Suggestion is powerful. You're tempted to eat ice cream after you see a commercial advertising that tasty product. A quintessential example of the power of suggestion is the placebo effect. A placebo can be an inert substance used to reinforce people's expectation they will get well. Twenty-five to 50 percent of people with anxiety reactions who take a "sugar pill" that they believe is a powerful antianxiety drug experience a reduction in their level of anxiety and attribute the change to the pill. But suggestion can create negative placebo effects. Your friend tells you that you look "ill." After the comment, you feel slightly sick. Some neophyte psychology students, while reading a text on abnormal psychology, will worry about having symptoms of mental illness.

Children live in a world of magic where words can suggest a false reality. A young child hearing about "ground fishing" (where you fish off the shore of a pond) may imagine fish coming out of the ground to chase a lure. Some children, after hearing that you can catch a bird by putting salt on its tail, will run after birds with a salt shaker.

Children are especially vulnerable to suggestion. Suppose you told a group of young children with runny noses that this is a sign of alien abduction. You add convincing details that aliens invade our minds in the form of dreams. Dreaming is the sign of alien abduction. Among this group, some children will be obedient to the authority who planted the suggestion. Within this group, the children may reinforce each other's expectations, and this alien abduction theme becomes a "collective reality" for them.

Suggestible people can be led to doubt themselves and to accept blame for things they didn't do. George tells Sally that she ruined his sex life because she lacks passion. Sally felt less passionate after George's comment. She resented George for blaming her and felt less sexy with him. George created a self-fulfilling prophesy.

If Sally had really thought it through, she may have realized that George's accusation lacked merit. Then she could have helped George find the true cause of his sexual dysfunction. Or she may have come to the conclusion that George's accusations did have merit and could have taken constructive steps to tackle the problem. Instead, by reacting to George's blaming suggestion, she deepened their sexual problem and added resentment to the mix. On the other hand, George may have leveled the blame at Sally because he sensed her suggestibility and willingness to accept the blame. It may have been easier for George simply to accuse

Sally—and have her accept the blame—than to explore the true causes for his problem.

Sensitivity

Sensitivity refers to your ability to tune in to what is happening around you or in to your own feelings and thoughts. It also refers to your awareness of other people's thoughts and feelings and how you impact them. This psychological process allows you to recognize such matters as other people's feelings, their sincerity, and their motivations.

If something doesn't feel right about a situation, your sensitivity may be at work. Although this *sensitivity* is a strength, oversensitivity can contribute to a troubled state of mind. Overly sensitive people have finely attuned emotional antennas. They are prone to blame others for hurting their feelings or they blame themselves for imagined inadequacies. They also are prone to worry. Because they present themselves as vulnerable, their friends tend to walk on eggs around them. In special cases of oversensitivity to anticipated loss, some people act self-protective to avoid intimacy, but their intimacy fears contribute to the feared state of abandonment and loss.

Sentimentality

Sentimentality arises out of emotional perceptions. You see a sad movie and cry. You hear a familiar song and feel nostalgic. Sentiment is a strength when your subjective views promote closeness with people who are important to you, but, when maudlin, sentimentality can get in the way of relationships.

Sentimentality can triumph over reason and prove handicapping. You hold on to possessions, such as an old blanket. By adding a tint of animism, you act as if you believe that the blanket would feel upset if given up. As a result, you might live in a cluttered environment where you fear getting rid of items that most people would discard.

The Dysfunctional Triple-S Pattern

People who are overly suggestible, sensitive, and sentimental risk magnifying situations out of proportion and feeling vulnerable. As autosuggestible creatures, we can invent far-fetched possibilities and then magically leap from these inventions to a false certainty where we believe we know who or what is to blame for something that may not have happened. When sensitive to such suggestive inner whispers, we can amplify our murmurings to suspiciousness as we weave often-unrelated bits of reality and fantasy into a logic-tight conviction. Further, when sentimentality propels these suspicions we become attached to those convictions, and often we are shocked when our taken-for-granted blame assumptions conflict with reality.

SUPERSTITIOUS THINKING

What do the following examples have in common? Step on a crack and break your mother's back. Avoid crossing a black cat's path. These magical solutions grow from a suggestion that we can appease the "fates" to prevent disaster. What purpose does it serve to knock on wood, carry a rabbit's foot, or hang a horseshoe over your door? These are magical solutions to bring luck. What do you gain when you wear a talisman such as a cross? Perhaps you can scare away a vampire. In these cases of magical believing, the wish is to gain advantage and avoid disaster and blame. Sadly, such superstitious thinking rarely does more than create a false optimism and paradoxical fatalism.

We see evidence of superstitious thinking every day. Some people wear the same socks for "luck." We might fool ourselves into thinking we have a "sixth sense," as when we avoid attending a sports event believing that our presence will cause our team to lose. If we stay away and our team wins, we attribute this to our sixth sense. Nevertheless, it is unrealistic to believe that by magically avoiding a certain event, we can avoid an unwanted outcome that is unrelated to our magical solutions.

Superstitious thinking grows out of suggestibility. It serves to explain reality, reduce uncertainty, assure a favorable result, and avoid personal blame. For example, we see early examples of this suggestible-superstition capability in ancient Greek folklore. Records suggest that many Greeks held superstitious beliefs of powerful gods ruling Earth from atop Mount Olympus. When displeased, these gods rained disaster on the people below. So the Greeks erected monuments to please the gods and to avoid provoking their wrath. Seen as capricious characters, the gods would blame and hold grudges. It was important for the Greeks to avoid blame to avoid destruction. Their magical explanations disappeared in Western culture when science provided real explanations for natural phenomena. Still, today we can visit "psychics" who proclaim they can foretell our future. Yet some of these same people may have been arrested by undercover police for fraud before they could see what was coming.

We are not far from our superstitious roots when we enter the world of the perfectionist. Perfectionism is a deficit philosophy based on a simple by unprovable assumption that to be worthy, one must be perfect. Perfectionism involves this superstitious insight: The reason that things go wrong and that one feels stressed is due to imperfection. The solution, then, is to attain perfection. There are variations on this theme. Some people hold to standards that they consider reasonable but that prove unrealistic. The person with a C average believes that obtaining a B-plus average would lead to prestige and respect and without that, one is a flop. The grade, then, is the solution for worth. But this contingency-worth insight is no more valid than believing that crossing a black cat's path brings bad luck. It just sounds more sophisticated.

Exaggerated levels of stress, self-induced feelings of being overwhelmed, and subjective feelings of failure frequently follow the counterfeit, extremist, superstitious quest for perfection. Incredibly, a superstition that promises protection from blame is a prime catalyst for blame. There is no reasonable way people can achieve excellence and enjoy their lives by straining to attain a state of infallibility. So, when life does not go perfectly, perfectionists feel primed to blame.

Let's look at another example of superstitious perfectionist thinking: "If only I always knew the right thing to say, the clear way to think, or the effective way to act, then all would turn out well." Now the perfectionist's quest becomes one of finding the right "way." Because we can have no guarantees about how people will react to what we do or say, this view sets the stage for frustration and blame. As long as we live in a world of variables, the *perfect-way myth* is about as valid as believing that angry gods destroy crops.

POSTSCRIPT

Mark Twain quips, "Truth is the most valuable thing we have, let us economize it." He was, of course, intentionally expressing an incongruous view. Blame is normally unpleasant. Because of this truth, many people bend over backward to avoid blame. Indeed, some panic at the prospect of getting blamed. In the end, magical solutions and false beliefs about blame subvert the economies of truth.

6

Self-Consciousness, Shame, and Guilt

> *Without inhibition we'd have chaos.*

Donna entered the room and sat uneasily in her seat. This was her first group therapy session. She joined this new group to help herself deal with her insecurity. The group theme was self-consciousness, and Donna wanted to discover how to free herself from her painful preoccupations about herself.

Donna normally felt isolated and insecure. She was painfully aware of these feelings as she sat quietly trying to appear inconspicuous. Then she reminded herself that this time she was not going to let her insecurity get the better of her. She was going to fight these feelings. Nevertheless, this declaration did not cause change—such assertions rarely do! Instead, she felt her heart beating and her mind numbing as she drew deeper into herself by trying to come out of herself. Then she told herself, "I can't let this happen again." She hoped that an act of courage would help her to break the ice. So she forced herself to look around at the other group members.

As she shifted her eyes, Donna saw some people chatting, others were reading, and some sat quietly and inactive. She continued to feel frozen. She imagined she stood out in the crowd and felt that people were aware of her presence. She could see this was a silly idea, but she still felt self-conscious.

The group leader entered, sat down, introduced himself, and described what the group would be doing. He asked the members to introduce themselves, say a little about why they joined the group, and what they hoped to accomplish. As the different members spoke up, Donna's attention lapsed as she preoccupied herself thinking "They all seem to know what to say. What if I stumble on my words when my turn comes? What if I make a fool of myself?"

The moment arrived. The spotlight was on Donna. She hesitated, recovered, and finished her description. Nevertheless, she felt very self-conscious. Her neck blotched red spots. Her mind whirled. She experienced a familiar wave of shame. "Why did I hesitate?" she thought. "How could I sound so inarticulate?" As her inner dialogue expanded, she was sure that she made a fool of out herself. She expected that the group would reject her because she sounded as though she didn't have any ideas to contribute. Then her attention shifted to believing that she had let the group down. She anticipated that she would again disrupt the group with her hesitations, have nothing worthwhile to say, and waste the group's time. She thought she deserved to die for this infraction. Meanwhile, no one in the group noticed what was going on in her head.

Does this scenario sound familiar to you? This process of self-blame based on self-consciousness, shame, and guilt is common; at its worst, it can paralyze you and diminish your perception of the choices you have in life. We'll break down how this process works and what you can do to stop it.

Donna's reaction illustrates the extreme edges of self-consciousness, fear, shame, and guilt, and how they lead to self-blame. When people feel shame, they act as if they believe their entire "self" is exposed, naked. Donna was self-conscious to the point that she became self-enveloped. She worried excessively about herself relative to others' opinions of her. She dwelled on her belief that she was a social misfit. She measured herself by her own stiff social standards—standards she assumed were shared by others. Her internal monologue percolated with shame and blame because she believed that she exposed weakness and impeded the progress of the entire group. She blamed and damned herself for intruding into it. Although she falsified and exaggerated reality, her feelings of insecurity that flowed from these self-deceptions were true to her thinking.

Donna experienced *convoluted guilt:* She anticipated causing the group future harm, and she blamed and damned herself for something that did not happen! *Extensions of blame* aggressively intertwined with Donna's social fears. Her self-consciousness, shame, and guilt formed an anguishing alliance that extended directly to self-blame.

Over a period of weeks working with the group, Donna came to recognize the importance of dealing with her insecurity. She felt relieved when she discovered that most other group members had similar insecurities. That awareness taught her that she was not unique. By learning how to parcel out and deal with the overlapping, interacting self-consciousness, shame, and guilt, and by learning new self-acceptance and expressive skills, Donna graduated from the group with greater command over her "self." Before she left, the leader asked where her insecurity went. Donna laughed, then said, "I don't care and I have no intention of inviting such an unwanted guest back into my life."

SELF-CONSCIOUSNESS

Our ability to become conscious of ourselves is hardwired. We begin to develop self-awareness as small children, around the time we can recognize ourselves in a mirror. This self-awareness separates us from other animals, with the possible exception of chimpanzees and orangutans, who also can recognize themselves in mirrors.

After we develop an ability to categorize, we begin to compare categories, such as pleasant and unpleasant. We like the taste of some foods but not others. As we evolve through the stages of cognitive development, we refine our ability to evaluate. We also proceed through an acculturation process. We learn what members from our social group expect from us. These expectations involve rules, roles, and responsibilities. Here we learn "right" and "wrong."

Reading, 'riting, and 'rithmetic are three Rs of school learning. Rules, roles, and responsibilities are three Rs that represent common standards against which we judge and evaluate. When we see someone violating the rules, or challenging our role, or questioning our responsibility, we might react with blame. If we believe we've violated one or more of the Rs, we could feel emotions such as shame, guilt, embarrassment, and humiliation.

Self-awareness develops naturally in a social group. This process is both conditionable and conditional. Some people learn to focus on goals, take initiatives, and follow a feedback loop where experience becomes knowledge that feeds invention that applies to the next set of challenges. They judge their efforts—and sometimes themselves—by how close they come to meeting their goals. At the other extreme, some people, like Donna, are preoccupied with how they feel about themselves, what others think about them, the potential for rejection, and personal inadequacy. They feel highly conspicuous. This is what we commonly call a global self-consciousness. The "ness" in consciousness separates a normal feeling of being ill at ease with aspects of the "self" from a conscious, subjective, global, uncomfortable awareness of self.

Depending on cultural conditioning, self-conscious reactions vary. A preadolescent Aboriginal girl runs naked through the village and jumps into the river with her friends. Meanwhile her father sits among the tribal chiefs, grabs a piece of meat from the fire, eats it with his hands, burps, and rubs his greasy hands on his legs to clean them. The tribal members pay no marked attention to either event but probably would to another one that they consider taboo, such as clacking sticks together. If the same event took place in suburbia, the child's mother might feel mortified and the child would quickly learn to become more conscious of what is expected of her. If her "middle-class" father grabbed a slab of steak from a grill during a neighborhood party, ate it with his hands, burped, and wiped his hands on his white slacks, eyes would roll. It is unlikely, however, that either event would occur in suburbia because of a long acculturation process that instills socially acceptable behavior.

Social Structuring

Social living is complex. To affiliate with others, we have to subordinate some of our impulses, interests, and wishes and act with restraint. Ideally, we do this without sacrificing too much spontaneity or personality.

Civilization's prime directive to people is that they give ground to gain ground. We give up some freedom to gain the collective advantages that an organized group provides. An organized society provides and requires an established and predictable degree of orderliness, uniformity, restraint, and structure. Indeed, it is the ability to organize and transmit information that probably gave our Cro-Magnon ancestors an edge over Neanderthals who seem, from archaeological remains, to have operated without passing down information in story form.

Established order binds the individual to routines. We enjoy structure in such forms as 1) different jobs for different people; 2) a fixed time for breakfast, lunch, and dinner; 3) government duties and obligations including obeying laws and paying taxes; and 4) standard procedures such as which side of the road to drive. Nevertheless, within socially prescribed structures, we have considerable latitude in expression and choice.

Self-Consciousness and Fear

People comply with authority to gain approval and to avoid feeling different. Psychologist Stanley Milgram's experiments in compliance show that humans have a strong tendency to go along with what they are told if the directive comes from someone in authority. In a series of classic experiments, Milgram's subjects were instructed to increase the level of an electrical shock they delivered to a person in an experimental room. They delivered the shock by a remote device each time the person in the experiment made a mistake. They started off delivering a mild shock. Then the authority told them to increase the shock. This escalation continued past the time the subjects believed the shocks reached dangerous levels. Sixty-five percent obeyed the authority and continued to the highest levels. Meanwhile the person receiving the shock wailed in pain and asked that the experiment stop. Unbeknownst to the person delivering the shock, the receiver faked the pain. Could the people holding the shock button know this was a fake? To eliminate this factor, the experiment was repeated with puppies that actually received a shock. The results were the same. A combination of compliance and a step-by-step process of getting used to inflicting pain partially explain the results. But are we a species that enjoys watching pain? Other explanations offer a higher level of plausibility.

Organizations of people would not have come into existence if suggestibility, self-consciousness, and compliance proneness were not built in to human psychology. Shame and guilt are expressions of punitive self-conscious emotions that powerfully shape what we do and do not do. Understandably, fear of blame, fear of the feeling of shame, a desire to avoid the nagging qualities of guilt, and fear of retribution assert a compelling internal control over the conduct of billions of people.

Babylonian kings, Egyptian pharaohs, Roman emperors, and other early rulers recognized that they could, in various ways, both shape human thinking and prescriptively channel people's choices by taking advantage of their subjects' biological proclivities to experience self-consciousness. They constrained them by using cultural structures to cause them to internalize rules and standards. Controlling behavior by having people shame or blame themselves for social infractions can result from this conditioning process.

The ancient Babylonian king Hammurabi established a code of justice and presented it in the form of 282 laws. He established punishments for antisocial behaviors, such as murder and theft, and for irresponsible behavior, such as failure to pay debts and taxes.

Hammurabi's primary genius was in how he influenced compliance by playing on people's self-consciousness.

1. Threats of punishment create self-consciousness. Hammurabi said that his laws reflected the wishes of the gods and whoever violated the laws, the gods would curse. So even if Hammurabi didn't see what was happening, a deity would and then would deal a lethal punishment at an unpredictable time. Hammurabi's threats of godly reprisals were important. They showed how authority figures could exert control over people's behavior by manufacturing myths and fictions that could play on their self-consciousness and fears.*
2. Blending self-consciousness with fear creates conditions for inhibiting behavior. Hammurabi's strategy involved drawing upon prevailing popular beliefs about powerful gods and declaring that the gods authored the codes; this added a dimension of fright to induce the population into compliance so that Hammurabi could maintain order.
3. People are suggestible, and this capacity cements the social contract. Once a belief in godly retribution enters everyday commerce and spreads, people tend to reinforce it among themselves. The "true believers" will pressure others toward conformity to the belief or rule. Adults will shape children's behavior such that they internalize the rules over a lengthy stepwise process that progressively moves them toward conformity. However, the illusion of the power of the gods must be maintained through ritual and reinforced through public punishment for this effect to hold up.

Social Casualties

When people have an exaggerated need for approval, does that represent a heightened sense of self-consciousness and a breakdown in social self-confidence? Probably. Those who suffer from unusually high levels of fear of disapproval straitjacket themselves to the detriment of their social experiences. They often cloud their social confidence when they:

➤ Concentrate on past negative social hurts and anticipate more of the same
➤ Expect rejection
➤ Obsess over feelings of inadequacy

---

*Early biblical injunctions included the Ten Commandments and assertions that God sees all. Rules of order also grew in the early days of Eastern cultures. Around 500 B.C., the Chinese sage Confucius suggested a way for the rulers of the Chinese people to move through life with morality and sound leadership. These "values" appeared in modified form in Japan circa 604. The regent prince, Shotoku Taishi, issued seventeen articles for living life. These values involve living in harmony with yourself and others; honoring the view that those who err can come back to the right path; leading a moral life; exhibiting clear judgment; promoting the common good; finding dignity in work; completing what you begin (even when it takes longer than you supposed); acting with loyalty; casting aside anger by recognizing one's own shortcomings; and examining the merit of the different positions that confound you.

➤ Feel helpless
➤ Experience a sense of social ineptitude
➤ Hold to an unrealistic need for control or guarantees
➤ Fear people or social situations for fictitious reasons

There is great power in a fear of rejection. To avoid this feeling, some people seek a false security by engaging in ongoing self-debates, such as "Should I say or do this?" "What will he or she or they think?" "I wonder if he or she or they like me, think I'm attractive, smart, witty . . ." This inner monologue reflects self-consciousness, but this self-envelopment solution invites social anxiety.

When you believe that the slightest nip of disapproval is an indictment against yourself, you're going to be overly cautious and increase your chances for what you fear occurring. Members of this subgroup create self-fulfilling prophesies. On the one hand, they fear disapproval, alienation, and devastation. On the other hand, because of their extreme social sensitivity, they limit their personal opportunities and self-induce the feelings of alienation and devastation that they fear. These oversocialized, self-conscious, individuals operate under oppressive emotional restraint because of an ill-guided fear of social sanctions. For example, these ideas include thinking of yourself as tongue-tied, socially inept, unattractive, or "sinful." This phenomenon occurs more often during adolescence. These thoughts ignite self-consciousness at a time when many people feel awkward as they shift from childhood to adulthood. Self-consciousness can, however, last a lifetime.

Social casualties include people who feel bottled up or fear to take social risks because they predict rejection, embarrassment, humiliation, disgrace, stigma, or shame. Interestingly, these reactions are often specific to certain situations. The more self-conscious among us can feel lighthearted and liberated from tension in zones of their lives where they feel confident of their abilities.

SHAME AND BLAME

Psychologists Nita Lutwak and Joseph Ferrari define shame as a socially involved self-conscious emotion that pivots on a negative evaluation of the entire "self."

Shame is rooted into our biology. It originates at a nonverbal level and eventually translates into a language that significantly mimics cultural expectations for the self. When shame links to language, words have the power to evoke the feeling. We see this in blame-shame cliché expressions we hear as children, such as: "Shame on you." "Look what you've done." "Bad boy." "Bad girl." "What's wrong with you?" "You're lazy." "Can't you get better grades?" "You're a disgrace." "How could you do this to me?" "Naughty." Such negative comments drip with criticisms that fire self-conscious feelings. After considerable social training, people often internalize and self-critically apply these clichés to themselves.

The power of self-consciousness occurs in shame cultures such as traditional Chinese families. People who follow tradition try to ensure they do not shame their community or ancestors. In traditional Iranian families, parents are responsible for shame brought about by their children's actions. Thus if a son goes bankrupt, the father is obliged to correct the wrongs of his son. That is because shame cultures tend to be collectivist cultures: The members of the group share the blame and shame. In individualistic cultures, such as the United States, the individual bears the brunt of the blame. Self-consciousness cuts across both cultural orientations. Blame and shame, of course, occur in degree in both collectivistic and individualistic cultures.

Some people adeptly get past shame clichés by realizing that these are alien ideas and refuse to accept them uncritically. In other instances, some people who are reared in largely shame-free homes and attend schools that deemphasize shame nevertheless develop irrational shame insights about themselves through their own invention or suggestibility.

Shame can have a lethal impact. The suicide rate for Japanese men who believe they disgraced their families or group is well documented. In that shame culture, shame has a stiff price. Over hundreds of years of social conditioning, there is a strong "moral" pressure to honor the group and do one's duty with honor, and there is great shame in failure.

However, you don't have to live in a culture of shame to cause yourself extreme distress. People living in a blame culture are vulnerable to equating their "self" worth with success. This irrational process can have pernicious effects. After the 1929 stock market crash, a small subpopulation of men who lost their fortunes—but not women—flung themselves out of Wall Street windows. For many people, avoiding blame and shame in the form of financial ruin was more important than life.

Inane Shame

Inane shame is a common source of needless emotional distress. It wails like wind through dark alleys of the mind, blowing mental debris in all directions. Within these alleys, shame and blame reach absurd limits. You feel ashamed of, say, your nose. You blame lost opportunities on that nose. It is the ridiculous, extreme irrationality of this shame game that makes it inane.

The founder of multimodal therapy, psychologist Arnold A. Lazarus, ponders: "To my mind, the shame game is predicated on views that are inculcated by parents and teachers. Nevertheless, it is far better, I think, to have someone who is capable of shame than to deal with psychopaths who have none. However, all therapists see those oversocialized neurotics whose lives are filled with needless shame, guilt, and self-consciousness. So many people are ashamed of their personal appearance, their parents, their homes, their cars and so on ad infinitum. Behind this lies another of my pet peeves—the ubiquitous emphasis on competition, of winning, of being number one and so forth. 'You should be ashamed of yourself!' is an oft-repeated parental admonition. The coach (parent figure) tells the team to hang their heads in shame for losing the match. Johnny is told that his parents are ashamed of him for failing his exam. It goes on and on."

When a person engages in an embarrassing and humiliating activity, Lazarus makes clear that shame can be an appropriate response. You deceive a friend and the friend discovers and confronts you with the deception. Lazarus also makes clear that people feel shame for inane reasons.

We can easily add to Lazarus's list. People self-consciously generalize about themselves because they disparage the shape of their toes, sound of their voices, physical conditioning, appearance of their mates, finances of their children's friends, acne or eczema conditions, bearing a disabled child, sexual performance, divorce, a dysfunctional relationship, and a drug or alcohol problem.

How is one to respond to recollections that evoke inane shame? Introduce some chaos into the shame process. Look for a factually accurate benefit derived from a re-called shame: What did you learn that is positive from the experience? Add a few positive clichés. For example, "The world didn't come to an end." "Life goes on." Feed yourself those clichés to balance other clichés about the woes of the shame experience, such as "I'll never live this down." Throw a little humor into the shame recollection. When you recall the shame experience, think of the song "It's the End of the World as We Know It." Done tongue-in-cheek, the song can produce a para-doxical effect that makes you feel more optimistic. Such activities counter inane shame perspectives.

Inventive Shames

We invent and inflict some forms of shame on ourselves. Three stand out: isolated shame, shame by proxy, and lingering shame.

Have you ever felt shame when nobody was around? When people feel shame without publicly exposing a deficiency, this shame represents an overly active sense of self-consciousness. For example, you look at your body in the mirror and focus on a feature you don't like. You feel shame and quickly try to hide what you believe is a fault. This shame is isolated because your shame reaction is a reflection of you judging you.

Shame by proxy is when an idea substitutes for a real event. You hold to lofty ideals where you expect perfection from yourself. You envision yourself erring before a group. You feel a twinge of shame as if you were performing before an audience.

What happens if you linger over a sense of shame that occurred in the distant past? You'll likely make yourself uncomfortable over a past event that you now have no ability to control. The lesson either has been learned, or it has not been. Like a pimple on the side of your face that turns to a pockmark, lingering memo-ries of a past event have their own emotional markings. However, the face is more than a pockmark. Focus on the mark and you'll see little of the face. Focus on the face and the mark means little. By analogy, focus on your memory of the construc-tive things you've accomplished, and a lingering shame can quickly fade into the background.

Inventive shames haunt the mind. Self-acceptance mutes their impact.

BLAME AND GUILT

You made a blunder and you don't feel ashamed but guilty. What's the difference? Shame involves generalizing about a perceived weakness of "self"; guilt involves self-criticism over a behavior. George Mason University psychologist June Tangney and her associates have noted that shame and guilt are distinct forms of moral self-consciousness. You feel ashamed of your "self" because you exposed a flaw or weakness, or violated a "prohibition." You feel guilt because you did the wrong thing. Are these reactions specific to situations? Tangney correctly found that whether a person responds with shame or guilt to a situation depends on his or her interpretation and evaluation of that situation. It's the way you think that makes the difference between guilt and shame.

You can separate shame and guilt. But these two states can still burn like two logs on the same fire of self-consciousness. It all depends on how you perceive, define, evaluate, assess, or judge yourself within the situation.

The Perils of Guilt

Psychologist Windy Dryden, Britain's leading proponent of rational emotive behavior therapy (REBT), describes guilt as "the enemy of understanding. Because when you blame yourself for what you did you are in no position to learn constructively from the experience."

People normally feel contrition, remorse, and regret for wrongful actions. These are healthy responses. Most reasonable people would then attempt to make amends, seek forgiveness, or act to undo the damage.

People with irrational guilt fall into a blame trap where they engage in extension-of-blame thinking: You damn yourself or proclaim yourself a slug for misbehaving rather than merely regretting the specific wrong.

Guilt can arise from how we act in different circumstances. A young woman believes that premarital sex is sinful. She experiences an orgasm during heavy petting. She enjoys the feeling but now believes she is a sinner. Caught in a conflict between a biological imperative and an irrational belief, she feels self-consciousness and guilt. You expect a certain level of performance out of yourself. You give a speech and your performance is less than what you expected from yourself. Now you add a few unpleasant self-critical ingredients. You declare that you should have done better, audience members wasted their time listening to you, you are a loser, and you might as well quit speaking in public. You feel guilty for wasting your audience's time. In both these cases, we see the cognitive signatures of guilt: rigid demands, failure to meet expectations, and self-blame.

Cognitive signatures are thought processes associated with a particular emotion. For example, the distress emotions of depression and anxiety have recognizable signatures. The cognitive signature of depression includes thoughts of helplessness, hopelessness, and self-blame. Anxiety involves both a premonition of disaster and a predicted inability to cope. Irrational guilt also has cognitive signatures that include a perceived violation of a principle or standard, an unrealistic demand that one should not have done what one did, and a sense of condemnation and intolerance. We'll look at how to defeat this form of guilt in the following section.

FREEDOM FROM SENSELESS SELF-CONSCIOUSNESS, SHAME, AND GUILT

Here are thoughts and exercises that can help people struggling to get beyond an overstuffed self-consciousness to break free.

Things to Think About

Here are ideas for defusing senseless forms of self-consciousness, shame, and guilt.

➤ When guilt links to unrealistic perfectionist standards, it pays to judge the definitions of the standards. Perfectionism involves two definitions that the person believes are true: 1) absolute definitions of what is right, wrong, good, bad, noble, and evil, and 2) contingency-worth definitions of the value of the "self" in reference to ability, appearance, or performance. If the first definition is false, then guilt for falling short is artificial. If the contingency-worth definition is false, blaming the "self" for operating outside of performance standards makes no sense. These two traps remind us of the word games that Zeno so aptly described in his paradox of the arrow that never strikes the target. The idea is seductive but unreal.

➤ Definitions do not have to reflect reality! They are not like indelible ink that won't come off. Just because you define yourself as "bad" doesn't make it so. If you are going to focus self-consciously on your "self," consider adjusting your definition of "self" to include all aspects of it, including all experiences past, present, and future. This creates a perspective that won't reasonably allow for a narrow definition of the "self." In this sense, a mistake can be thought of as similar to an instrument off pitch in a large orchestra. It is not so notable when you listen to the rest of the ensemble.

➤ When you make a good-faith effort, you are less likely to experience shame even if you fall short of accomplishing what you determined to do. So why not pick good-faith standards that you can stretch for and often attain? For example, many times you can meet the standard to do the best you can within the time and resources you have available.

➤ When in a self-conscious state of mind, you take an inward view. If you find yourself in this trap, make a radical shift. Watch the many events that take place around you. Note that you are not the center of the universe. When you recognize this, you may view yourself as better able to manage what you see taking place around you.

➤ When you feel self-conscious, instead of focusing on your insecurities, force yourself to refocus on what is going well in your life. Under the most miserable of circumstances, something is going well. As the psychiatrist Viktor Frankl discovered when condemned to a Nazi death camp, you can always find a basis for hope. Sometimes the smallest thing, such as watching an ant carry an item many times its size, can take your mind off a grim reality and help you focus on the positive.

➤ An irrational self-consciousness frequently represents shame and or guilt about your "self" and behavior. Separate the emotional blend of shame and guilt into manageable parts by separating the cognitive signatures of shame and guilt. For example, what do you tell yourself about your "self" that fits with your experience of shame? What cognitive signatures characterize the extension-of-blame ideas you apply to evaluate your conduct when you generate guilt? Now, can you find any ideas to disconfirm the self-critical dimensions of shame? Can you find a way to disconfirm extension-of-blame ideas associated with guilt?

➤ Extension-of-blame thinking turns inward to evoke guilt when you damn yourself. However, by accepting responsibility and accountability, and by refusing to damn yourself for your mistakes, you increase your chances to stop bedeviling yourself with self-punitive extension-of-blame thoughts. Free of irrational guilt, you have more personal resources available to manage the problem.

Stepping Out of Character

You wear an odd pair of socks in public and, upon recognizing this, feel shame. Psychologist Albert Ellis, who pioneered REBT, suggests that people perform shame-attacking exercises to simulate shame conditions in order to inoculate themselves against such reactions. The idea is to intentionally create conditions to show yourself that self-consciousness is a manufactured misery and that many of the things we feel embarrassed by or shame over fall into the same category. When you prepare yourself by developing a coping repertory for surprise exposures, you are less likely to react self-consciously. For example, wear odd-colored socks for a day. Put a bandage on your nose. The idea is to show yourself that you are not disgraced or embarrassed unless you believe you are. True, some discomfort may occur. However, through this process, you'll find that most people don't notice if one sock is blue and the other is brown; of those who do notice, most won't care. However, even if the whole world thought less of you for wearing odd-colored socks, you still have the power to accept your "self" and assert your right to be different. Although you may feel uncomfortable initiating social actions, intentionally bearing discomfort can help inoculate yourself against discomfort fears. As you build tolerance for discomfort, you are likely to develop social self-confidence.

Here are stepping-out-of-character exercises to help accomplish those results:

➤ Go to the local diner for breakfast. Ask for the unconventional one fried egg and one scrambled egg instead of two eggs the same style.

➤ If you want to work up to the two-eggs exercise, ask the food server to warm your cup before pouring your coffee, tea, or hot chocolate.

➤ Take off your watch and, in a matter-of-fact style, ask thirty different people for the time at a busy shopping mall. You'll probably note a broad range of responses from friendly to matter-of-fact to obvious avoidance. Such a range of responses can show that different people have their own social styles that are quite independent from what you do.

➤ Put on two different-colored shoes for a day.

➤ Wear an unusual hairstyle for a week.

➤ Wear a hat with a turkey feather for an afternoon.

➤ Whistle "Row, Row, Row Your Boat" as you walk down the street.

➤ Change your appearance. If you normally dress sloppily, dress sharply. If you often frown, force a smile. If you don't compliment people, do so. In other words, try to change some external things that you do.

➤ Ask for change in a busy store with a sign reading "No change given." Ask the proprietor to explain the rule. You don't have to be hostile or aggressive, just matter-of-fact.

The type of social desensitization exercises you try will depend on your situation and your local culture. People in New York City normally have more latitude in the types of social risk they can take than people in a small New England village.

Some exercises have greater applicability than do others. You can order two different eggs "any style" anywhere. Although you may not want to wear two different shoes to a business meeting, you might consider wearing two different-colored socks to a bowling alley or to a movie.

If you feel embarrassed stepping out of character through these exercises, ask yourself: "What is wrong with temporarily exercising my right to be less conventional than normal?" Well, what is wrong with that?

Many people with social discomfort worry about feeling uncomfortable in social situations. Some things are uncomfortable to do! That's the point. When you can experience discomfort without fear or avoidance, you may wonder, "Where did the anxiety go?" You also may be less prone to inventive forms of shame.

POSTSCRIPT

The English poet John Keats had a thought for the self-conscious: "There's a blush for won't, and a blush for shan't, And a blush for having done it: / There's a blush for thought and a blush for naught, And a blush for just begun it."

We are conscious of many things about our "self." To steer away from a single judgment of "self," it helps to expand our perspective. The nineteenth-century German philosopher Georg Wilhelm Friedrich Hegel asserted that self-consciousness is a necessary condition for fulfilling social responsibilities. Hegel then spoke of levels and types of consciousness. He categorizes consciousness into sensory, perceptual, understanding, alienation, duty, freedom, spiritual, philosophical, and absolute where love, harmony, wisdom, social responsibility, and experience converge into one.

Inane shame, guilt, blame, and angst decrease agape (a healthy sense of wonderment with life). These self-consciousness conditions are the enemy.

Self-consciousness plays the same parts as we move across the public stage. An exaggerated sense of shame, embarrassment, humiliation, guilt, and blame are main actors in this "enemy" script. Those who know about and can separate and defuse the elements of a burdensome self-consciousness have an advantage in defeating this enemy.

7

Breaking the Circles of Blame

> *Circular blame leads to logical anemia.*

Evil spirits are credited with causing the Black Death in the Middle Ages. The Indian government gets blamed for not doing enough to prevent the Bengal tiger's decline. University professors blame high school teachers who blame middle school teachers who blame elementary school teachers for poor student performance. Blame the British for the destruction of ancient sites. Blame liberals, conservatives, moderates, and the courts for a rising crime rate. Ducks and pigs get blamed for the flu. Socialists blame capitalism for promoting alienation. What do these situations have in common? Each involves generalized blame.

On an everyday level, we hear examples of *externalized generalized blame.* "You *never* listen to me." "You *always* try to get away with something." Alli, for example, saw George wipe grains of sugar from his hands. She shouted, "You slob! I work hard to keep this house clean. All you do is mess things up." That said, George waved his battle flag and a war ensued.

Some people who listen to themselves hear *internalized generalized blame:* "I can't do anything right." Brad, for example, tells himself he is a complete failure and fake. He makes up excuses to himself to avoid challenges and uses different excuses to justify his procrastination to others. His generalized blame statements are irrational and illusory.

In this chapter we'll probe generalized forms of blame. We'll start with propaganda, stereotyping, and blame. We'll finish with techniques for breaking circular reasoning patterns that so often form the core of generalized blame.

PROPAGANDA AND BLAME

The term "propaganda" began in holy quarters. In 1622 Pope Gregory XV applied "propaganda" to missionary work when he said, "Sacra ongregato de propaganda fide," which means "Go forth and convert."

Propaganda has not changed much in the past 378 years. The propagandist wants to influence you to feel and behave in a particular way. Today we see less missionary work to convert people to Catholicism and more propaganda-based advertising designed to influence choices such as what beer to buy or what candidate to support.

Some propaganda is positive; some is not. We have many examples of positive propaganda where people encourage us to watch our diets, exercise, stop smoking, get regular health checks, and engage in activities to improve the quality of our lives. But propaganda is best known for its dark side. The propagandist intends to manipulate people's beliefs, emotions, and behavior in a way that serves the propagandist's ends. We clearly see this propaganda-blame process at a national level. During World War I the British government used negative propaganda to cause Britons and their allies to feel hatred for the Germans. The British propaganda machine described Germans as "huns" whose soldiers would cut off the hands of little Belgian children and the breasts of nurses. There was no evidence that this was ever done.

During World War II, Nazi propagandist Joseph Goebbels, borrowing from Adolf Hitler's *Mein Kampf,* said that if you tell a lie often enough, it will sound like truth. Nazi propaganda coalesced a nation against common enemies and extolled "Aryan" superiority as a rallying point.

People also can use disinformation strategies to get a fair-minded picture. By looking for exceptions to the "big lie," you can teach yourself to see through propaganda.

THE AGITATOR AND GENERALIZED BLAME

Demagogues typically dramatize life as a struggle between good and evil, or paint things as either black or white, or appeal to national pride in order to create a common enemy to blame. The agitator intuitively knows and exploits this knowledge. At the extreme of the propaganda continuum, we find agitators who use "blame" to inflame public emotions. The agitator also knows that appeals to greed, status, safety, sex, oppression, or power are likely to to evoke an emotional reaction.

The agitator's rhetoric is stirred by loaded words and phrases that convey blame. You can deal with the agitator's generalized blame approach by eliminating loaded words and generalized ideas from agitator statements. In that way you can cut to the core issue. For example, remove the emotionally arousing extension-of-blame nouns, adjectives, and phrases from the following agitator statement, or substitute "balderdash" for each.

> We are ripped off by the debauchers and slick politicians who diddle with our feelings. They laugh at us behind our backs. They pay lip service to law and decency and subvert these principles whenever they think we don't see them. We are blocked from action by bureaucratic crackpots and dregs who think only of their retirement check. We are

cheated by a phony justice system that conspires with the crooks to make mockery out of fair play. These sinister powers pull our chains at will. Like parasites, they feed on our life-blood. They surround themselves with stooges and scabs. They will walk over the flesh of our children. Alone, we are powerless to stop their menacing underhanded tactics. I say we must unite. For too long we have been fleeced. Who will say no to the spoilers? Who among you will join me and wear the sign of the wolf?

When you strip emotionally charged adjectives and phrases from his propaganda, what remains is fragmented or indecipherable. Little remains when you substitute "balderdash" for the following terms: ripped off, debauchers, slick politicians, diddle, laugh at us behind our backs, lip service, decency, subvert, bureaucratic crackpots, dregs, cheated by a phony justice system, conspire with the crooks, make mockery out of fair play, sinister powers, pull our chains, parasites, feed on our life-blood, stooges and scabs, walk over the flesh of our children, menacing underhanded tactics, fleeced, spoilers. Despite its "sound and fury," the agitator statement, when stripped of loaded language, sounds silly and is completely lacking in meaningful content. Its power lies in its deceptive language.

Agitator appeals occur in public forums and private conversations and sometimes even when we're denigrating ourselves with harsh accusations. But if we become propaganda conscious, we may, in time, develop a measurable degree of immunity to the half-truths and vacuous emotional appeals that have the power to evoke hostility and hatred.

STEREOTYPES AND BLAME

Our ability to abstract is a natural way of making life comprehensible. The word "abstract" comes from Latin and means to draw away or to take from. When we abstract we simplify (take away), lose information, but gain efficiency. However, efficiency may not be effective when reality simplifications catapult us along mental paths leading to "upset." You can feel *abstractly upset* when you blame yourself for who you think you are.

Harvard University psychology professor Rudolf Arnheim, in his book *Visual Thinking,* argues that seeing, thinking, perceiving, and reasoning flow together. Instead of feeling a table, we think table. We add meaning to events by defining them as good, bad, fair, unfair, just, unjust, pleasurable, and painful. These value labels help organize reality. For example, abstract principles, such as freedom and responsibility, represent important assumptions and truths that we can use as standards to match against behavior. They also impel behavior. People have died for *freedom.* If you value the abstract concept of *responsibility,* you will strive to arrive on time, follow-up on commitments, and make yourself accountable for your actions.

Most of our abstractions are incomplete, descriptive representations of reality. For example, when we call a person a redhead we realize the person is more than that. Still, we need to summarize through abstractions if we are to communicate effectively.

We use abstractions when we describe people as philanderers, monsters, teasers, procrastinators, selfish, greedy, corrupt, drunkards, and braggarts. These stereotypes are abstract beliefs about the characteristics, attributes, and behaviors of individuals or groups. Nerds, eggheads, Gypsies, convicts, pot-heads, alcoholics, hippies, philanthropists, psychologists, mothers, and accountants also refer to stereotyped groups. If you think of an accountant, are you more likely to think of "the life of the party" or a dull, bookish number cruncher?

We judge stereotyped group members on the basis of comparisons between the individual and the stereotype. Some stereotypes are generally predictive. Women frequently are more verbal than men and normally have less upper body strength. However, some women are less verbal and have greater upper body strength than some men. The 16 Personality Factor (16 PF) test, a psychological measure that applies to both men and women, amply shows the great diversity between temperamental patterns among both sexes. Some patterns seem classically masculine, yet we most frequently see them occurring among women. Some patterns associated with sensitivity and warmth show a higher frequency among men. However, all 16 PF patterns include both men and women.

Repeated often enough, a pejorative label, however unfairly conceived, will tend to stick. When we stigmatize in this way, we brand people. Stigmatization sets the stage for scapegoating. For example, during the "cold war," various Soviet dictators used "capitalist" as a pejorative term that meant corrupt, evil, exploitive, and subhuman. Through repetition, they conveyed the image that America was wrecking the communist economic system when, in fact, the decline of that socialist system had other complications including the dictator Joseph Stalin's slaughter of potential opposition, which significantly depleted the numbers of people with special skills and management ability. From the other side, former U.S. President Ronald Reagan labeled the Soviet Union "the evil empire" and communism a defective political-economic system. The view of the Soviet Union as an evil empire with a dangerous ideology existed from the 1917 Bolshevik Revolution. Its focus on world domination fortunately failed.

To maintain cold war support of their respective populations, and to demonize the other guy and his ideology, both the Soviet Union and the United States had talking points, cartoons, photographs, documents, and other propaganda to dress the other side in stereotyped garb. Each did this because stereotypes are easier to blame and hate than are individuals. Ultimately, the "cold war" was decided by economics, and the Soviet system failed.

The beginning of the First French Republic is well known for the reign of terror that led to the guillotine deaths of thousands of people, including city magistrates and members of the aristocracy, because of their stereotyped social roles. Under the propaganda banner of "liberating the people," the terrorists confiscated great wealth from the aristocracy, clergy, and "people."

STEREOTYPING PARADOXES

Stereotypes reflect overly generalized thinking. For example, the traditional mother stereotype is that of a nurturing and protective person. This stereotype is positive, and the vast majority of mothers try to do their best and typically do well. But not all mothers fit the stereotype. Some act in opposition to it. In rare instances, mothers have Medea complexes and murder their children. Others suffer from Munchausen syndrome by proxy. Munchausen mothers feign or produce illness in their children to attract medical attention in order to gain attention and reassurances from medical authorities. Some women abandon their children to keep a new "boyfriend," to avoid child-rearing hassles, or to pursue a substance abuse habit. Some are neurotic individuals who shift in a moment from oozing praise and affection to cold, hostile, rigid, scowling, scolding irrational outbursts triggered by the slightest inconvenience. The message: Stereotypes tell us little about an individual.

Most people who stereotype also will accept the concept of individuality, which is to say, we are not all alike. Stereotypes, however, rob people of their individuality. Here is the paradox: How do we justify grouping people under narrow stereotypical labels and yet still believe each person is diverse and individual?

We help ourselves get beyond blame inferences and blame extensions when we judge people's behavior rather than stereotype them. People do engage in blameworthy acts, and the punishment should fit the crime. However, we add little of value by using blame labels to defame someone's character and then to justify extending blame based on the label. Normally we are wiser to see people as fellow humans. When they engage in blameworthy activities, we can hold them responsible and accountable without ascribing to a single generalized label.

You can help yourself break free from the generalized blame stereotyping trap by breaking down the stereotype into subgroups. Let's take "psychologist" as an example. Here are some substereotypes for psychologists: The man with the beard behind the couch. The woman doing brain research on rats. The man testing a learning theory with elementary school children. The historian studying how psychology evolved. The clinician actively engaging a client in self-examination. The social scientist studying persuasion and influence on public policy decisions. When you think of psychologist, which of these substereotypes applies? Now, substereotype by role, responsibilities, and relationships. Next, substereotype by interests, values, attitudes, or religious beliefs. Then substereotype by motivation in different contexts. Through this substereotyping exercise, you can better see people as individuals as it becomes clear to you that there are almost innumerable permutations under any single label like "psychologist."

CIRCULARITY AND BLAME

Traditional family values are declining. Because they are declining, the crime rate is rising. Now, what have we learned from this declaration that can change either effect? If we decrease the crime rate, does this lead to increased family values?

In a circular thinking trap you may believe that you can feel relaxed about yourself only by getting control and that you can be in control only by being relaxed. There are at least two major flaws in this thinking. First, you need to feel relaxed, and second, control is the means to this end. When you think you need to be in control, you probably are teetering on losing control.

People get caught in a circular loop that includes extension-of-blame thinking when they tell themselves they are worthless and then do little to change their image. Here the circle of thought includes: I am worthless, and because I am worthless I deserve nothing, and because I get nothing, that proves I am worthless. This vague, stereotyping extension-of-blame statement has no end until this reasoning tautology is cut short.

We see this blame circularity in other contexts: You believe that you are distressed today because you had unloving parents. The circularity becomes clear when you complete the loop: "I feel distressed because I had unloving parents, and because I had unloving parents I feel distressed."

You can disrupt the blame circularity by shifting perspective. For example, do all people with unloving parents feel distressed? Do you have anything to do with your distress? Do you disturb yourself because of what you tell yourself about your parents or what you tell yourself about yourself? By stepping out of the circular loop, you position yourself to stay out of the loop.

POSTSCRIPT

The Indian political and spiritual leader Mahatma Gandhi said, "Truth never damages a cause that is just." But just as snowflakes have an identical composition, each pattern of truth is unique in detail. This uniqueness allows us to recognize both the general quality of "truth" and, at the same time, the specific uniqueness of each truth.

Often generalized presumptions of truth float in the cloudy world of abstractions. For example, although we may find some basis in fact for saying that ducks and pigs cause the flu, there are immediate causes, such as an opportunity to contract the virus and an inadequate immune system response to it.

Unless we work to ground vague abstractions to a concrete reality, we make ourselves vulnerable to ambiguous circular messages that can entrap us in an emotional maelstrom punctuated by unresolvable conflicts. By focusing our attention onto separating fact from fiction, we move further from generalized blame, which is, after all, no more than a stumbling block to development and personal growth.

8

Piercing Patterns of Blame

Extend blame to yourself, the world,
or events, and you distort reality.

If we had only one form of blame to contend with, this would be a very short book. Sadly, blame appears in different guises. In this chapter we'll look at self-blame, externalized blame, and victim blame and what you can do about them.

SELF-BLAME

Self-blame is likely to emerge when you've done something wrong. In this sense, self-blame is a form of internal control. For example, you blame yourself for speaking harshly to an associate. When next you meet, you make a point to be more positive. Self-blame can be a stimulus for making amends or for taking corrective action.

Some of us go too far crediting ourselves for the blame for conditions in which we have limited or no control. You blame yourself for not anticipating a shower on the day of your picnic. People blame themselves for very abstract reasons, such as for not living up to their potential. But what does it mean to live up to one's potential? At the extreme, some people foolishly blame themselves for being not adequate enough, successful enough, rich enough, beautiful enough, or smart enough.

On the extreme end of the self-blame continuum, we find people who believe that the locus of control lies exclusively within themselves. Within this mind-set, the rape victim thinks that had she been more careful or fought back harder, she would not have been raped. The battered wife tells us that if only she were a better wife, her husband would not beat her. The grieving son tells himself that he should have seen his mother's illness sooner and done more. Others believe they have a fatal flaw and blame themselves for that. Because of this assumption, they also believe they are fated to fail and so make halfhearted efforts, only to bring about the prophesy they feared.

When you generalize blame to your total self, you place yourself on a sticky web. You have no reasonable way to escape other than to stop internalizing and generalizing blame to yourself. However, by studying this process, you can understand how self-blame can dominate thought and how to substitute corrective actions for blameful preoccupations. The good news is that people who internalize blame normally have a better prognosis for making positive changes than do those who hold themselves faultless while blaming outside conditions for their troubles.

A TRAGIC TALE

It is sometimes helpful to put the matter of personal control and accountability into perspective. For example, in some situations it is completely implausible that one can have control over a situation, yet the individual will take the credit for the blame. Let's take Randy's tragic case to put the issue of controllability and self-blame into a sharp focus.

A state division of child and youth services referred Randy to me after the child's fifty-year-old alcohol-dependent father forced her to participate in a kiddy porn flick in which he had intercourse with her. She was three years old at the time. The producers paid him money for the performance. Beyond the kiddy porn rape, Randy later witnessed a drug-related murder, barely escaped from her mother's apartment after a drug pusher set it on fire, and repeatedly was returned to her mother when the police found her wandering unattended on the streets. Once alerted, the state's department of children's services removed the child from the environment and placed her into a foster home.

I first saw Randy in counseling when she was five. The state's children's services people and foster home parents were most eager to help Randy and provided much helpful background information.

Randy first presented herself as a hyperactive child who jumped from chair to chair and showed great difficulty in attending. She required much time to learn to stay focused and to develop rudimentary psychological coping skills. After she had learned a broad range of such skills, she started to talk about the rape. (Children often do far better when then they first learn, test, and refine psychological coping skills.) When she related the incest experience, Randy showed a very clear and almost photographic recollection of the event. The images haunted her. She felt deeply ashamed. She faulted herself and believed she had brought it upon herself.

Randy needed to get past her self-consciousness and shame. To establish a foundation for helping her cognitively restructure her recollections, I asked Randy if she could control whether the sun would rise in the east or rise in the west, whether she could stop the wind from blowing, and whether she had any control over when and how much it would rain. Could she raise her hands to stop ocean waves roaring to the beach in advance of a storm? She acknowledged that these were matters outside of her control.

I next asked if she could force her foster mother to buy an army tank for transportation. Could she cause her teachers always to teach how to build houses rather than reading? Did she have the power to make a grocer sell bicycles instead of groceries? She acknowledged that this was easier than changing the weather, but it wasn't very likely the grocer would sell bicycles.

Next we looked at how much influence she had over what home chore she would do first, her preferences for supper, the cartoon show she would watch later that day, or the kind of pictures she would draw. Here she admitted that she had considerable latitude.

With these conditions set, I asked her whether what happened with her father when she was three was more like controlling the wind, having her foster mother buy an army tank, or deciding what type of picture to draw. She was understandably very emotional. Nevertheless, she acknowledged that she had as much control over her father's behavior when she was three years old as she had over the direction the sun set. She could no more stop her father than she could stop the waves at the beach from rising in the wake of a storm. I asked, "If you do not have the power to stop the ocean waves, then how are you to blame for something that was clearly outside of your control?"

That day she developed a radically different perspective. She understood that it made no sense to blame herself for what she could not reasonably control. Although the event was understandably traumatic, she need not worsen the harm by declaring herself the perpetrator, then blaming herself for what happened.

Randy could not forget and would not forgive her father. She was able to put the matter into a different perspective. She dramatically reduced the time she spent blaming herself and feeling shamed. She progressively came to accept herself and to find herself acceptable.

Eventually Randy was adopted by her foster parents. Her therapy ended around the time she was eight. I periodically followed her progress until she was about sixteen. As far as I can tell, up to that point she did quite well psychologically, socially, and academically.

Self-Blame and Change

Most people would endorse this item on a test: It is important to act responsibly to others and to keep one's promises and commitments. However, self-blamers also have a responsibility to themselves to recognize that they do have control over the cognitive processes they engage when they put themselves down.

As a practical matter, we can accept ourselves for having the attributes that arrived with us at the moment of birth and the influences of our social environment and still recognize that we have the responsibility to develop our most constructive capabilities. Sometimes what we think can get in our own way, especially if we follow irrational thought patterns that bind us to an unpleasant existence. The chain-of-pain exercise is a helpful way to visualize and override an irrational self-blame process that evokes emotional pain. Try it as an experiment.

Imagine self-blame as a chain of interlocking ideas involving frustrated expectations and thoughts of powerlessness, inferiority, and blameworthiness where each idea flows in sequence and interlock. These ideas form the links that tighten around you. Now imagine this snakelike chain wrapping tighter and tighter around your body. Next switch perspectives. View the chain as a holograph and the ideas that form the links as hypotheses.

➤ To weaken the links in the chain of pain, pretend you are a scientist tracking the direction of your self-blame thinking. Recall and in a notebook record a specific self-blame event. For this process, write down the event, what you were thinking, how you felt, and what you did, and your afterthoughts. This gives you a running commentary. Graphically chain this sequence together to create a visual picture. Then put the notes aside.

➤ After about an hour, go back and review your notes. Evaluate each of the ideas that form the links. For example, how valid were the thoughts that you had about the event and your afterthoughts? Next accept only factually verifiable statements that would hold up in a court of law. Exclude the rest. Through this exercise, you may discover that the links of the chain of pain are weaker than you previously thought.

➤ Wait another hour. When you are by yourself, look at your graphic and speak out loud the sequence of thoughts that go into your self-blame pattern. When verbalized, the words can sound different from how they do when locked in your mind. You may quickly discover that the thoughts do not have as much impact as before.

➤ If you have a video recorder, videotape yourself verbalizing your chain-of-pain script. Review the videotape. Now rewrite your script twice. In the first revision, you doubt and question the chain of pain on videotape. The second time, assert a self-affirming script on videotape. Next, go back and review the two tape segments. Chances are you will choose to practice the self-affirming script.

➤ For four minutes on the following day, recite and repeat your chain-of-pain self-blame scripts in a deliberate monotone. (This phase of the exercise may cause you to bore yourself with the self-blame thoughts.) Immediately after that monotone phase, define then challenge the assumptions that hook each link in the chain. If you think this way, ask yourself, "where is the absolute proof that you are a thoroughly blameworthy, unredeemable individual?"

You have many ways to put a self-blame pattern of thought into perspective. The right-now intervention can help. If you feel caught in a chain of pain because of self-blame, tell yourself: "Right now I feel stressed." By reciting how you feel in the present moment, you paradoxically open opportunities for feeling better about feeling bad. That is because right now is not forever.

Living through the feeling complements the right-now exercise. When you accept living with an unpleasant feeling until it changes, this act of acceptance can add to your sense of tolerance.

The concept of the apple barrel also can help to put self-blame into a sharper perspective. No human is without shortcomings and flaws. Negatives, such as errors of judgment, ignorance, and selfishness, blend with positives, such as altruism, insights, diligence, persistence, and character. This is part of the human condition. With this background in mind, the concept of the apple barrel can help put "self-blame" attitudes into perspective. Suppose you had a barrel of apples. Some were bruised. Would you throw out the whole barrel because of a few bruised apples? The concept of the barrel of apples applies to the "self" in this way: Blaming your "self" for imperfections makes as much sense as throwing out a barrel of apples because of bruises on a few. In this self-development situation, the truism "One bad apple spoils the bunch" is false.

EXTERNALIZING BLAME

Some events are externally caused and some people may behave in truly blameworthy ways. That is not what we are talking about here. A habit of externalizing blame is where one has an automatic reaction to exonerate onself by dumping the blame elsewhere.

Externalized blame sometimes wrongly falls on women. Japanese "educational moms" feel the pressure and get the blame when their children's academic performance falls below standard. There is an ideological tendency in the Mexican culture to blame women for social problems.

In the world of the externalized blamer, you have nothing to do with the stress you feel. People are always starting up with you. Life could be wonderful if you would only have your way when you want it. People thwart your interests. The core of your troubles lies with your mate, boss, "bad breaks," lack of opportunity, racism, a rotten childhood, parents, and unfairness. Teachers tend to blame the kids, parents, or school administration for their troubles. Parents blame their children's grades on both the child and the teacher. What do these examples have in common? People in this blame trap too often believe that their only option is to change external events or the fates. That is not likely to happen!

At the extreme, externalized blame can become a painful, entrenched, habit with violent consequences. Jack beats his wife because, he says, she is not tidy enough, sexy enough, and attentive enough to make him happy. His solution is for her to change. He believes he has nothing to do with how he feels. Then his wife gets a restraining order. He blames her for doing that. Thereafter he blames her by saying that she is unfair because she won't give him another chance.

Habits of externalizing blame to others can quickly alienate them and disrupt, damage, or destroy relationships. June is a quintessential blame externalizer. She broods, obsesses, and bitterly complains about what people do to her to make her life miserable. June will quickly tell you how her ex-husband ruined her life and how he now holds back on alimony payment so she only has scraps of food to eat. Her employer is cheap. Her salary is not enough to support her suburban home. Her grown children are ungrateful. They practically never come to visit. Her current lover is a worm for not spending enough time with her. Her friends won't return her phone calls. Her coworkers have a clique and unfairly go to lunch without inviting her to join them. Because of their clerical errors, the bank screwed up her credit. Even her therapist is incompetent. The list goes on. If you try to question June's list, she'll tell you where you are wrong and why. She is skilled at negating.

If you feel powerless to change and still need to do something to explain your plight, externalizing blame falsely exonerates you from responsibility because you can now explain how outside forces cause events in your life to go wrong. However, a habit of externalizing blame has disadvantages. Externalized blame can give one a sense of powerlessness.

EXTERNALIZED BLAME AND CHANGE

Blaming spirits, the fates, bad luck, or a palm reader for not accurately foretelling the future is not likely to get you into serious difficulties with people around you. Keeping blame abstract, general, and vague also is not likely to bring you into direct conflict with others. For these reasons, few people will have a strong incentive to change these ways of thinking. Indeed, some will embrace generalized blame externalization as a way to reduce tension.

Women in some cultures seek external causes to blame for their troubles. Psychologist John Burdick found that Brazilian working-class women who seek religious help to cope with domestic conflict have access to the authorities of three religious faiths—Catholicism, Pentecostalism, and Umbanda. Pentecostalism and Umbanda allow them to place the blame for their domestic conflict on spiritual entities. Catholic authority, however, emphasizes placing blame for domestic conflict on themselves and their mate. As a result, most women seek advice from Umbanda and Pentecostal religious authorities. This act of blaming entities takes the edge off of a current conflict. But, predictably, attributing problems to spirits won't get to the core issues.

In situations where blame directly damages relationships, the pattern may not be readily seen by the externalizing blamer, who has a vested interest in denying accountability. Even when externalized blame has a mildly negative impact on relationships, it makes good sense to put oneself in a position to choose to externalize blame or to stop the process. Here are some thoughts about disrupting an externalizing blame habit:

➤ People with illusions of insight (if you feel it, it must be so) and judgment (if you believe it, you can't be wrong) do well to look at the results of their blaming views. If they repeatedly have conflicts with others over who is right, they can suspect these dual illusions are present. To change the pattern, look for evidence to disconfirm the view that one cannot possibly be wrong.

➤ Externalizing blame is often a quick-fix solution for denying accountability for one's emotions or for escaping penalties. However, this habit runs counter to self-development. Building on personal strengths involves imposing reason between an impulse to blame and its expression. By training oneself to extract exten-sion-of-blame thinking from an externalizing blame process, one's options and choices broaden to include self-development.

➤ Externalized blame becomes a form of victim thinking when complemented by a sense of powerlessness. This powerlessness thinking correlates with emotional turmoil. Enveloped in the belief that you have no control over your emotional turmoil and its causes, you may feel reduced to complaining. But there is practically always something that one can do to take charge of part of an otherwise untoward situation. By focusing on what you can do, you may discover that you have power of inner con-trol. That awareness can give you a feeling of liberation from victim thinking.

Practice in debunking false and irrational external blame ideas can add signifi-cantly to your clear-thinking ability. At the same time, you reduce the risk that you will succumb to negative suggestions built into a generalized and externalized blame situation.

VILLAINIZING THE VICTIM

Unscrupulous people attempt to exonerate themselves from responsibility by mak-ing a villain out of their victims. For example, senior citizens are too often easy tar-gets for bum deals by used-car salespeople, unethical contractors, contest-driven mail-order magazine sales, telephone companies, and quacks. Those who perpetrate a fraud against this group rarely view their victims as senior citizens deserving con-sideration. Rather they blame label them "old fogies," "patsies," or "jerks." A mug-ger views his target as having *his* money. The mugger feels justified getting his money from the victim. When the mugger uses *blame labels* such as "dupe," he avoids blame in his own mind: He was only going after what was his and what he needed, and he took it from a dupe.

People are villainized for other reasons. In the remainder of this section, we'll look at people who speak up for what they believe is right only to find themselves the subjects of blame, repression, and retaliation.

BLAMING THE MESSENGER

The term "whistleblower" comes from the factory setting where a person would blow a whistle to stop a production line when something went wrong. The term now de-scribes people who speak up in the public interest to expose waste, fraud, unsafe con-ditions, dangerous health conditions, costly error, and so forth. From one perspective, this conscientious reporter is a hero who saves money and possibly lives. The whistle-blower, or conscientious reporter, is unique. Most people tend to look the other way.

In a healthy organization, people who identify problems—even unpopular problems—make unique contributions. Problem identification, clarification, and good solutions help improve the health of a society or an organization.

But what if the authority is part of the problem? In such a case, those people who speak up in the public interest may find themselves villainized for doing the right thing. When a conscientious reporter calls attention to the use of shoddy materials in a building project, or points to a pattern of excess medical care billings, or reports abuse among elderly people in a nursing home, rather than triggering an investigation of the complaint, he or she may become the subject of investigation and retaliation.

In a celebrated whistleblower case, the U.S. Department of Labor awarded Marvin Hobby $2 million and job reinstatement. The agency determined that Hobby's employer, Georgia Power, caused him considerable damage in reputation through retaliatory actions calculated to cause a loss of reputation and, thus, his credibility. Then, in an ironic twist, Georgia Power officials vigorously argued against Hobby's reinstatement, saying that Mr. Hobby now had a bad reputation. They conveniently omitted mention of the fact that they had created the illusion that Hobby was unfit. Georgia Power illustrated a common blame-the-messenger pattern.

Just as brainwashing does not follow one set pattern, retaliatory practices also vary. However, there are some common features:

➤ The conscientious reporter identifies a problem. Following that, he or she often receives negative memoranda that include false or misleading information designed to criticize and blame them for their performance. It doesn't matter if the person had thirty years of a clean work record and performance awards. Suddenly the record tells a different story.

➤ This repressive process normally includes a joint illegal enterprise where several people focus their efforts on fault finding, blaming, and harassing the conscientious reporter. Members of this repression support group need not receive direct orders but act as if they knew the result to bring about.

➤ Blame labeling is an integral part of the repressive retaliation process. This labeling process often begins with describing the conscientious reporter first as disgruntled and malcontent and later as crazy. These blame labels are distractions that disparage. The "crazy" label falsely explains why a previously conscientious person suddenly changed.

➤ Once blame-labeled as crazy, some conscientious observers are ordered by their employers to undergo psychological testing or psychiatric examinations.

➤ Conscientious reporters are made the subject of discriminatory actions that make it tough for them to do their jobs. These administrative actions can include loss of secretary services, phone, pager, computer, and so forth. Their office may be relocated. They are sometimes transferred or suspended, making it easier to isolate and ostracize them. This harassment also can include public ridicule.

➤ When there are written disciplinary rules, the repressive process can include fabricating cases against the reporter under the guise of progressive discipline. This is a prelude to suspension, demotion, and dismissal.

➤ Some reporters receive anonymous death threats, physical threats, or damage to property. The intent of such practices is to frighten and intimidate and to force the reporters to retreat.

➤ When someone is the subject of repressive conditions, his or her work associates often separate themselves from the individual to avoid becoming the subjects of the same repression.

This retaliatory pattern can seem unbelievable to those who have not been subject of a reprisal process. One common question is: What motivates this repressive process? There are no simple answers and many possibilities. In some cases, the administrator is corrupt or a crook and fears personal exposure. The problems escalate from there. Image-conscious people in positions of power who seek to keep up good external appearances often externalize blame. Normally they tend to villianize the messenger to save face. Others have a good deal of arrogance. They believe they are untouchable, independent of what they do. At the extreme, we find people with power pathologies who feel in control when they can assert power. The conscientious reporter and reporting authority may also develop a personality clash. They start a dispute with each other that neither can let go of. These conditions, of course, can interact.

There are simple solutions for dealing with conscientious reporter claims. One listens and corrects what is reasonable to do. However, a crook can't afford to back off. A person with an externalized blame outlook will tend to abuse the process to support his or her views. People who think arrogantly are tough to get through to. People with a power pathology are rare but unrelenting in their quest for control. They are the wild cards of the human race.

Why would anyone go through a reprisal process when they could quit and work elsewhere? Conscientious reporters may get drawn into the process as they face conditions that put them between the proverbial rock and hard place. When encountering a reprisal system for the first time, many will feel confused and uncertain before they realize what is happening. By the time they understand the situation, they may have become personally invested in righting the wrong and safeguarding their reputations. Furthermore, to maintain their sense of integrity, dignity, and identity, conscientious reporters typically continue to stand up for the principle they initiated as well as for their personal rights.

Conscientious Reporter Emotional Survival Kit

For those conscientious reporters who intend to follow through, I offer the following techniques:

➤ The first line of defense is to recognize the repressive process before it gets too far along. This awareness can help conscientious reporters to decide to continue or to stop pursuing the opportunity to help protect the public interest through a quest for justice.

➤ Log and document all relevant events and their dates, times, who said what to whom, and what was the result. Maintain copies of documentation in more than one secure site.

➤ Establish a support team. Capable allies are among the most valued possessions in the conscientious reporter's survival kit. You find these allies among people who have influence, integrity, and power who want a safer world. This team can include people who have followed this trail before and know many of the traps and pitfalls.

➤ Knowledgeable legal counsel and a psychologist with whistleblower experience can provide useful direction and support. The attorney can advise you, for example, about your rights and responsibilities. The psychologist can help you to cope emotionally with adversity.

➤ Keep focused on problem issues and constructive goals.

➤ Blame labeling is often a part of a retaliatory process. This needs to be taken seriously but not personally. Repeatedly remind yourself that you are not the same as the label.

➤ Recognize that it is often wiser to focus on discovering ways to solve the problem than to focus on the character of the repressive authority.

➤ Be prepared for unpleasant surprises.

➤ Don't expect people who have acted repressively suddenly to act fairly. This would be a most unusual occurrence.

➤ People who are the subjects of repressive actions can and do get emotional. Their writing can reflect this. The emotion then becomes the message, to the detriment of the issue. Consider all that you express in words or writing as if you were preparing to present before a court or independent tribunal. If you wouldn't want a particular statement or report presented before a jury, don't make it public.

➤ Factually respond to all allegations of "wrongdoing" directed toward you. Identify inconsistencies and false statements. Present your statements in a constructive tone. Support your statements with facts. Normally this activity requires considerable time.

➤ As you proceed, stick with the data, work from the facts, and operate from this foundation. You don't have to say everything that you know, but you'll do better when what you do say is verifiable or highly plausible. Avoid exaggerations or slanting the truth. Remind yourself that the "truth" normally proves friendly.

➤ As Sergeant Joe Friday in the show *Dragnet* said, "Just the facts, ma'am." However, how you put the facts together and connect the dots can make all the difference.

➤ When you are the subject of negative actions, systematically follow administrative remedies and appeals processes. While initial appeals may be biased against you, they are a part of the process.

➤ Know what you can economically and emotionally tolerate and know when to quit. Health and sanity are probably more important than vindication and justice or even a cash award. Knowing when to quit involves an objective cost-benefits analysis. This analysis will normally include your subjective feelings, sense of dignity, and family and financial responsibilities. But—

➤ Often when you feel "at wit's end," the other side may be wobbling and cannot restabilize. However, remember when there are corruption or criminal issues, repressive people will risk doing the most outrageous things rather than risk a loss of image or jail.

Although Mark Twain was probably right that "A lie is halfway around the world before the truth gets out of bed," truth can run fast when supported and repeated. Calmly but persuasively repeat the truth in different relevant forums.

POSTSCRIPT

Shakespeare muses, "The world is a looking glass, and gives back to every man the reflection of his own face. Frown at it, and it will in turn look sourly upon you: laugh at it and with it, and it is a jolly kind companion; and so let all young persons take their choice."

Self-blame, externalizing blame, and victim blame all project the same sorry face. Changing the face involves developing a realistic perspective, getting past a just-world illusion, and concentrating on what is important for you to accomplish free of extensions of self-blame, illusions of external control, and victim thinking. Improvements in these areas will feel rewarding.

PART TWO

Relationships and Blame

9

Blame and Intimacy

> *Intimate relationships require*
> *cooperation more than work.*

When you fall romantically in love, you probably will look at your beloved through rose-colored glasses. As the glasses age, they clear. In time, you will see faults that were not so obvious or important.

Perfect relationships exist only at the tip of a romantic author's pen or in fantasy. That's because people have foibles and flaws. However, it is how you and your partner manage your differences, your faults, and the inevitable changes in perception that take place over time that predicts the quality of your relationship.

Intimate relationships can be quite complex. A big challenge is to reduce the complexity by keeping needless blame out of the picture. In this chapter I will tell you about thirteen blame practices to avoid and fourteen characteristics of couples who enjoy a special, happy, long-term relationship.

THIRTEEN DEADLY WAYS TO DESTROY A RELATIONSHIP

Your clock strikes a midnight chime, and a raven appears at your door. You invite the bird in. After all, you are an Edgar Allen Poe fan.

The raven gets right to the point. It says, "I know thirteen ploys to totally wreck a relationship. Each relies on blame. If you are successful with these blame tactics, you might convince your partner that he or she is at fault for all the havoc in your relationship." As you listen to the raven, you decide you really don't want to practice these tactics but think it is wise to know what to avoid. So you bid the raven to continue.

The raven tells you that you can follow blame rules that practically guarantee contention. You can get into power struggles, flirt with others, assert unrealistic demands, and sabotage your friendship, companionship, and sexual interests with your partner by behaving sullenly, silently, and argumentatively. Because people are imperfect, you can easily find a reason to blame your partner. Use your defect detection talent. Take something small and turn it into a federal case. With this strategy firmly in place, you are sure to promote a counterattack and cause the game to rise to complicating new heights. "But since thirteen is an unlucky number," the raven says, "the following thirteen sicktricks can turn your relationship into a waking nightmare."

1. Play the Judge

Define yourself as flawless and faultless. As the perfect person, you can judge your mate. After all, who is better qualified? Now you can confidently blame your partner when anything goes wrong. This tactic has the power to keep your mate's blood boiling. With this blame strategy, you don't need to change. It is your partner who needs to change.

2. Throw Tantrums

Throw a tantrum when you don't get what you want. Act with indignation. Flip out. Get hysterical. Convincingly show that you must have your way or your partner will rue the day. When you meet with resistance, feign giving up by using *sign-off statements* such as "All right. All right. You win. I give up." These sign-off statements express this blame sentiment: Your mate is to blame for not being fully receptive to your views. Then you figuratively beat a dead horse by continuing the same explosive argument.

In this extension-of-blame contest, admit to nothing negative about what you are doing. Keep the tirade going by using blame labels such as "crazy," "stupid," "you're just like your mother (father)." When your partner puts up the white flag, don't stop. Cast more blame through dredging up the past. Explode over those "hurts." Keep fueling those emotional fires until you both get burned out.

3. Keep It Abstract

Abstractions allow us to think efficiently. Abstractions also can be vague and tough to pin down, such as when we say "I want you to make me happy."

To keep blame alive, resist any attempt to be specific. For example, demand of your partner such things as "I want you to make me happy." Now you can blame your partner whenever you feel unhappy. Make sure that you conveniently forget that happiness is a by-product of doing something else first. Definitely reject the idea that only you can give the gift of happiness to yourself.

Abstract, nonspecific demands practically guarantee that you will keep your partner off balance and frustrated. That is because satisfying anyone's vague and changing demands is practically impossible, especially if the rules keep changing. Your partner soon will find that whatever he or she does is not going to be good enough. Now your partner has cause to blame you.

4. Use Exaggerations

Exaggerate by using "allness" phrases. Examples: "You *always* ignore me." "You'll *never* be successful." These accusatory phrases can infuriate your partner. He or she is likely to show you that your exaggeration is incorrect. Then you can confidently say, "You always want to get in the last word." "You never try to understand what I am saying."

5. Stick with Your Illusions

Illusions are ideas that you believe to be true but are not that way at all. Here are two illusionary traps: 1) Tenaciously stick to the "if you love me illusion." Tell your partner, "If you love me, you will do _____." (You fill the blank.) Keep changing the requirement to keep your partner off balance. 2) Act like your partner should have ESP: "You should have known what I wanted." These expressions translate into something like this: It's your fault that I'm unhappy. You are too dumb to know what to do. These negative expressions can get your partner's emotional juices swirling and get you considerable negative attention.

To keep your illusions alive, never look at the negative results in your life that follow the same sorry extension-of-blame themes. Instead, blame it on the fates, an uncooperative mate, a sorry childhood, or bad breaks in life.

6. Play on Guilt

Guilt can have a big payoff, so exploit it at every possible opportunity. Use inferred blame expressions such as "You didn't keep your promise. How can I ever trust you again?" You also can play the role of the long-suffering martyr: "Look at all that I've done for you, and how unappreciative you are." Such indirect blame assertions can provoke guilt in your mate.

7. Hit the Hot-Buttons

Find your partner's hot-buttons, then keep pushing them. For example, play on your partner's insecurities by criticizing his or her foibles and faults. Nitpick and badger him or her for bodily imperfections. Denounce his or her interests and hobbies as trivial. Defame your mate's favorite relative. Say that he or she makes a lousy lover. Be sure to accuse your partner of having poor taste (according to your standards, of course) or general ineptitude.

8. Blackmail Your Partner

Use emotional blackmail to fuel your conflicts with your partner. For example, threaten to do something radical if you don't get your way. Say you will walk out, get a divorce, have an affair, get drunk, or make public complaints. Follow this pathway, and you can experience many hours of strife and conflict.

9. Exercise Your Manipulation Skills

Use coercion, past grievances, and intimidation to cause your mate to feel blame-worthy and bend to your will. Then act manipulatively. *Sweetly* declare that you are only acting in your partner's best interests because you are the only one who cares. For that reason your partner should give you what you want. In reality, you are act-ing in your own self-interests. But you deny this to yourself and to your partner. Af-ter all, who wants to admit to looking like the emperor without clothing?

10. Stay in the Love Addict Trap

Play out a love addiction role: Practice clinging dependency. Show intolerance for being alone. Demand constant attention. Follow your mate everywhere, even into the bathroom. Blame your partner for not paying enough attention to you.

In a state of dependency, you act as if you believe that you absolutely must have your partner's complete attention. When your partner resists, then you can feel insecure and convince yourself that someone else will sweep him or her away and you will be left with nothing. So you work all the harder to keep track of your part-ner's movements. Diligently follow this pattern, and your possessiveness turns your relationship into a prison.

11. Bury Your Partner's Head in the Sand

In the wake of the above ten tactics, and to keep the blame game going, keep telling your mate that your relationship will improve someday and that he or she will just have to wait out troubled times. Suggest to your partner that if he or she were more tolerant and understanding of your problems, things would get better. Of course they never will as long as you insist on manipulating and blackmailing, but don't tell your partner.

12. The Control Ploy

Act like a controller. Here you micromanage your relationship. You act like a parent to your mate. You strive to have the last word about the roles and rules your partner should follow in his or her relationship with you. You continually show your mate that he or she must follow your prescription for living or face big troubles. Work to turn the relationship into a reform school. Act to force your partner to live according to your expectations and rules. Use your own roles and rules to justify dominating the relationship and then to blame your partner when he or she falls short.

13. The Thirteenth Ploy: Accusation, Escalation, Justification

The number 13 is associated with bad luck. So it is only natural that there is a thirteenth ploy. The raven wouldn't have it any other way. This is the accusation, escalation, justification ploy. To put the thirteenth ploy into play, you do such things as accuse your partner of any fiendish thing that comes to your mind. You do this to put your partner on the defensive. When your partner counterattacks, you justify your initial accusation to escalate the conflict to new heights of bickering and strain.

You can exploit this game at any time. He or she arrives later than expected. You find food-encrusted dishes in the sink. Your child did poorly on a test. You dredge things up from the past. If you are especially articulate, you may reduce your mate to grumbling and muttering incoherently.

If your partner successfully sidetracks the issue by blaming you for your foibles and faults, you will have another opportunity to defend yourself. Then the game goes on until someone leaves in a huff.

A final bit of blame advice. You do not have to feel limited to the thirteen relationship ploys. You can play one-upmanship games where you show your partner you are better in every way. You can go from a state of hostility, yelling and reeling out of control, to one of reasonableness, caring, warmth, creativity, and optimism: That tactic often proves confusing and can destabilize your mate's sense of direction in the relationship. That will keep your partner feeling ambivalent and on edge.

FOURTEEN POSITIVE CHARACTERISTICS

We are now left with the challenge of coming up with non–blame game alternatives to building a solid intimate relationship. For this purpose, let's start by looking at the durable qualities that make for a solid, lasting, quality relationship. By developing these conditions, you crowd out blame.

Couples with consistently warm and loving relationships communicate clearly, care about each other, and have positive concern and regard for each other. Specifically, the following fourteen characteristics are largely present in such relationships.

1. Enjoy Your Partner

Is your partner someone you like to be near? Do you like to share similar experiences? Do you routinely lighten up and have fun with each other? Can you laugh together? Do you feel playful around each other? If you could no longer make love with your partner, would you continue your relationship as special friends? An answer of yes to these questions suggests that you enjoy your mate.

Unfortunately, after settling into their relationship, many couples get caught up in daily routines, obligations, and private pursuits. Some act as if individual tasks and pursuits should rule over relationship time. The challenge is to find ways to break from routines and to make time to enjoy shared activities.

When you enjoy your partner, you will find ways to create opportunities for relating in meaningful ways. Trying to create such opportunities raises the probability that you will have more enjoyable experiences and fewer hassles.

2. Trust

When you trust your partner, you believe the person is someone you can count on and can take at his or her word. You know where he or she stands on matters that are important. More important, you have confidence that your partner won't brush you off when you face severe challenges, such as a serious illness, disabling accident, job loss, death in the family, and other tragedy. You know you will be together for the duration.

3. Empathy

Empathy is where you have an emotional understanding about how other people feel. This highly important human tendency revolves around your ability to put yourself in the other person's shoes. If most people could not empathize with each other, we'd have little basis for communicating and maintaining attachments. Through this "feeling understanding," you experience a type of connectedness. When you recount a sad part of your past, you sense your partner knows how you felt. This empathy builds bridges between people.

Acceptance flows from empathy. This acceptance fuels good social relations. People who feel accepted normally will think well of those who accept them. However, you can understand and accept a person and still strongly disapprove of certain of that person's actions. Thus, separating a person's global worth from highly specific actions is challenging yet often rewarding.

4. Common Causes

Couples with a common cause stand out from the crowd because they share something truly special. A common cause is an activity, or an ideal, that both partners feel a joint commitment to support.

A common cause is more than having "something in common." It's a jointly held, vitally absorbing set of interests. This common cause can relate to a broad range of activities including raising children, restoring old houses, exploring new places, dancing, and the relationship itself.

You have a genuine common cause when you join to do something important to both of you. In this growth atmosphere, you look beyond the moment to put aside petty, discretionary complaints and feuds that could impede that common cause. That perspective includes finding ways to resolve personal differences equitably in the service of the greater good.

5. Compatible Social Styles

Sometimes people with stable and conservative views team with free spirits. She wants him because he's uninhibited. He wants her because she is stable and grounded. Sometimes these once-charming attributes lose appeal and become the foundation for clashes if each later tries to reform the other.

Common social styles often make for firmer relationships. Two outgoing people, for example, may share more in common because of their compatible social styles. Compatibility is even more important, however, when it comes to morality, or your sense of right and wrong.

6. Mutual Morality

A person with a subjective moral value system eventually is going to disagree with a partner with a more objective moral outlook. Here is why: People with an extremely subjective outlook believe that anything goes. Their actions are arbitrary and based on the whim of the moment. This "means justifies the ends" promotes patterns of deception and distrust. People with an extremely objective outlook value such things as keeping one's word, doing the right thing, acting with integrity, and being a responsible citizen. Couples with two radically different value styles invariably clash.

As a practical matter, couples with markedly different values styles rarely team up. However, since these variances exist in degrees within all of us, we can normally expect some value conflicts. However, partners with a shared sense of morality, based on common social experiences, are likely to have more stable relationships. That is because they will have more points of agreement on moral and ethical matters.

7. Care, Concern, and Positive Regard

Mature love exists at a level of care and concern for the hopes, wishes, and welfare of the other. Couples who show care, consideration, and positive regard for each other are going to find it easier to relate to each other. That is because positive acceptance encourages positive acceptance.

The importance of this idea is seen in its opposite. When you disrespect what your partner stands for and show little consideration for his or her wishes, wants, and dreams, you fertilize the grounds of contention.

8. Tolerance

This is a keystone to a solid relationship. The ability to accept one's partner's foibles and faults is an important condition for increasing the probability that the partner will reciprocate in kind.

Tolerance is based on acceptance. Acceptance means you understand and act on the idea that any relationship will ebb and flow. Some moments will be less than idyllic; others will feel great. Nevertheless, when you act with tolerance, you realize that your partner remains a worthy and important person throughout the rougher moments. This perspective means that you can see your partner's positive attributes even in a potentially unpleasant situation. With this mental attitude, conflict resolutions are simpler.

9. Openness

A sense of openness helps bind a relationship. In this state of mind, you are willing to let down your guard, share your feelings, express your disagreements, and non-defensively reflect on your role in the relationship. In this atmosphere you feel free to defend your position without having to defend yourself.

Openness is an important part of communications. In an open state of mind, you clarify and reconstruct your views through your ongoing dialogue with your partner. In this way you build a platform for improving the quality of your relationship. You also avoid many of the impasses people get into when they defend themselves and repeat self-sabotaging patterns.

10. Authenticity

This is the courage to be yourself without losing sight of the values, desires, and wants of your partner. When you feel and act naturally you normally will project a positive and congruent sense of self. In this atmosphere, you are likely to say what you mean in a way that evokes receptivity.

When you and your partner feel natural with each other, your thoughts and movements flow comfortably. You feel free of the sort of artificial constraints that come from projecting an image that is different from what you feel and deeply believe. You project depth and maturity.

11. Support

This involves putting yourself on the line to support your partner's rational interests; also, to comfort or protect. Support involves advocating for your partner when this is clearly in the partner's interest and in the interest of the relationship.

You and your partner both know that you can go forth independently on your own. Still, you share a mutual sense of dependence without falling into the dependency trap. This is the trap where you think you are nobody and nothing without the other, or that you can't do anything on your own. That is a hallmark of self-centeredness. In an enlightened state of support, you know you can go it alone. Nevertheless, you strongly prefer and value the help you gain from a partner who keeps your interests in focus, whom you also will support.

12. Harmonious Problem-Solving Style

In premarital counseling, a psychologist may give both partners individual IQ tests and observe how each independently goes about solving the problems. Thereafter, the couple takes the test together. We call this "interactional testing."

Sometimes one person dominates, and the joint IQ score reflects that person's score. In a second case, the couple may argue over answers, stubbornly refuse to bend, and spoil the result. Their couple IQ score may dip lower than the lower of the two. In a third common situation, the couple work cooperatively, pulling on each other's strength. Their averaged IQ is higher than their individual scores.

Couples with the stronger relationships bring different perspectives to bear on finding the best solution. Both members of this "team" feel a sense of satisfaction that he or she contributed to the solution. Under these circumstances, you and your partner will have a greater sense of investment in the processes and the outcomes and in making your joint problem solutions work.

Cooperative and compatible problem-solving styles give the couple an advantage. They will be motivated to work together because their experience shows them that the joint output is normally better. However, in cases where the partners have different preferred problem-solving styles, each can still decide to use his or her knowledge and approach in a complementary but effective way to formulate a "relationship" solution to a problem.

Successful joint problem solving usually involves: 1) a solid problem analysis; 2) an agreed-upon, concrete, and achievable goal; 3) a plan for reaching the goal; 4) a sensible way of organizing efforts such as deciding who will do what; and 5) flexible adjustments based on changing conditions. When you both cooperatively work together on solving problems, your "couple IQ" will be higher than what it would be if one person worked alone on the same problems.

13. Communicating Emotions

Communication is one of those vague terms that means more than it appears. When you communicate effectively with your mate, you do so from a point where your impressions are clear and realistic and your expressions represent that inner clarity.

Your communications take many forms. Positive emotional expressions involve your ability to say what you feel without unnecessary fear or risk. Saying "I love you" may involve some risk but also carries the promise of reciprocity.

Communicating emotions carries an often-unforseen risk. While what you feel is always correct, the perceptions that propel the feeling may or may not prove valid. Thus, a feeling is a fact but the beliefs and perceptions that evoke it may or may not prove valid. It is the wise person who recognizes this difference and has the emotive vocabulary to give meaning to feelings.

A key part of communicating emotions involves active listening. (You'll learn more about this communication style in chapter 12.) Active listening can help smooth many of these rough spots. Here you listen to understand the point your partner is making. Look for the positives in the statements. You don't have to agree with your partner's position, but people who feel understood will often reciprocate in kind.

14. Specificity

Specificity is a vital part of good communications. This is the ability to articulate what you want using words and ideas that the other can understand and act upon. It involves describing what you want in operational terms. "I want you to go for a walk with me" is an example of a specific, achievable, and measurable goal.

Specificity begins with being clear in your own mind about what you want. But specificity is more than that. It involves your ability to balance your wish with reasonableness and reality.

POSTSCRIPT

And what's romance? Usually, a nice little tale where you have everything As You Like It, where rain never wets your jacket and gnats never bite your nose and it's always daisy-time.

—D. H. Lawrence

An intimate relationship is as much an economic enterprise as it is a social unit. Romance may be there at the start, but economic and family conditions soon come to the forefront. It is how we manage these changes that can stabilize or destabilize a relationship.

You can practically always find a constructive challenge for improving the quality of your intimate relationship. These challenges include planning for the future, deciding on where to live, creating joint visions for the education of children, selecting mutually appealing home decor, deciding on purchases and savings, compromising on different sexual appetites, managing health crises, and balancing affection with responsibilities. This is an active, constructive, progressive process.

Can most people take steps to improve the quality of their intimate relationships? Definitely yes! Many times the place to start begins with the self.

10

Triumphing over Family Blame

> *The family is a source of stability that wobbles when under the weight of blame.*

Looking back over their lifetime, most people report that their greatest satisfactions came from their relationships with their families and friends. Indeed, some find that the time spent with their families is of such great importance that they will not accept career advancement opportunities if the opportunity threatens their family life.

At the other extreme, family life is far from paradise and is a source of repeated stress and strain. Predictably, the more strained families are those with surplus problems because they weave blame into their relationships. Although blameworthy actions do occur routinely within a family, when we embellish them with putdowns, blame labels, personal attacks, and tongue-lashings, these activities can quickly sour relationships.

Approximately half of all people who go to a therapist arrive because of marriage and family problems. Blame is common in such troubled relationships. This chapter can have special value when family blame is the issue. We'll look specifically at ways to keep needless blame out of family interactions and how to build positive alternatives. This can help reduce the need for therapy.

FAMILIES IN TRANSITION

The traditional family is becoming exceptional. As traditional structures change, we have fewer stabilizing guidelines. In the past fifty years, U.S. culture has undergone dramatic changes. Family expectancies are in transition and we don't quite yet know the shape they will take across diverse subcultural groups. The divorce rate has steadily risen to about 50 percent, despite our improved knowledge about family dynamics. Single-parent families are common and dominate some communities. Stepparenting programs have proliferated. Adolescent depression has risen tenfold since the 1950s, and substance abuse rates have risen sharply among that group. Family values have become a nondefined political slogan. Meanwhile, the traditional family appears against the ropes.

Culture, religion, past experiences, emotional styles, and other social-personal conditions influence the expectations, behavior, and style of family members. We can characterize some family systems as stoic, and others as emotional and volatile. However, it is not exclusively the social changes, emotional styles, cultural views, or religious bearing that separates families that function well from those that habitually interact in a dysfunctional manner. Often the degree of extension-of-blame thinking contributes to family satisfaction or problems.

Low extension-of-blame interacting forecasts higher family satisfaction. Predictably extension-of-blame bound families will feel stressed.* The inevitable conflicts that are part of any family are resolved more readily when family interactions are relatively free of needless forms of blame.

FAMILY CONFLICTS

Technically, the word "conflict" refers to a state of disharmony between incompatible persons, ideas, or interests. Conflict is a common result when we believe we are not getting what we want or feel "shortchanged." In this atmosphere, it is easy for people to fall into *blame traps* and blame others for denying them their "just due." However, each family member's perceptions of his or her "just due" will vary and often include competing beliefs and interests.

Family conflict is common. Among parents, the three major points of conflict involve money, children, and sex. Other conflicts occasionally may rise to the top of the list: trust, appearance, cooperativeness, work habits, and home maintenance. The way primary family caretakers resolve their personal differences about such matters teaches children how to manage conflict.

Since most people strongly prefer to fulfill their desires and interests, some family conflict is inevitable. Dad wants to take the family to the beach. The kids

---

* A blame-oriented family atmosphere has many interacting causes. People frequently imitate what they experienced in their own families. Family members on drugs or alcohol are more likely to engage in blame and defense. Emotionally disturbed family members can strain families' emotional resources and participate in a reciprocal pattern of blame. Families with attention deficit hyperactive children are typically more strained and prone to criticize and blame. Classic time-urgent, driven, hostile, competitive, controlling, and achievement oriented families. "Type A" fathers will tend to act critical, blame, and promote this same behavior in their sons. "Type A" mothers tend to use punitive, nonpositive controls with their children. Both sons and daughters of Type A parents report more frequent and greater distress due to family conflicts.

want to go to the amusement park. Mom wants to go to the movies. Each can compromise and make trade-offs to resolve the conflict. However, when differences in desires turn into a contest of wills, predictably someone will take the brunt of the blame. Inferred blame assertions such as "I can never do what I want to do; you always have to have your way" can promote an unresolvable conflict.

Other conflicts are possible. Siblings will play music too loud, try to control the television set, argue over who will sit in the front seat of the car, hog the computer, confiscate each other's personal property, hit and scream, tease and put down, and find ways to get each other into "trouble." Not only do they get into conflict with each other, they also put themselves into conflict with parents who want the behavior to cease.

The lessons we learn about resolving conflict within our own family can translate into skills that are needed to negotiate effectively in a competitive world. Conflict may even strengthen family relationships. That is because learning to deal with conflict within the family translates into learning how to deal with it in life outside of the family—a crucial skill, to be sure. Conflict can be positive when we reach for reasonable goals and learn to deal with others through this process. But while resolution removes a particular point of conflict, people are likely to feel dissatisfied with getting less than what they want. Nevertheless, through this stretching, responding, asserting, and compromising we add to our social strengths.

Positive Modeling

The family is not a group characterized by democratic consensus. A five-year-old normally doesn't make family financial decisions or vote on how to pay back debt or invest income surpluses. Many times whoever has the superior knowledge and holds the power in the family has the final word on such matters. A five-year-old can, however, choose what game to play, choose among outfits to wear, or participate in age-related decisions. Since the adults are in charge, they are the models.

Aristotle taught that we learn by watching what others do and then by imitating their behavior: "Man is the most imitative of living creatures and through imitation learns his earliest lessons." Mates who respect each other, who create a constructive home atmosphere, present as models worthy of imitating. Predictably, modeling healthy ways to resolve family conflicts can affect the conduct of future generations in constructive ways.

An important message in this conflict resolution process is that of articulating the problem, identifying solutions, and gaining agreement about a solution. Conducting this problem-solving venture with the intent of resolving the conflict (perhaps preventing future conflicts of the same kind) can prove productive. This approach provides a model for other family members to imitate.

Parents who typically model rational and spontaneous behavior take a positive step to improve the lives of future generations as well as the quality of life for their children and themselves. What are the critical ingredients of this positive modeling? Effective models strive to eschew extension-of-blame thinking, teach responsible behavior by example, provide a supportive atmosphere for experimentation, protect against dangers, express empathy and warmth, act attentive, educate and support, maintain emotional availability, balance control with flexibility, show common-sense judgment, demonstrate personal problem-solving skills, communicate clearly and effectively, show perspective, exhibit frustration tolerance, follow through, keep their word, act firmly, discipline when required, use humor to defuse needless conflict, exhibit reciprocity, and persevere. Since there are no perfect people and perfect ways to model, a noble quest is to seek ways to do progressively better in these areas.

Defining and Reframing the Conflict Process

Behavior rises to a destructive level when family members repeatedly engage in self-defeating behavior. Caretakers can provide negative modeling by enacting blame traditions that can haunt future generations.

If you don't like a pattern, understand it and change it. For example, behavior has a reason. It may not be a good reason, but there is a reason. Figuring out the basis for recurrent behavior can help put conduct into context to set the stage for finding meaningful solutions.

When we define a conflict process, we spell out what happens. For example, Johnny's mom wants him to start his homework immediately after returning home from school. Johnny stalls and acts frustrated when repeatedly told to do his homework immediately or no television. He blames his mother for causing him to feel upset and for depriving him of TV. However, he knows sometimes he can escape his homework responsibilities by whining about feeling fatigued or by saying he really doesn't have much work to do. Mom blames Johnny because he doesn't try hard enough. She also penalizes him by keeping him in after supper so he cannot play with his friends. Mom and Johnny are repeatedly in conflict, often leading to yelling and tears.

Once we reframe the situation without blame, both parties are likely to think more receptively about changing their respective contributions to the problem process. Instead of blaming Johnny, we can look at his part of the conflict as difficulty in managing frustration over doing an unpleasant task. Instead of blaming Mom for acting demanding, we can reframe her part of the process: Mom believes she would fail as a parent if her child didn't perform well in school. She believes that when Johnny completes his homework right after school, she is helping him to succeed in school and in life.

Once beyond the conflict-of-wills phase of the process, compromises become feasible. For example, Mom might agree to focus on helping Johnny build frustration tolerance. She could give Johnny a half-hour break to do what he wishes after he returns from school providing he does what she wants, which is to study without complaining. On this basis, Johnny may agree to finish his homework before supper so that he can play with his friends afterward. Both can learn, through this process, to change their internal blame-filled monologues to accommodate this idea: Power struggles frequently put both parties into a quagmire where they feel rotten and have no way out. Both people can win if they find a way to exit their logic-tight compartments to find a way to give ground to the other.

The Want-Something, Do-Something Strategy

Adolescents have their means of control. They are often A students in understanding how their parents are likely to react. The typical teenager also understands that beyond a certain point, parents have little control over whom they date, how much they eat, and their school grades. Teens can act to hold parents hostage by implying that they'll do something radical unless they get their way. Such conditions challenge parents to come up with workable solutions.

Parents normally have leverage. Money, the family car, time on the computer, and clothing purchases provide leverage. Most know this but misuse the leverage. They can reframe this leverage in a way that gives the teen a responsible choice.

The *want-something, do-something* strategy reframes the issue. Driving the family car, for example, is a privilege, not a right. If one's adolescent son or daughter wants to exercise a driving privilege, a reasonable parent can require reasonable trade-offs. Either the daughter or son avoids doing something negative or does something positive. So if the teen decides he or she would rather, say, skip school than have access to the automobile, the adolescent signals that he or she wants the time off from school more than the use of the automobile. The want-something, do-something technique gains its validity from a parent correctly insisting on responsible, disciplined behavior and making clear to teens that they control the outcome by what they do.

MORE TIPS FOR IMPROVING FAMILY RELATIONSHIPS

Here are some additional tips for improving the quality of family relationships. Note that they can also help improve the quality of other relationships.

➤ Avoid forging threats in the heat of conflict. Back off and cool down when you are inclined to say something that you may later regret.
➤ Use "I" messages over the accusatory "You" message. For example, "I feel sad" will normally lead to a better outcome than "You make me feel depressed."
➤ Practice constructive values such as tolerance, integrity, and responsibility.
➤ Even a superficial display of care and concern normally will go farther in creating a positive atmosphere than repeated rumbles based on gripes and complaints.
➤ Express perceptions as perceptions: for example, "I believe this to be so."
➤ Family members typically understand that others have hot-buttons and how to push them. Avoid pushing hot-buttons. Pushing those buttons normally evokes a counterattack.

➤ Every day find something kind to say about your mate or family members. Express these sentiments.

➤ Find something about each family member that provokes a sense of empathy. People who feel empathic are less likely to overreact in a negative way. People who feel understood are also less likely to make strong, negative, emotional assertions.

➤ Create desirable outcomes for discussions where participants are all likely to feel like "winners." Seek common ways to solve problems where mutual cooperation promises a "win-win" solution.

➤ Do something out of the ordinary that is helpful to another without keeping count of who is doing the most.

➤ Arduously avoid issuing insults or blame labeling.

➤ Whenever feasible, defuse personality conflicts with humor.

➤ Keep promises.

➤ Find something positive in a normally negative situation.

➤ Avoid creating needless crises.

➤ Clarify expectations and assumptions.

➤ Listen, ask clarifying questions, seek proof and evidence for assertions, and separate the person from his or her actions.

➤ Determine the advantages and disadvantages of either fixing a problem or forgiving versus defending and blaming.

➤ An alternative perspective to "my way or no way" might include yielding ground to gain ground.

POSTSCRIPT

"Things perceived as real will be real in their consequences," wrote W. I. Thomas. The real belief that family members can expel extensions of blame from their interactions will yield a perception of reality that is radically different from that of the family that acts as if its members are powerless to do any differently.

Within a family, extensions of blame are both a problem and a primary symptom of dysfunctional conflict conditions. By addressing these and other needless blame patterns, families can help liquidate blame thinking and, perhaps, simultaneously expose core problem issues to an enlightened review.

11

Understanding Blamers

> *Prejudicial thinking is at the root*
> *of the extensions of blame.*

Practice blaming and you get better at it. In a sense, this practice is like the children's nursery rhyme "Jack and Jill":

> *Jack and Jill went up the hill to fetch a pail of water.*
> *Jack fell down and broke his crown and Jill came tumbling after.*

Let's look at a possible contemporary translation of the lyric. Jack: "Did you know you left the light on in the garage and left the door open?" Jill: "You were in there with me." Jack: "See, you won't admit to anything." Jill: "You're a bore." Now, who broke the crown and who came tumbling after? Neither Jack nor Jill is likely to admit to blaming. Perhaps that is why they both took a tumble.

You might think, "Me a blamer? No. That's the other guy's problem." On second thought you might consider, "Perhaps, sometimes, but I'm no worse than anyone else." However, in a blame culture, practically everyone will, from time to time, fall into blame traps. We can't avoid them, but we can curb them somewhat. The trick to curbing blame patterns is first to recognize our own distinctive blame style and the blame styles others will likely exhibit. Then deal with them!

In this chapter we'll look at two general blame styles, blaming complaining and discrimination. We'll look at some options to address these blame processes.

As a prelude to what follows, it helps to view blame styles as generated from automatic thought processes where the blame habit occurs without much forethought. This view can help reduce a major stress caused by blaming people for their blame style or blaming yourself for having a blame style. Superimposing one misery onto another serves no sane purpose and can only worsen an unfortunate situation.

BLAMING COMPLAINING

Complaints are common but complaints need not involve needless blame. Legitimate complaints about services, complaints about the continuation of a problem, or complaints about unwanted situations can stimulate us to fix the cause. Abraham Lincoln, for example, had a justifiable complaint about the Confederacy breaking from the Union. He acted to preserve the United States through military force.

You have a justifiable complaint if you buy a new automobile and it drives like a lemon. You return it to the dealer for repair. If your state has a lemon law, you get your money back if the automobile dealer can't fix the problem. Although you are likely to feel frustrated by purchasing a lemon, then having to deal with getting it fixed or replaced, extension-of-blame thinking won't fix the car.

Complaints also can symbolize helplessness. Some people feel powerless and whine and complain in the hope that the complaint will make a problem go away or that they might feel relief. Some get themselves into a rut when they spin their wheels by complaining, complaining, and then complaining some more about one thing or another. They spend so much time and energy complaining that they deprive themselves of the time to put energy into what is most important for them to be doing.

Blaming complainers have a different agenda. Wendy, for example, compulsively carps about people rejecting her and how these despised individuals ruined her life. Indeed, she routinely speaks on the phone with friends who also complain about their lacks and disappointments. She and her complaint club members enable each other to continue their distress by reinforcing each other's gripes. To break this cycle of blaming complaining, Wendy would best pause and reflect upon these questions:

1. What do I mean by "ruined"?
2. In what way has my life been irrefutably ruined by some past rejections?
3. What do I hope to accomplish by blaming others for ruining my life?
4. What purpose does it serve to tell members of my telephone circle about others ruining my life?
5. Do I have anything to do with how I feel?

As Wendy answers these questions, she quickly discovers that her blaming complaining did nothing to change her life for the better. Indeed, her preoccupations with her complaints added to her distress. If she chose, she could refuse to engage in blaming complaining and concentrate on taking action to improve the quality of her life. Wendy chose to lead a different life when she put herself in charge of her own happiness.

Carl entered counseling for work stress. He believed management was unfair to him for failing to promote him. He complained that people who get ahead are suckups. He believed he was overlooked for promotions because his boss was blind to his true skill, and that his company's management could easily make the Peter Principle "Who's Who" list. (The Peter Principle states that people rise in an organization to their level of incompetency.) He nitpicked about what others do and griped about too much noise in his office complex. Although he did not overtly blame and complain to his coworkers and employer, he often looked tense and discontented as an outward expression of his negative thinking.

Sadly, Carl sabotaged himself through his covert blaming complaining practices. Although he was extraordinary when it came to job knowledge and solving complex technical problems, his style was self-defeating for a person who sought advancement. Meanwhile, locked in a world of blaming complaining, Carl lead a life frothing with inner misery that translated into a sour external appearance.

Carl had a brilliant ability to grasp complex concepts when the concepts were mathematical, technical, or scientific. So, as part of his positive change program, he agreed to turn this strength against a "vulnerability."

1. He applied powerful scientific thinking methods by converting his complaints into hypotheses, such as people treat him unfairly because he is competent.
2. He sought ways to disconfirm the hypotheses. When your goal is to develop an objective outlook, disconfirmation is often more powerful than trying to prove your point. In proving a point, you look for ways to support a bias.
3. He applied his problem-solving skills to interpersonal areas. To do this, he tested a hypothesis that by taking an initiative to daily greet his coworkers, make positive statements, and increase his smile rate from zero to twenty times per day, his coworkers would voluntarily approach him with greater frequency.
4. He assessed this voluntary approach outcome variable by first taking a two-week baseline, where he recorded the frequency of voluntary approaches. Voluntary approaches included asking social questions, making general comments, telling jokes, small talk, and invitations to lunch. His baseline was zero.
5. He initiated the experiment for two weeks. The voluntary approach rate went from zero to an average of ten contacts per day.

In the process of conducting this experiment, Carl discovered he could 1) profitably use his scientific ability to disable his blaming complaining, 2) adopt a more open manner and style that made him approachable, 3) find strengths in people when he looked for them, 4) refocus from blaming complaining to taking action steps, and 5) significantly improve the quality of his coworker relationships.

Part of Carl's blaming complaining was linked to social anxiety and related rejection fears. The experiment helped him to reduce his fear of rejection significantly. The idea of an experiment also enabled Carl to view what he did as a plan. Now he could test the effectiveness of the plan, thus reducing his ego involvement in the outcome. For example, in a scientific experiment the results are friendly in the sense that the results point to what to do next. Although Carl began this experiment by following a mechanical procedure, he finished feeling natural.

Every so often, people awaken and act as if they were going to find someone or something to blame. Laura awoke, jumped out of bed, walked to the bathroom, and then darkened her day. The water wasn't hot enough. The cap was off the toothpaste. She saw a bathtub ring. Now smoldering, she walked back to the bedroom, shook Tom out of his slumbers, and screamed: "How could you be so irresponsible?"

Laura's bewildered mate sat up, initially speechless. Then, almost instinctively, Tom blamed Laura for her tone and complained that she was "making mountains out of molehills." Then he went on to say that she was like her crazy sister. At that comment, the wick to the power keg was lit and short. Both thought about divorce.

Laura is confident that she is right about her complaints. However, she is not happy about the results of complaining. She can act to deal with her blaming complaining by 1) considering the importance of her complaint, 2) specifying what she expects to accomplish by her complaints, 3) determining if her tone and attitude convey extension-of-blame messages and, if so, how are such messages predictably received, and 4) doing a short- and long-term benefit analysis to get an articulated perspective on the pros and cons of blaming complaining. Tom can act to deal with his blaming complaining by 1) recognizing that the root cause of Laura's blaming complaining and then dealing with the core issue, 2) dealing with each complaint individually, 3) addressing and fixing what he is responsible for, 4) without judging Laura, expressing how he feels about her blaming complaining, and 5) refusing to engage in cross-accusations. To the extent that both Laura and Tom put reason between their blame impulses and reaction, predictably they will decrease the frequency, intensity, and degree of blame-related conflict. Since it takes only one person to stop an argument, either Laura or Tom can defuse the conflict.

We've all met people like Jack and Jill, Wendy, Carl, and Laura and Tom. They are not bad people. Rather, they are people with highly prejudicial but correctable blaming complaining habits. Change, however, rarely comes easily; normally it requires learning alternatives and then implementing the alternatives. Fortunately, this book is filled with alternatives to blaming complaining.

GENERAL TACTICS FOR DEALING WITH BLAMING COMPLAINING

People who fall into the blaming complaining trap often have a partial truth to justify both the complaint and the blame. They will, however, be hard-pressed to justify the extensions of blame that mingle with this pattern.

Blaming complaining often has a paradoxical effect of alienating an audience. Alienated people eventually will turn a deaf ear to the complaints. The blaming complainer will correctly interpret this as rejection and probably feel a sense of self-alienation that turns to desperation to be heard. At this phase, the blaming complainer rotates around a circle of misery.

Should you encounter a blaming complainer, you have many choices, including the following:

➤ When receiving a blaming complaint about someone else, say Joe, you can ask, "If Joe were here, would he see the situation in the same way?" "Would he have any valid point to make?" "If so, then what?" This form of inquiry can help clarify the blaming complaining issue while at the same time let the blaming complaining individual understand that accusations are subject to legitimate questioning.

➤ If you are not in a position to do anything, you might inquire, "What do you anticipate that I can do to help you in this situation?" As complainers make most blaming complaints about other people for either cathartic purposes or to cause you to think badly about the subject, this question can help to put the matter squarely in perspective.

➤ It is normally wise not to give unsolicited advice. Because some blaming complainers appear desperate, you may feel tempted to give advice. Someone who makes a legitimate complaint may apply the advice if it seems valid. Blaming complainers have another agenda. They present themselves as victims and normally are more interested in playing out their version of the blame game than focusing their efforts on self-development and self-improvement. Suggesting responsible actions doesn't gel with what they want to hear. A true blaming complainer is likely to say "I already thought of that, it won't work." "*Yes, but* you don't really understand the problem." This "yes but" form of negation is so common as to represent a partial cognitive signature for a blaming complaining syndrome.

➤ In the world of the blaming complainer, reassurances that life may someday be better typically fall flat. When you reassure, you are, however, engaged. That signal encourages the blaming complainer to continue and the game goes on.

➤ Avoid irritating yourself by listening to the same complaints. I have told friends who have repeated the same blaming complaining problem that I did not want to talk about the subject. There was nothing I could do other than to feel irritated. I have taken this action after I have responded and given advice when asked.

➤ Some whistleblowers fall into the blaming complaining trap. Believing they did the right thing, some will not only expect but demand that others defend them whatever the economic, personal, and emotional cost. Since blaming complaining is likely to turn away potential allies, demanding whistleblowers weaken their own cause. For this reason, many follow the man of La Mancha (Don Quixote) into jousts with windmills. Potential allies are normally more impressed and confident in supporting people who can ably fend for themselves, keep focused on the issue, and persist.

➤ If you find yourself surrounded by blaming complaining types, you might ask yourself what you truly gain from these affiliations that you could not gain by engaging tolerant people who are willing to take necessary steps to solve their problems.

If you have any illusions that you can easily change a habitual blaming complainer into a thoughtful, empathic, congenial companion, you have a noble challenge.

Blaming complainers routinely seek ways to justify their complaints and to justify why they cannot improve their lives. As a group, they follow a pattern of negation in which they find reasons why they can't improve. They typically suffer considerably, repeat the same sorry patterns, attribute their powerlessness to past hurts, preoccupy themselves with current crises, or focus on conditions they believe are impossible to change. It is only when they get sick and tired of complaining and act to improve that they start to get better by doing better. This is a task that only they can do for themselves. The best anyone can do is give guidance when guidance is requested.

DISCRIMINATORY BLAMERS

A preference for asparagus is a personal choice. If you'd "rather drive a Buick," date a "blond," or eat steak, that's your choice. Indeed, it's your right to have a positive prejudice toward automobiles, foods, people, and most other matters. Blame is typically absent from such preferences.

Same-sex members have some qualities in common. Sex typing of behaviors means that a majority of the people who behave in a certain way are of one gender. There is no blame involved in the objective description of certain sex differences. For example, women have, on average, better fine motor coordination than do men. That's an empirical observation. If you want to discriminate on the basis of fine motor coordination, the discrimination favors women.

Most of us will occasionally poke light fun at ourselves because of our foibles or at other people because of their features, characteristics, or work. That's a form of discrimination, but it often doesn't amount to much. The most politically correct people may blamefully object to this form of levity, but such complaints are not likely to quickly promote a widespread change.

Practically any group can be the brunt of light levity: "blonde" jokes, lawyer jokes, mother-in-law jokes, or psychologist jokes. Such jokes are based on prejudice and an inferential form of blame that rarely amounts to much among reasonable people. Indeed, the person who tells lawyer jokes may be abstractly prejudiced against lawyers in general and yet have close friends who practice law. While sometimes in poor taste, the jokes are common.

Prejudice occurs when people have preconceived stereotypical ideas about another person or group's race, religion, height, weight, shape of glasses, sex, age, intelligence, achievements, education, parents, type of work, "social class," marital status, country of origin, political beliefs, disability, hobby, and appearance. The prejudice can be favorable, but when we think of prejudice, we normally assume that the attitude is negative. Mentally ill people, for example, often are stereotyped in the movies as mad killers. As a generalization, the "mad killer" prejudice is flatly wrong.

Although clinical populations such as psychopaths and pedophiles are dangerous people, the vast majority of people with mental health problems experience excruciating anxiety and/or major depressions, suffer from self-concept disorders, or manifest other exaggerations of normal human stress.

Some epidemiological studies suggest that over half the American population have or will have a noteworthy mental illness over their lifetime. So most people who are negatively prejudiced against other people with psychological problems will surely either personally have a significant emotional challenge or will have a friend or family member who experiences some form of intense prolonged psychological distress.

We enter a serious arena of generalized blame when prejudice is adverse and condemning and leads to discrimination. Generalized extension-of-blame thinking sets the stage for discrimination when a bias rises to a level of behavioral expression that disadvantages another. Harassment is an extreme form of discrimination, as when hostility or hatred motivates intentionally harming another through causing a loss of status, loss of friendships, loss of work, loss of privileges, or loss of educational opportunity. Often subtle and cloaked in official-sounding denials, the exoneration ploys for discrimination fall flat when viewed in the context of their results.

Extensions of blame based on extreme prejudice motivate violence. At the limit of this process, we find terrorism and ethnic cleansing (state-inspired hate killings of a population based on race, religion, politics, or other common quality) and mate battering. Let's look at people who batter other people. They start with hatred, follow up with belligerency, and end with physical assault.

To assuage criticism and to protect their public image, people who batter predictably put aside their real motives and employ hypocritical exonerations that sound detached from the event:

➤ The anger overcame me.
➤ She (he) made me do it.
➤ I was provoked.
➤ The argument got out of control.
➤ I was venting.
➤ Alcohol made me do it.
➤ People pushed my buttons.
➤ I had a lot of stress and things built up in me.
➤ I just went ballistic.

Predictably, if people who batter overcame their extremely prejudicial extension-of-blame thinking and exoneration ploys, they would stop battering (discriminatory assaults). For example, identifying the erroneous elements in the prejudicial battering logic by looking for extension-of-blame thinking is a good start.

Using the first three of the above examples as an illustration, we can say:

➤ How does anger overcome you? When you feel angry, what do you tell yourself to fuel the anger?

➤ How does she *make* you assault her? What were you telling yourself about "her" behavior? Can you find elements of extension of blame in that thinking?

➤ People are provoked every day without getting physically abusive. What excuse did you give yourself to justify your actions? Where is the extension of blame in the excuse?

This analysis often goes further in highlighting areas to change in one's thinking than one gains in uttering a blanket exoneration. Exonerations normally serve as a weak attempt to abrogate personal responsibility. Predictably, people who excuse harmful behavior are more likely to repeat what they excuse. Those who truly accept responsibility and carefully examine and change the underlying prejudicial extension-of-blame process will engage in fewer assaultive behaviors and can train themselves to stop altogether.

DEALING WITH PREJUDICE AND DISCRIMINATION

Most everyday forms of prejudice are manageable. The extension-of blame process does, however, require awareness, perspective, and action to change. Here are a few thoughts on this topic:

➤ If you are black, white, yellow, or brown; Catholic, Protestant, or Moslem; Democrat or Republican; liberal or conservative; labor or management; man or woman, you will find some people both within and outside of your reference group that you simply would not want as your best friend. People have different interests, styles, values, abilities, ethics, cultural heritage, degrees of trustworthiness, and problem-solving styles. If these conditions are instrumental to solid intimate relationships, they also are instrumental to friendships. The problem arises when extending blame to people outside of one's reference group because your group defines them as different, unacceptable, condemnable, and expendable. A special commitment to "take people as they are" brings about relationship selections on the basis of specific individual qualities rather than on the basis of generalized blame or idealism. The world would be a better place if we took people as they are, rather than grouped them.

➤ When extension-of-blame thinking engages our prejudices, then the path to change is to seek and root out ideas of condemnation affixed to the target of the blame. You stubbornly refuse to allow yourself to accept others' condemnation of "you" because you are a member of a different reference group from theirs. Most people can learn to separate what they like or don't like about a person. They can avoid falling into a condemnation blame trap if they remind themselves to do so.

➤ Identifying and defusing extensions of blame has great value as a tool to help people improve their mental health. In a blame culture there exist numerous extension-of-blame examples, including fault-finding, inferential blame, subtle putdowns, discrimination, or blaming complaining. Selective examples provide opportunities to develop and practice critical thinking skills to discriminate between fact and fiction. When this lesson translates to a realistic tolerance, tempered by the observation that people are normally responsible for their actions, people are more likely to think better of their own personal problem-solving abilities and tolerance.

➤ Treating blameworthy acts as blameworthy without flowing them into extensions of blame will promote greater objectivity and a greater willingness to correct problems. In such cases, I predict we will find a lower incidence of emotional and behavioral problems normally associated with self-concept disorders, insecurity, inhibition, depression, anxiety, or other stress states that correlate with extension-of-blame beliefs.

COULD-BE ALCHEMY

"Could-be alchemy" refers to the idea that people could be and therefore should be different or act differently from the way they do. In other words, if something could be, it should be! This belief is a prime catalyst for inner misery and animosity between acquaintances, friends, kin, neighbors, coworkers, and strangers.

Just as the ancient alchemists couldn't turn the baser metals to gold, the could-be alchemist frequently suffers the same fate. They fail. For example, how can demanding that a person in a grumpy mood act pleasantly change the person's demeanor when such changes are discretionary? When we pose the question in this way, we discover that there is no alchemy. The other individual has to find an incentive for change, and our wishes won't make that so!

We have reasonable expectancies for how we'd like others to treat us, for equal opportunity, and for a safe and secure life. However, when we expect, demand, or require what we'd prefer, this could-be alchemy has predictable outcomes. We are likely to condemn those who do not comply with our demands. In this process we are likely to preoccupy ourselves with hostile and vengeful thoughts, feel tense, and shrink our perspective. By keeping expectancies (probability statements) separate from expectations (absolute statements), we act to escape the negative effects of thinking in could-be alchemy terms.

The could-be alchemy prescription is a prelude to bias, extension-of-blame thinking, and discriminatory actions. In a sense, this is like the Midas touch in reverse. We get the opposite of what we expect. (In the King Midas myth, the king wished that he could have the power to turn everything to gold. He got his wish; everything he touched turned to gold, including the food he touched to eat.)

The simple act of using the label "could-be alchemy" can help signal us to think about the benefits of avoiding rigid demands. We also can remind ourselves that predictably we can get farther in improving our relationships with people through reason, tolerance, and cordiality than with magic.

POSTSCRIPT

The English novelist Charlotte Brontë knew well of the influence of prejudice when she wrote, "Prejudices, it is well known, are most difficult to eradicate from the heart whose soul has never been loosened or fertilized by education; they grow there firm as weeds among stones."

Blaming complaining and discrimination rely on prejudicial forms of thinking that have growth-stunting potential. Perhaps education is our best hope for positive change. The question then is: What type of education? Understanding how prejudice feeds extension-of-blame thinking, which then feeds discriminatory actions, sets the stage for thinking in opposite but positive ways.

12

Communicating Powerfully with Impact

> *Communications twist through our lives from the*
> *beginning until the end. The magic happens in between.*

Have you ever heard the phrase "We need to communicate better"? This interest is high on the list of things that most people want to improve. Effective communications can go far in keeping channels open between intimates, reducing family squabbles, and relating to acquaintances and strangers—some of whom might appear difficult if we don't communicate our ideas clearly.

Communications mean more than the dictionary definition of the term. When we communicate we do such things as convey information, describe feelings, present and learn of others' interests. In a broader sense, communications are a form of making connections with other people. Unless we are willing to share a connection with others, we learn little about ourselves and about them.

I designed this chapter to give you tested techniques for expressing yourself in a friendly, confident, blame-free manner. The means for accomplishing this result revolves around this idea: What we perceive and believe (impressions) are the platform for effectively conveying what we mean (expressions).

IMPRESSIONS AND EXPRESSIONS

Your inner impressions influence your outward expressions. When you tune into your inner voice and understand the meaning of the messages that you send to yourself, you'll come to see how these ideas influence your emotions and actions. When your expressions reflect a set of negative impressions, you tie yourself to a turnstile. To make positive personal changes in your impressions and expressions requires taking responsible, concrete actions to build tolerance, acceptance, and social skills. This is a most powerful alternative to blame: communicating powerfully with impact.

Our impressions connect with our perceptions and expectations of reality to form the first conscious level of our understanding of what is going on around us. For example, when we touch something that is cold, we feel it in our brain yet find the source in our bodies.

We create our own impressions of the world. This is not a new idea. The eighteenth century philosopher George Berkeley correctly noted that we have an endless variety of ideas and impressions that are part of the mind, spirit, and self. The inner impressions that Berkeley noted gain outward *expression* through our words, phrases, gestures, grimaces, tears, laughter, and other visible messages.

EXPRESSIONS

The world of expressions is a world of action where we speak, gesture, inform, persuade, hug, greet, or seek. This action process occurs in the present moment. Since we think in the present, past, and future tenses, our expressions also will reflect these capabilities.

We can't escape the reality that our expressions will partially influence how the public sees us. A person who exhibits aggressive, pushy, lecturing, arrogant, critical behavior acts distinctively different from one who beats a wimpish retreat from normal conflicts. Although these extremely different social styles represent visible attributes, they only scratch the surface in defining the complexities of how a person perceives and responds to events.

Our expressions normally are toned by our personalities, emotions, and beliefs. Because our expressions are so fundamental to our social interactions, it is easy to see how our colorful expressive abilities partially tie in to who we think we are, our social role, and our sense of control. For this reason, some people strive to adopt a socially desirable public image and to follow "safe" paths to avoid any form of disapproval—even the normal or necessary kind.

Emotional Expression

Your emotions resonate from your impressions of reality. Thus, part of the process of expressing yourself with impact involves understanding and trusting your natural feelings. For example, if you feel comfortable or ill at ease around someone, perhaps you have a valid reason worth exploring. Clear expression also involves recognizing and overcoming misleading feelings that come from false ideas.

How effectively we express ourselves partly depends on our emotional state of mind. When we feel natural, confident, and happy, we are likely to present ourselves as personable. When we doubt our feelings or worry too much about embarrassing ourselves, we hinder ourselves and risk dampening the more congenial parts of our personality.

Feelings are part of experiencing. Expressions such as "I felt happy when you remembered my birthday" can help you to connect with another person in a positive way. There are many appropriate times when "I feel" expressions can defuse a needless conflict. For instance, a friend forgets your birthday and you note, "I felt bad when I did not receive a card from you on my birthday." This is a straightforward expression of how you felt and why. However, sometimes even the most gentle emotional assertions can put another on the defensive.

"I feel" or "I believe" statements can go far to defuse defensiveness and prevent blame counterattacks. Blame tied to expressed beliefs gives others opportunities to explain. Blame tied to certainty can spur defiance.

LEVELS OF COMMUNICATION

People who feel warmly toward you may touch your arm. People who stroke their chins while listening to you may convey a judgmental attitude. While some signal their attitude through body language, others play on words. A double entendre, for example, is a word or phrase that conveys a double, often risqué, meaning.

Secondary verbal communications occur when the message has a deeper meaning, such as when the meaning is in the tone. We hear secondary communications in which we hear blame questions with a twist. A mother infers blame when she asks her child, "Where is your coat?" She knows the coat's whereabouts, but her intent is to blame the child for not wearing the coat. "Why didn't you call when you were supposed to?" is another example of a blame question with a twist. Here the message is to chastise the respondent by putting him or her on the spot.

Secondary communications represent interesting challenges. Do you respond to a secondary communication with a secondary communication? In cases where you receive a secondary communication and you want to establish parity, a statement such as "I'm not clear about what you mean" provides one of many optional responses. Do you want to identify the communication for what it appears to represent? The choice depends on the context.

ACTIVE-REFLECTIVE LISTENING

How are we to build communication bridges? The answer to this question begins with an answer to another. How do we listen with sensitivity and awareness? You will find part of the answer in active-reflective listening.

People who listen actively and reflectively interact through identifying, clarifying, and confirming the meaning of a message. The system gains value when it is important for you to 1) convey to the speaker that you understood, 2) comprehend subtleties, 3) grasp a complex message, 4) sort out a mixed message, or 5) verify your understanding when a message sounds ambiguous.

As a practiced active-reflective listener, you'll read people and their ideas with greater clarity. Normally you will get your ideas across because you can tie what you say to the other person's frame of reference. However, you will limit yourself in your active-listening skills unless you have a plan that involves an attentive effort to decipher what a speaker intends to say as well as what is overstated and what is missing from a communication.

Active-reflective listening is not a plan of "silence." Active-reflective listening includes talking with the person to clarify and comprehend the messages that you hear. Through this process, you seek to understand the meaning of a speaker's message, interests, desires, expectations, judgments, positions, attitudes, beliefs, and actions. As an important phase of this plan, you arduously avoid responding with skeptical tones, negative body language, and subtle and inferential expressions of blame. Such blame messages can dampen a conversation quickly.

Using the active-reflective listening plan, you normally operate from an a posteriori framework: You go from gathering facts and impressions to using this information to evolve general ideas about people and their messages. This is radically different from the alternative a priori framework that involves prejudging a speaker's message on the basis of your theory about the speaker. Although past behavior is a predictor of current and future behavior, most people dislike feeling pigeonholed. An a priori judgment can cause a speaker to feel slotted.

When people feel understood, they are likely to rate the communication well. Interestingly, most people point to active-reflective listeners as the best communicators—and conversationalists—even when the "listener" had very little to say.

Here are some general guidelines for this active-reflective listening process.

> ➤ Focus on what the speaker says. Resist inserting your thoughts into the subject until you understand the issue. (Most of us skip this step.)
> ➤ Avoid presenting information prematurely. Try to blend your message into the conversation in a way that fits naturally.
> ➤ Develop eye contact early but do not stare. Look into the person's eyes and not just at his or her face.
> ➤ Maintain a "comfortable" distance. In U.S. culture, three feet is a comfortable distance for informal discussions.
> ➤ Match the other person's body language against the words you hear to assess the veracity of the statement.
> ➤ Use questions that yield concrete answers so you can use the information you glean.

Paraphrase for Understanding

At cocktail parties, social gatherings, or informal luncheon meetings, we often see communications where active-reflective listening is rare. In such circumstances, where people keep skipping onto different topics for social reasons, an active-reflective listening style may have limited value.

In settings where understanding and clarifications are important, active-reflective listening often yields benefits. The interviewer who does most of the talking, for example, learns little about the other's views, principles, and abilities.

Even when you are confident that you have tuned in to the meaning of a speaker's message, you might want to confirm what you think is happening to ensure that your assumptions are accurate and to let the speaker know you understand.

The active-reflective listener may start this clarifying process by saying "I heard you saying . . ." or "It sounds like you said . . ." or "Is this what you mean?" Then he or she restates what the speaker said.

Paraphrasing has several benefits:

➤ It offers listeners the opportunity, at frequent intervals, to confirm what they hear.
➤ It tells the speaker that the listener actually is listening.
➤ It gives the speaker the opportunity to hear an "instant replay," so he or she can clear up inaccuracies or misconceptions.

Self-Checking

When you actively and reflectively listen, you keep focused on the issues. These self-monitoring questions can help you maintain your focus:

1. Am I concentrating on the speaker's issues?
2. Am I linking my experience to these issues as a reality check?
3. Am I clarifying my understanding of the speaker's message?
4. How is the person responding to my actions?

NONVERBAL EXPRESSIONS

New information flows into your mind through all your sensory channels and through the visual channel more than any other. For example, body language gives added meaning to a speaker's words. For example, does the person's posture convey a message? Does the posture loosen up or change with time? Does she squirm in her chair? Does he lean forward toward you?

Ray Birdwhistle, a body language expert, estimates that we project 65 percent of our communications through nonverbal expression. The reflective listener knows this and pays special attention to this body language and to word inflections. These gestures convey messages about the person's interests, attitudes, and state of mind.

Any part of the body can display a message that can support or run contrary to a spoken message. Hand gestures normally congruently flow with the person's ideas. When a person's hand gestures go out of rhythm with his or her speech, what might this mean?

Active-reflective listeners pay close attention not only to what speakers say but to how they say it. To the active-reflective listener, body language—along with word choice, tone, and inflection—is part of the message. For example, if you heard your neighbor say, with a furrowed brow and clenched teeth, "I feel very happy today," would you think that person felt overjoyed? A person who glares at you after saying

"So glad to see you again" displays an attitude of mind that goes beyond the words. Gestures, such as finger-tapping, could convey impatience. Here your sight becomes part of the listening process. The eyes can reveal the thoughts behind them. Are his pupils open more than expected for the lighting? (Pupils may dilate with interest and contract with anger.) In "singles" situations, does the person who interests you maintain eye contact while you are still at a distance? Eye contact can suggest interest.

Swallowing and gulping may convey a message about speaker tension, as do tightening of facial muscles into a grimace or licking the lips. (Anxiety can include a dry mouth and lips, but some medications produce this as a side effect.) However, signs of anxiety are equivocal when it comes to sending truthful messages. A person can appear ill at ease and the message can be quite honest. Anxious people may squirm while telling the truth because they are uncomfortable with a certain reality. On the other hand, a pathological liar can look you straight in the eye and use words that sound convincing. Practiced deceivers, for example, might show little body movement when they tell an untruth because they don't want their body language to give them away. It is only when you know the truth that the deception becomes obvious.

People may smile when they feel pleasure, amusement, or derision. Psychologist Paul Ekman describes the smile as a doorway to a speaker's thoughts. He describes several examples. The *felt* smile conveys genuine pleasure. The *contempt* smile, seen in the tightening of the corners of the lips, may reflect disgust. In the *fear* smile, the lip muscles pull horizontally toward the ears. This smile projects the person's sense of impotence.

We can add to Ekman's list. In the *dampened* smile, the person tries to subdue visible signs of tension through pressed lips. The *miserable* smile suggests resignation where the person simply "grins and bears it." We may masquerade our emotions through fake smiles. In the *listener* smile, the "listener" substitutes a smile for the usual uh-huh responses. Here the speaker may take the smile as an urging to continue. The *dictator smile* appears on the pictures of the faces of tyrants such as Saddam Hussein. Intended to convey a message of benevolence, the smile hides the darker sides of these personalities. This is an effective deception when the viewer thinks that anyone who looks that kindly can't be that bad. But history tells a different tale.

While you observe the body language of others, consider your own body language: 1) Are you maintaining good eye contact (neither staring nor looking out of the corner of your eyes)? 2) Are you leaning toward the other? 3) Are you showing an open posturing? These three body language signs convey a message of interest.

EMBLEMS

Emblems are nonverbal signals such as head nodding, shoulder shrugging, winking, twiddling thumbs, hand flipping, and other. There are cultural variations in the meaning of some emblems. In the United States, a bowed head may be a sign of shame or guilt. In Japan, bowing one's head may also convey respect. In the United States, twirling your index finger near your temple signifies that the object of this gesture is acting crazy. In Denmark, the gesture is a signal that you disapprove of another driver's performance.

Your knowledge of culture-specific signs is important in situations that require such knowledge. The former president Richard Nixon went to China and gave a "thumbs-up." He didn't expect the reaction. "Thumbs-up" in China is like giving "the bird" in the United States. In 1997 when Chinese premier Jiang Zemin visited the United States, he gave a thumbs-up when he spoke at Harvard University. You can bet that he intended this as a signal of friendliness.

In observing emblems, watch for patterns that appear congruent or incongruent with what you hear. By doing so you will have more confidence in the accuracy of your understanding of the other person's communications. For example, emblems take on special meaning when the person acts them out with unconscious intent. Such actions reveal the spirit of the "true message." A person who says yes but nods her head no probably means no. A person who nods his head in an affirmative manner after making a statement may want the listener to give a sign of agreement. When a speaker sounds calm but points his finger at you, you might question the disparity between voice and emblem.

POSTSCRIPT

The French philosopher Simone Weil described communication thus: "Two prisoners whose cells adjoin communicate with each other by knocking on the wall. The wall is the thing which separates them but is also their means of communication."

Indeed, "communication" is a single word with many shades of meaning and many means of transmission.

In this brief sojourn, I've highlighted important parts of this "communications territory" map. In this journey we've stayed away from blame. Instead, we've looked at a different way to understand what is going on.

PART THREE

Overcoming Blame

13

Improving Your Life Story

> *We are the authors of our stories*
> *and our destinies.*

A single word can ruin a life. Does this sound a tad radical? Suppose you truly believed that you were worthless. Would that word convey a message about your self-image that could shape your future in the worst of ways? Now suppose you blamed another person for being inept. Would the word "inept" influence how you viewed and acted toward that person? Such inference-of-blame characterizations can influence how we feel and what we do. Indeed, the linguist Benjamin Whorf asserted that our language is like a warped lens through which we know our world. He argues that our language has tricked us all our lives.

Your words symbolize reality. They are not the real thing! Nevertheless, as we define ourselves, so we view ourselves. For example, when you believe the word "powerful" applies to you, you are more likely to experience confidence. Apply blame words, such as "worthless" and "inept," to yourself and you can easily slide into a blame trap. Fortunately, if you don't like the label, you can change it.

Shakespeare said that "a rose by any other name would smell as sweet." A name is not the same as the entity it represents. A frog doesn't know it's a frog. We could call it by any other name and it still wouldn't know. But we know it is a frog because of its greenish skin, webbed feet, and long tongue that it uses to strike unwary passing flies. We use the label to communicate. So the word "frog" is a useful descriptive term. However, when you make yourself the name you call yourself, you fool yourself. People who think they are "wonderful" or "losers" convey a false message to themselves. Unlike the frog, who knows not what it is called, we take labels seriously. Such is the power of words that we use them to create illusions.

Categorizing through blame labeling can powerfully influence the story of your life. By examining this blame-labeling process, you'll learn alternative ways to shape your future. You can confidently add a positive direction to your future by editing out the subtle and not-so-subtle extension-of-blame categories that can dominate perception. By developing knowledge in this area and developing alternative ways of dealing with extension-of-blame categorizations, you can prepare yourself to create conditions that make for an exciting, satisfying, and fulfilling life story.

In this chapter we'll look at why blame labeling can color both our outlook and the way our life stories unfold.

CATEGORIES AND ILLUSIONS

Most people realize that an individual is more than one trait or another. That is why characterizing a person through a single word or phrase is an illusion. Nevertheless, few people complain when called "pleasant," "friendly," or "ingenious." But pigeon-holed with uncomplimentary terms such as "fool," most of us will bristle. We won't, for example, locate many who feel joy after hearing that their neighbors think they are "fools." Not many like to have their entire character shoved into a narrow category.

We think in categories; we can't escape them. They simplify and describe and thus yield great communications advantages. Every day we use these abstract categories to describe people: man, woman, child, elder. Most of these groupings work well. What we can escape is the messy misuse of categories that represent extension-of-blame thinking and generalizing about complex personalities.

Applying names and labels to people creates an illusion that we can know a person through the categories that we use. However, we misuse categorizations when we make a character generalization through blame labeling, express extension-of-blame thinking, or label the motivations and intention behind behavior without ever doubting the validity behind the label.

Using character generalizations such as "fearless," "disgruntled," "bold," or "bad," we taint the person for better or worse. For example, Tommy shut the kitchen window and the glass shattered. Hearing the noise, his mother ran to the scene. Upon seeing the mess, she yelled, "Bad boy! Look at what you did. Clean up the mess, then go to bed without your supper."

"Bad" categorizes motivation and intent. Did Tommy break the window because he is "bad"? Following this reasoning, if Tommy were not bad, the window would not have broken. And because the window broke, Tommy is "bad." This circular thinking represents an emotionally charged chain of blame leading to punishment in the form of no supper and isolation (bed). The silent and more damaging outcome predictably includes a temporarily diminished self-concept.

Blame labeling is a common shorthand way of characterizing a person's entire "being." But that process is highly misleading and flatly wrong. We think we can explain a person's "being" in a single word! But members of what group would accept themselves as having only one quality?

We use categories as shorthand character descriptions for people. As we do, we normally skip important steps. To use a label objectively with people, first we'd have to accept the label as an abstraction; next we'd have to verify it; we'd need to justify using the label in specific situations; and we'd have to be wary of exceptions. We'd also have to view the significance of a label as existing on a continuum. This form of conditional analysis serves as a validity check against putting people into limited categories, especially the extension-of-blame label variety.

Aristotle deserves either the credit or the blame for extending categories into either/or extremes. In Aristotelian terms, we can place people into categories of "good" or "bad," "sick" or "healthy," "aggressive" or passive," "strong" or "weak," "blameworthy" or "innocent." If you are healthy, you are not sick. If you are passive, you're not aggressive. If you are not blameworthy, you are innocent.

We can confidently divide life according to either/or categories such as plant and animal kingdoms. We divide people according to sex, age, or race. We also label people according to trait categories, such as gregarious, moody, or witty. But these traits invariably exist on continua. However, you can be partially to blame, so the either/or view also does not prove valid in such instances. Here "and/also" reasoning is more accurate, provided we know where on the continuum for each variable category one may fall temporarily.

We often have choices when we categorize character or behavior. Your neighbor borrows your lawnmower. You are not home when he comes to return it, so he locks it in his garage. In his rush to catch an airline connection for a three-week vacation, he forgets to return it. Your newly fertilized lawn is setting a growth record, and seeing the long grass starts a chain of thought that evokes a feeling of irritation within you. Now, do you judge the neighbor as conscientious, forgetful, or both? Do you define the neighbor as an irresponsible worm for not returning your lawnmower promptly? Or do you define him as a considerate friend for his efforts to secure your equipment? Whatever your judgment, you are making a categorical choice.

Taken to an extreme, we might argue that we need to eliminate character labels entirely because they give a misleading picture. However, some can represent general truths, as when we say that Jill is normally industrious, warm, and inclined to act stubbornly when challenged. Supported by behavioral data, this characterization provides information about some of Jill's distinctive features. Realistically, we can't eliminate characterizations, but we can choose how we will characterize.

Nouns, Verbs, and Blame

Categorization is inevitable. Our language burgeons with words that describe categories. For example, labeling someone as lazy, especially when his or her activities show differing motivations and levels of activity, misuses the descriptive category "lazy." I use categories in this book such as "blame trap" and "comfort junkies." Used descriptively, such categories are informative. It is the misuse of categories for extension-of-blame purposes that perverts reason.

When we say something like "Len is a crook," we categorize him. When we say he is "a dirty rotten crook," we make the category include an extension of blame. We add validity to this charge when we give an example that provides a context for this assertion, such as "Len took a newspaper without paying for it." Even if the example is valid, "one breeze does not accurately predict a storm."

People can tarnish the reputations of others by falsely applying pejorative "blame" labels to them. However, if Len is in jail for embezzling, the label "crook" clearly applies to the embezzlement. Dirty rotten crook, however, gets us into extension-of-blame thinking. The danger of this thinking is especially obvious when we apply it to ourselves. If you were to think something such as "I am a worthless failure," you've categorized, characterized, and blame-labeled (condemned) yourself in a five-word phrase. This is definitely ridiculous. But millions fall into this blame trap daily, scarcely aware of what they are doing.

We fall into blame traps when we categorize with negative nouns, characterize with adjectives, and compound the error with verbs that generalize. The Spanish-born American philosopher George Santayana succinctly noted, "The little word 'is' has its tragedies. It marries and identifies different things with the greatest innocence; and yet no two are ever identical." The founder of General Semantics, Alfred Korzybski, argues that the verb "to be" distorts one's identity. (For readers interested in how to eliminate the verb from written expressions, I wrote chapter 20 without the use of the verb "to be.")

This brief analysis shows the folly in generalizing about people through the use of an abstract label such as "crook" and how the "little" verb "is" compounds this blame-labeling distortion. Our language structure, social conditioning, and experiences are such that we probably shall never fully keep extension-of-blame labeling and generalizations out of our minds. However, through growing our awareness about how this blame-labeling process works, we educate ourselves. By taking steps to gain progressive mastery of ourselves by reshaping our language to limit extension-of-blame labeling, we are less likely to fall into circular thinking, blame traps. This clear thinking development process sets the stage for more enlightened choices, emotional freedom, and advantages.

COMPOSITE VIEW

The "self" is a patchwork of changeable self-impressions that can strengthen or unravel with changes in perception or situation. For example, our composite view of "self" represents our self-concept. But self-concepts come in different forms. You can have a high social self-concept about how you get along with others. You can have a "work" self-concept where you judge your "self" against the work you do. You can have a "sports" self-concept where you see yourself as a star, klutz, or something else. Because of our human complexities and variances, you may act constructively at times. But this does not make you a complete angel any more than acting self-defeating makes you a worthless worm. Truly, we have many ways to describe ourselves and other people.

People are complex and have numerous attributes, and their behavior will vary. This is the composite view of people. It has special validity when applied to people who exaggerate by falsely boosting themselves as "perfect" or who put themselves down for minor faults. However relevant this view may appear for self-development purposes, the composite view carries little weight in a court. There the focus is on determining guilt or innocence and ascribing penalties and punishments. It may carry less weight in a corporate setting where performance counts. However, this view is important from the standpoint of "self" understanding and acceptance. Since this is a psychology self-help book, a composite standard has utility here.

Through the composite picture of a person, we see virtually thousands of characteristics, traits, emotions, and patterns of beliefs and actions. Our lives consist of millions of thoughts and actions, many of which involve learning and changing. We have hundreds of attributes and qualities called abilities. Intelligence, for example, consists of dozens of different abilities and variations in them. Abstract reasoning, verbal ability, and spatial ability are a few of the many parts of "intelligence." People also vary in the way they express their attributes to their mates, family, friends, and coworkers. From this perspective, we cannot legitimately shrink a person down into a single label.

Fixing a single global label on a person is irrational. However, separating a person from a situation does not mean you have to give up your preferences and interests about people's behavior. You can legitimately judge a person's behavior without judging a composite person. However, the sooner you are able to separate person from action, the quicker you broaden your choices about how to respond.

How is the "self" to be judged? The philosopher Immanuel Kant tells us that people have value because they are rational creatures able to determine right from wrong. More recently, psychologist Albert Ellis persuasively argues that you cannot legitimately determine the global worth of a person. He cautions that although people can and do rate themselves as worthwhile or worthless, this global rating is both arbitrary and changeable. Ellis professes that if you insist on determining your personal worth, you can say you are worthy because you are alive.

CONTINGENCY WORTH

Contingency worth thinking involves these beliefs: Do well and you are worthy. Do less well and you have less worth. Commonly, when people fall short of contingency worth standards, they are likely to get defensive or engage in self-blame. Here is an empirical way of looking at contingency worth and of getting beyond this blame-riddled process:

> Doc limped home feeling deeply in despair. He was behind in his ordering of supplies, his nurse was out ill, and he was unable to find a fill-in. He felt rushed and flustered all day. By the time he reached home, he felt like a loser. However, by taking a composite view, he reminded himself that he labored long and hard to earn his medical degree. His three grown children had careers that fit their abilities. His quick ability to diagnose had saved many lives. He routinely volunteered his services to a free clinic. By regaining the composite, Doc regained his normal sense of equilibrium.

You can choose to rate yourself as worthwhile as easily as you can choose to rate yourself as worthless. However, a positive global definition is likely to be as flawed as a negative one. For example, you may make a great decision on a stock investment. You buy Fidget Widget stock and it gains four points the day you make the purchase.

You glamorize and glorify yourself for the wisdom of this choice performance. The next day Fidget Widget files bankruptcy. You now have a virtually worthless investment. You are the same person on each occasion. The main difference is that when you make a profitable decision, you have advantaged yourself; when the decision leads to undesired results, you have disadvantaged yourself. Your performances are an extension of yourself. But to what extent can you judge your total worth based on any performance? What if you win the 100-meter dash in the Olympics? Does that make you *a* winner or *the* winner of the race? While you can relish the victory and garner advantages, what then of your human worth long after the victory has passed?

From a composite view, performance counts but your performances do not define your global worth. For example, can you improve your performances? Can you possibly perform worse? In either case, your global worth does not change, only the quality of performance.

If you are still challenged to break loose from the contingency worth trap, here is another way to confound such thinking. The *Oxford English Dictionary* defines the word *floccinaucinihilipilification* as a habit of estimating something as worthless. People who habitually blame themselves often fall into this worthlessness habit trap. Self-blame can spill over to a total renunciation of the self as worthless. Since this extreme self-denunciation represents a clearly disputable problem habit, think floccinaucinihilipilification when you self-blame. Pronouncing the word may be sufficient to get your mind off a negative train of thought.

SELF-STORIES

There are three levels to most novels: The situation, happenstance, and people's motivations that drive the characters' involvement in the story. The characters' beliefs, values, aptitudes, attitudes, traits, drive, motivation, incentive, desire, and emotions are instrumental to the tale.

We all have life stories. As the story evolves, you might want to improve the text to incorporate a confident self-view, ability to cope with the unexpected, and will to create and meet challenges. Your understanding and application of the composite view can free your mind of the negative impact of artificially inhibiting thoughts. With a clearer perspective, you can better identify and take profitable risks. Such changes promise new opportunities for creating interesting new twists to your life story.

If you concentrate your efforts on changing the external conditions in your story, you believe in restructuring your environment. If you concentrate on changing your inner condition, you believe that you can self-improve through restructuring your perspective. However, this need not be an either/or decision. Different situations involve acting to improve both external and internal conditions simultaneously. It is how you apply yourself that adds quality into your narrative.

Narrative Role Taking

If you don't like parts of your story, change them! Psychiatrist Eric Berne found that people follow scripts that represent a replay of their history. So it should not prove startling that most admonish themselves for doing the same self-defeating things. For example, John appears overly eager to date Samantha. He presses her to go out with him and behaves anxious and insecure in her presence. He knows he'd like to act less pressured and to appear "cool." Yet John follows the same pattern with any woman he finds attractive and wishes to date. After he defeats himself with his pressuring tactics, he dumps on himself for what he sees as his "social ineptitude." He then rehashes his history around his negative experiences and indicts himself as a loser. How does John change the process that spurs the pattern? Rather than blame himself, Berne would suggest that John focus on solving the problem.

Psychologist George Kelly's approach complements Berne's position. Kelly asserts that we construct our versions of reality. We are capable of changing our more unrealistic and self-defeating interpretations through questioning the ideas, beliefs, and values we have about the event. Changing an extension-of-blame outlook, for example, would involve planning and executing a new antiblame role. This approach leads to the development of a new construct. The non-blame construct can lead to healthier behavior.

John can apply Kelly's system to help himself progressively overcome his fear to the point where he can approach attractive women confidently. By following Kelly's role prescription, John defines what he would like to accomplish, identifies the traits or qualities he has that he wants to project, plans out a new script, and then tests the new role. Kelly says that people who employ his approach act like scientists seeking to make new discoveries.

If you wish to test Kelly's method for change, do the following:

1. Write a brief narrative outlining a realistic theme you want to see unfold and behavior changes that support the theme.
2. Pen a nonblame theme into the narrative. For example, tolerance and understanding involve looking at people from the perspective of a kindly and forgiving friend.
3. Implement your plan but consider your modified role as an experiment. Let the results guide your subsequent actions. By following this experimental approach, the results are neither right nor wrong, but instructive.

When you are open to experimental feedback, you are more likely to make adjustments to revise causes and produce more positive effects. Few novels are written without revision!

The psychologist Edward Thorndike correctly pointed out that practice without feedback won't cause improvement. If you blindfolded yourself and attempted to draw a ten-inch line, chances are that you'd continue following a trial-and-error pattern and have no idea which trial brought you closer to meeting the standard. However, with visual feedback and a ten-inch standard to compare your work, your accuracy would improve quickly.

You can't realistically expect to draw an accurate ten-inch line blindfolded. How then can you expect to improve your self-development opportunities without objectives, guidelines, and feedback? The objectives define the category. The guidelines outline the standards. Feedback provides directions for evaluation and change.

This feedback is all the more important in situations that involve relating to other people, where the level of complexity is considerably greater than in trial-and-error line drawings. So when you write your script, build feedback into the process.

Our stories go beyond a selected expository description to the joys, victories, defeats, loves, camaraderie, quiet moments, challenges, feuds, friendships, altruism, disappointments, sadness, and frustrating experiences that inescapably parallel this evolution. Our psychological stories incorporate learning, changing, developing, and growing. By experimenting with ways to express our positive attributes, we refine our knowledge and shape our stories with positive experiences. Following this experimental approach, we come to know more about ourselves and of the personal meaning of discovery and knowing. It's an endless story.

Optimal Social Scripts

Within the role you've prescribed above, if you could be the best that you could be, what would you be like? The answer to this optimal performance question involves engaging your solid inner strengths. Since this description represents qualities that you already possess, your challenge is to put these resources to good use to support the role you've chosen.

An optimal strength analysis can provide you with information that you can plug in to your new narrative role. You can use this four-step framework for optimal social performance situations.

1. Write down the environmental conditions. Where did the event take place? Was the situation challenging? What type of people were present? What made the surroundings conducive to your peak performance experience?
2. What qualities did you present? For example, did you feel relaxed or charged up? Were you expressive or attentive? Did you convey an attitude of acceptance? Did you operate at a high cerebral level? What emotions did you experience or express? Were you focused on the events around you to the point where you forgot about focusing on yourself?
3. Describe what made this experience a peak experience that you did not list in items 1 and 2.
4. In testing your new theme, imagine yourself operating at your peak. Try to capture that optimal state of mind to create a positive mental atmosphere.

POSTSCRIPT

The U.S. poet Robert Frost understood the power of choice when he wrote:

> *I shall be telling this with a sigh*
> *Sometimes ages and ages hence:*
> *Two roads diverged in the wood, and I—*
> *I took the one less traveled by,*
> *And that has made all the difference.*

Categorical thinking strongly influences our choices and the composite view of "self." Our view of who we are and the choices we make tone the tale that we tell.

If we could snap our fingers and afterward change what we wish about ourselves, we'd hear a lot of finger-snapping. Meaningful personal change is not so simple as snapping our fingers. Nevertheless, editing needless blame processes out of our life story is an important part of creating positive new scripts to test on the stage of life. This process involves penning in positive attributes to add desired qualities and experience to our lives. It also involves red-lining conditions to delete that can do us more harm than good. Increasing the positive and reducing the negative contribute substance to promote an enlightened life.

14

Beyond the Boundaries of Blame

Change touches everything. Yet when we voluntarily attempt to change, this sometimes feels impossible.

In a strange case of alien abduction, an advanced species, the Minervians, whisk you to a planet they call Walden III. Welcomed as an honored guest, you have the privilege to see how this species deals with blame and change.

You learn that a green-clad group called the "teachers" freely wander the planet with blame detectors that cue to any form of needless blame. Their job is to teach alternatives. You are interested in this approach, so you team up with a master teacher named Thorpe.

Thorpe explains that his people learned that by bringing blame awareness close to the event and by understanding the mental content of blame, they increase their chances for staying out of blame traps. Minervians who are interested in this form of self-development volunteer for the program. Participants then qualify to receive on-the-spot assistance. Before he can say more, Thorpe's blame device signals "event." You both transport and instantly arrive at the scene of an accident.

Two Minervians, standing beside dented spacecrafts, point fingers at each other. Each shouts that the other deserves blame for the accident. Thorpe jumps into action. He says, "Although it is important to identify fault for insurance purposes, blame stress has greater consequences. Let me demonstrate." In a twinkle, Thorpe projects a holographic image of each Minervian's brain. The holographs depicts the firing of neurons and emotional chaos. The part of the brain where reasoning resides glows blue to show that rationality has gone cold. The holograph further shows the vulnerable body organs that stress affects. In both cases, stress affects coronary functioning. That demonstration gets the combatants' attention.

Thorpe follows up with custom visuals on the statistics on life-reduction expectancy that come about as a result each individual's blame-stress profile. This second intervention results in Minervian contemplation, where each thinks about the destructive effect of distress and the advantages of coping to reduce the stress. Both Minervians agree to cope in a constructive way. Next, Thorpe engages both in an instant playback of their thoughts and emotions so each can connect thoughts to the blame-stress emotions. He encourages each to create an alternative perspective to restructure thoughts from a stress to a problem-solving mode. Each tests the problem-solving ideas. That change instantly promotes calmer feelings. Although both are frustrated by the accident, each stops the double-trouble sequence and feels quite a bit more in charge.

The next phase involves problem resolution. With double-troubles, extensions of blame, and finger-pointing out of the picture, the resolution proves simple.

You are impressed. You ask Thorpe, "How did you discover that solution to dealing with the extensions of blame?" "Simple," Thorpe responds. "We took ideas from writers from your planet. Ralph Waldo Emerson's *Walden Pond* taught us to keep it simple. Burrhus Frederic Skinner's *Walden II* showed us the importance of working cooperatively and using positive reinforcement for change. Albert Ellis taught us about the importance of how our thinking affects our feelings."

Thorpe goes on: "We're not perfect. As you note, we just observed a conflict over an accident. But we can create conditions that make a compelling case for positive change. As a result, we've come a long way shifting from a culture of blame to one of accountability and choice. We are still working to do better."

You return to Earth with these thoughts in mind: 1) dealing with problems sooner than later is beneficial; 2) seeing the benefits of change is motivational; and 3) progressive mastery over false blame, needless blame, and extensions of blame requires a sustained action. You now feel ready for a radical shift in how you manage blame.

A RADICAL SHIFT

Personal change and development are processes, not events. The question following a personal change is this: "What has happened that is different?" To make positive changes, we normally direct our attention toward eliminating negative habits as well as developing positive attributes. We stretch our positive resources while working to eliminate personal blame traps and extension-of-blame thinking.

Self-change often challenges us fully, yet practically everyone can learn to advance their key interests by focusing on a desired change, evolving a plan, and persisting and changing the plan through feedback. But it is important to be realistic. Personal change normally takes time; progress often is matched by setbacks; a simple declaration to change is not worth much unless followed by purposeful action.

Some changes appear simple yet carry unforseen complications. Even a seemingly minor change, such as deciding to change one's hairstyle, involves a resolution of inner conflict about the change. Many self-changes where you put energy into breaking a problem habit are far more challenging to bring about than changing a hairstyle. Choosing between two hairstyles is a one-time decision at the time it is made. Self-development involves ongoing adjustments in changing circumstances where regression competes with progression.

Although guidelines exist for personal change, this process does not follow precise universal rules. Yet you may want to know the rules of self-change. How should I think? What should I do? How can I make it happen, you wonder. Passive inquisitive efforts reflect a well-meaning attempt to reach out for a solution that must come from another place. The self-change process typically involves actively testing frameworks for change. This occurs in the service of creatively unraveling or destroying dysfunctional ways of knowing and believing that is part of creating something new. This switch in perspective and action often occurs initially with resistance but becomes simpler with time and practice.

FIVE PHASES OF CHANGE

What can we learn from cognitive-behavioral psychotherapists who are effective in their efforts to help people make positive changes? Productive therapists raise *awareness* and serve as catalysts for *action*. They understand that positive personal change is a process that takes place over time and that the important changes are those that occur within the person. Through the therapeutic process, people make adjustments in their thinking, develop a sense of acceptance, and extend what they learn into their daily lives. What people think, feel, and do is something that only they can decide for themselves. The following describes the phases of a process I observed people go through on their way to making enlightened changes:

1. *Awareness* involves a consciousness of the linkages between what we think, feel, and do.
2. *Action* involves practicing with new ways of thinking and doing.
3. *Accommodation* is where you make and integrate new connections. Conceptual changes take place at this level. Here you adopt functional new ways of thinking and believing. In a sense, accommodation is a deeper level of awareness.
4. *Acceptance* is where emotions are congruent with thinking. This is the emotional integration phase of change.
5. *Actualization* is where you make the new learning an extension of what you do. You are no longer testing ideas and actions but have adopted and now use ones that best serve your enlightened interests.

This five-part framework serves different purposes. In a stepwise fashion, it organizes information to use to advance your ability to take charge of your life. It enables you to organize your change strategies in a logical and progressive direction.

It serves as a checklist you can use to see where you are at in the process of change. The model also suggests how to build motivation to do better.

You can apply this change process to a broad spectrum of challenges. Starting with this chapter, you'll see how to use the approach to uncouple needless blame from your life. In the following chapters, I use the framework to show how to develop alternatives for needless blame. They outline a program for building perspective, debunking false beliefs, overcoming blame-related anger, building tolerance, asserting your interests, and overcoming procrastination to avoid blame that often follows needless delays. Collectively they provide a grand convection of thought you can use to direct your efforts to take charge of your life by beating the blame game. Since positive self-change normally begins with awareness, let's start there.

1. Awareness

Awareness is a conscious recognition of the events that take place within and around us. It involves acquiring information and being able to describe to ourselves what is happening.

Awareness is the first phase of a process for making life-saving connections. For example, imagine walking through a darkened wood. You hear the sudden flapping of wings in flight and a faint crinkling of fallen leaves though the wind is stilled. You see large claw marks on the trail. Your awareness, in this instance, involves alertness to different bits of sensory information that become transformed through thought and reason to emotionally feed your judgment to secure your existence. When information comes directly through your senses, your intellect rapidly goes to work to understand the meaning. How you piece these bits of information together involves use of your intelligence and experience.

We're excellent at piecing bits of information together, developing understanding, and acting on that understanding. It is important to reflect and make connections, to incubate on ideas, and to take time for creative thinking. Nevertheless, this natural and constructive ability misfires when we withdraw within ourselves, don't validate our beliefs, and unintentionally cause ourselves to distort reality.

We can close ourselves off from valid information by delving too deeply into our inner world to the extent that we lose sight of what is going on around us. This often comes at the cost of our relationships and limits the expression of our abilities. Analogously, you sit on a log in the darkened wood engrossed in thoughts about a world gone mad. In a vortex of deepening tension, you screen out the sounds of a nearby brook and bird's wings in rapid flight. You have no awareness of claw marks on the trail. The evening chill and rising moon fall silent before your thoughts. You preoccupy yourself with your "self." Through this self-focus, you captivate yourself with your fears and tensions as well as with your dreams of glory. You easily miss much of what takes place around you. On the other hand, when people focus on what they are doing rather than on their navels, they normally feel better and do better. They have less time for talking themselves into feeling powerless, victimizing themselves, or blaming others. When you take sensible actions and absorb yourself in what you do, you are going to learn more about yourself, about what you can do, and about the world around you.

Levels of Awareness

Our challenge is to reduce and manage the burdens of the needless form of blame in order to accelerate our command over what we think, feel, and do. Coping with blame begins with self-understanding. This starts with an awareness of the scope and impact of blame on your life.

Awareness exists at different levels. In a state of *oblivion,* you don't know what you don't know. You repeat problem blame patterns. However, by reading this book, you are unlikely to be in a state of oblivion for long about how blame impacts your life.

In the *twilight zone* of awareness, you have a fluctuating awareness of the relationship among problems, how you think, and what you do in troublesome zones in your life. You still may watch yourself go through the motions of thinking in extension-of-blame terms, but you also recognize that such processes are habitual. In this ambivalent state, you may both believe and doubt the validity of extension-of-blame assertions.

In an *enlightened state* of awareness, you have a more developed understanding of the relationship between extension-of-blame thinking and exoneration ploys. You can see them in yourself and in others. You have begun to figure out ways to stay out of blame traps when they impede your self-interests.

Awareness Guidelines.   Blame awareness is strengthened through practice. Routine self-monitoring helps us keep our ability to exercise problem-solving alternatives in shape.

Unless we think about our thinking (metacognition), silence limits awareness of the background messages we give ourselves. The background is our words, language, beliefs, principles, images, and other cognitive processes. We make them audible by focusing attention on them, saying them, writing them, or highlighting them in other ways such as through art and music.

Self-monitoring helps you recognize and separate groundless from verifiable assumptions. The process involves following the relationship among an activating event, perception, beliefs, emotions, and action responses. Thus, self-monitoring involves observing the event and observing yourself negotiating it. For example, what are you doing to meet the challenge of overcoming extension-of-blame thinking? What are the results of these efforts? Factual answers to these questions can quickly broaden your perspective and self-understanding.

To expand upon this awareness, pretend you are a detective with a case to solve. But first you have to know what it is that you are seeking. Assuming you are going to solve an extension-of-blame case, look for the trail that leads through unrealistic assumptions to adverse results and exoneration efforts to deflect from those results. In this self-study approach you observe what you think, how you feel, and what you do in extension-of-blame situations.

By understanding and watching out for the mechanisms for extensions and exonerations of blame, we move a step closer to wiping out senseless blame habits.

2. Action

Awareness ushers in opportunities for an enlightened outlook that we can use to guide constructive *action*. Action is the process of doing what you are thinking. The philosopher Hegel argues that acting extends the consciousness of mind where the individual becomes real through doing.

Levels of Action

Three levels of action help propel our positive self-change efforts: mental rehearsal, behavioral rehearsal, and psychological activity assignments.

Mental Rehearsal. In the blame zones of life, the actions we take involve dealing with blame thinking as much as changing blame conduct. A mental rehearsal is a time-honored method to simulate problem conditions in order to work on solutions. Here you define problems, figure out solutions, and mentally rehearse ways to respond to blame and to express blame constructively. You can use this rehearsal to help rid yourself of inane shame, guilt, and extension-of-blame thinking. Here are some examples:

➤ You refuse to use blame clichés. Instead, you spell out your thoughts to include context and content presented through an enlightened formulation. If you are at fault, you imagine stating the context and content, define your plan of correction, then carry it out. If you are the subject of false blame, you imagine pithily stating your position without resorting to counteraccusations.

➤ You refuse to engage in extension-of-blame thinking or to accept extension-of-blame references to you. You imagine articulating the joint problem as you engage the other person in ways to solve it.

➤ When others use blame clichés and extension-of-blame referencing about other people, you imagine refusing to allow yourself to be swayed by blanket declarations. Instead, you ask and insist on concrete examples that you can verify. Then verify or disconfirm them based on evidence.

➤ To counter inane shame, you imagine yourself psychologically inoculating yourself by doing something reasonable that others would normally do but where you would feel uncomfortable. Critique your thinking. Consider alternative perspectives.

Behavioral Rehearsal. You extend mental rehearsal through behavioral rehearsal. Enlist the help of a friend who role-plays different blame cliché and extension-of-blame approaches. In this way you get live practice discovering ways to cope that best fit with your personality, style, and objectives.

Psychological Activity Assignments. Psychological activity assignments are at the heart of any active self-change approach. Here you put your insights into action in real-life settings. You engage in an active, constructive process where you test and measure the results of what you do. Normally these activity assignments are intended to solve problems and build risk-taking skills, confidence, perspective, and tolerance.

Insights can lead to actions but actions also spur insights. So if you want to develop your insights in specific zones in your life, it is important to test new ways of thinking and behaving in these areas. The activity assignment, or actions that you take to develop your personal resources, provide experiences that can give birth to positive new self-insights.

Measured, directed, or spontaneous responses are woven into every phase of your waking hours. You are going to do something. The question is: What is that something? Even procrastination involves a form of action—an avoidance action. The actions you take are an extension of your thoughts, values, perception of reality, and reactions to the realities that surround you. The more focused and realistic your thoughts, the purer your actions that give feedback to your thoughts.

As you test new behaviors, each advance you make along the path you want to take provides food for conscious thought. In this process, expect to adjust to new information and to unexpected happenings. Setbacks will occur and have the advantage of teaching what doesn't work. We also learn to appreciate the role of chance in change.

Action Guidelines. We can decide the actions we take and how we will take them, then test the effectiveness of our plan through those actions. The following action guidelines illustrate how to promote a radical shift from blame to problem-solving through action.

➤ Develop a vision for how to operate positively in a blame culture.
➤ Create a metaphor that can serve as a guiding principle as you traverse a sea of blame. For example, hydroplaning above a wind-swept sea of blame symbolizes rising above blame.
➤ Devise a detailed plan. Declarations without visions and plans last as long as New Year's resolutions.
➤ Treat your proposed constructive actions as experiments. When you experiment you learn what works and what doesn't. There is no failure, only discovery. This positive view provides a radically different form of motivation than deficit motivations to avoid failure, blame, and shame.
➤ Accept no extension-of-blame or blame cliché as valid.

3. Accommodation

Why don't people with self-defeating blame habits just quit the blame game? Can they not see that it makes no rational sense? Perhaps not! Experience doesn't always teach, or by itself teach very well. We can and do repeat self-defeating patterns. It's in our nature as much as is our ability to learn, develop, and grow.

Although we can take steps to segment what we see from what we expect to see, we can easily filter new information to meet our expectations and biases. This information can twist along the labyrinths of the mind through the most peculiar of operations to distort experience. For example, people who regularly feel justified to fault and blame can find it hard to see their contribution to a conflict when they think others have the problem and need to change.

Because most problem habits take knowledge and practice to break, it shouldn't surprise us to discover that getting beyond blame proves challenging. Here the accommodation process to shift from leaning toward blame to explain, to one of understanding involves work. Yet in the U.S. culture, we often expect quick fixes to break deeply established habits such as a blame habit. Quick-fix solutions for positive psychological development frequently fail.

Accommodation is a point of truth in learning. We can parrot slogans that make us think we've found ways to divorce ourselves from blame. We can create external impressions of cordiality and politeness to disguise our inner feelings. These experiences may be preludes to accommodation, but they do not represent accommodation. We have accommodated to an enlightened way of thinking about blame when we shrink the frequency of needless blame within our minds and actions.

We can aid and promote accommodations through paradoxes, incongruities, images, humor, contrasts, and other forms of juxtaposing reality ideas. For example, in shifting from a self-blame to a tolerant self-view, you can take the blame belief and twist it. If you blame yourself because you think you are psychologically weak, you remind yourself that it takes a great effort to maintain that view. Effort is a form of strength. By rationally resolving this type of incongruity, you take a step to strengthen your analytic thinking and reasoning skills. You also are less likely to follow that part of a habitual self-blame script.

Levels of Accommodation

Breaking any problem habit involves problem awareness and actively keeping new, positive beliefs squarely in conscious awareness. For our purposes, the process includes decreasing the negatives by repeatedly challenging reality-distorting blame-conditioned thought.

In making personal changes, our adjustments can occur at different levels. We become aware of the importance of making a change. We have a vision for what the change will look like. We act to modify our blame views. Doing so often involves the mind arguing with itself.

We have biases, prejudices, attitudes, and defense mechanisms that compete with our growing new awareness. We pit these views against our more rational ideas. We sort, think out, reconcile, and propel our views to create positive experiences. Thus we do more than react and adjust.

When we have both a rational and irrational belief on a topic, a sensible accommodation involves strengthening the rational idea and weakening the irrational one through internal debate. With practice, our views shift in a more positive direction.

Accommodation Guidelines.　You can accelerate your ability to accommodate to nonblame concepts through practicing making new connections that filter experience through mental channels of tolerance and understanding.

➤ Consider the extent to which your old beliefs dictate your interpretations of blame situations or whether you are assessing the results using extension-of-blame–free reason. Since there is no such thing as perfect objectivity, your determination is going to be based on degree of bias rather than freedom from bias. Nevertheless, you lessen unreasonable bias by expanding your repertory of reasoned judgments.

➤ Label experiences that go counter to prior blame experience with a positive phrase or term. Since we think in categories, this positive label practice can compete with the old blame labels.

➤ Look for incongruities, paradoxes, and other ways to put blame and non-blame thinking into perspective.

➤ Look for examples to support positive thinking.

➤ Generalize the new learning by intentionally creating conditions to apply it. This generalization phase of accommodation raises knowledge to a higher level.

4. Acceptance

As you accommodate to the ebbing and flowing of change, you become accepting of the inevitability of change and of the power to direct change through the development of your personal resources. This acceptance gives you a sense of emotional integration.

As an integral part of the five phases of change, acceptance implies tolerance and understanding. It does not mean giving up, giving in, or resigning. The American author Henry Miller said it well when he described acceptance thus: "Life has no other discipline to impose, if we would but realize it, than to accept life unquestioningly. Everything we shut our eyes to, everything we run away from, everything we deny, denigrate or despise, serves to defeat us in the end. What seems nasty, painful, evil, can become a source of beauty, joy and strength, if faced with an open mind. Every moment is a golden one for him who has the vision to recognize it as such."

Levels of Acceptance
Most people feel unsure of themselves from time to time. Accepting the inevitable ambivalence that can accompany a change and accommodating to changing ideas involves a sense of tolerance for this learning process. In this phase, we recognize that while it is often easy to return to extension-of-blame ways and to exonerate rather than to correct, development and growth requires a different price: building realistic awareness, acting on that awareness, and creating functional new awareness through action.

An enlightened acceptance includes accommodating to the view that we will never be finished products, error is inevitable, and some selfishness, envy, jealously, anger, anxiety, disappointment, and depression will periodically invade our mental landscape. However, we have the choice to do something about such states of mind. Accepting your human foibles and faults is a good, basic, forward-looking phase of positive change. With this outlook, often you can prepare yourself to change what you don't like.

Acceptance Guidelines.   These guidelines begin with a tolerance awareness.

➤ Acceptance involves knowing and believing that we will not live a nonjudgmental, ego-free life devoid of all impulses toward extension-of-blame thinking. Such things are more likely in an isolated temple on the peak of Mount Everest than in the day-to-day life within a blame culture. Nevertheless, you can work with yourself to stretch for improvement knowing that you are unlikely to reach perfection. The advantage of reaching for excellence is that you can find more ways to live comfortably within yourself.

➤ With an accepting viewpoint, you can appreciate people for who they are, value the constructive things they do, and still refuse to acquiesce to any harmful actions. For example, you don't have to put up with someone's blame assertions and poor behavior. The spirit of acceptance includes refusing to acquiesce to harm.

➤ Acceptance often involves role taking. You ask, if you were in the same position, what type of understanding would you prefer? If you wouldn't blame yourself, why blame another?

➤ If you, or someone else, violate a legal or social standard, part of the spirit of acceptance involves recognition of consequences. This is partially accomplished by taking corrective actions.

➤ In a state of self-acceptance, you recognize that you are the only *self* you will ever be. You don't have to like everything you do, but you don't have to blame yourself punitively for lapses or errors. Instead, you can make amends or try again, perhaps with a different plan.

5. Actualization

Actualization means to realize through action or make real. In an actualization phase, we absorb ourselves in healthy, purposeful, and productive activities.

Levels of Actualization

The idea of actualization has existed throughout the ages. The ancient philosopher Aristotle used the term to mean that living things grow or move in a natural manner without ever arriving at their ideal. This position is positive. It implies that people evolve through a continuing process. We can argue with Aristotle by saying that the "ideal" is a judgment, "natural" is a definition, and there are peaks to development as well as declines. Nevertheless, we evolve. When we cease to evolve in one way, we can evolve in another.

The nineteenth-century German philosopher Friedrich Wilhelm Nietzsche portrayed the ideal person as the *Ubermensch*—a person with a will to channel rather than suppress passions. In *Thus Spake Zarathustra* Nietzsche observed, "He who cannot obey himself will be commanded." Nietzsche adds this ingredient to Aristotle's actualization process: ". . . Will a self and thou shalt become a self."

In the mid-twentieth century American psychologist Abraham Maslow presented his theory of the self-actualized person. This person promotes health over deficit and focuses on such matters as developing potential and making choices to improve growth. Maslow describes self-actualized episodes where the person experiences a feeling of integration, spontaneous expression, and a sense of naturalness.

We cannot realistically expect that we will become fully actualized in all ways, but we can work to actualize ourselves in important zones of our life. These zones can involve improving communications, gardening, writing poetry, advocating for the less able—practically any healthy pursuit will do.

In your actualization zones, you continually stretch your resources to discover more about your interests and abilities. As you concentrate on what you are doing, you move away from concentrating on yourself. Paradoxically, through learning and contributing, you discover more about yourself.

Like the nautilus, as you develop your resources, you keep adding chambers to support future growth. As a by-product, you are likely to feel more authentic, capable, motivated, and alive. In this state of actualization, you experience yourself as natural, spontaneous, and acting in concert with your finest values. Whatever your age or stage of life, you can find actualization zones where you can express and develop your talents or where you can discover interesting parts of your personality.

Actualization Guidelines.   When engaged in actualization, the changes you make are a positive extension of your "self." Here are some actualization zone guidelines presented in the form of questions:

> ➤ Am I directing my efforts toward purposeful and meaningful goals?
> ➤ Are my efforts based on a healthy outlook?
> ➤ Am I stretching my capabilities to learn and contribute?
> ➤ Do I feel absorbed and committed to what I do?
> ➤ Are my thinking, feelings, and actions congruent?
> ➤ Are my expressions a natural and genuine extension of my beliefs and "self"?
> ➤ Do my actions benefit my group?
> ➤ Do I experience tolerance for ambiguous and unusual events I encounter?
> ➤ Do I make opportunities to express my imagination, visions, insights, and creativity?
> ➤ Do I experiment with promising new ways of thinking and behaving?
> ➤ Do I maintain an openness to my experience where I don't exclude what I don't like to see from my conscious awareness?
> ➤ Do I rise above self-consciousness and accept the different parts of my personality while expressing the best?
> ➤ Am I taking reasonable risks to learn and develop?

THE FIVE-ONE-FIVE PLAN

Throughout life, two paths will rise before you. These are an ancient pair: threat (distress) and challenge (exhilaration). You choose the path to travel.

Tension due to blameful thinking counters your potential to actualize your abilities and to meet challenges. This is the path of threat. To break free of blame extensions and false exonerations requires acting against these negatives. But this is only half the story. To move forward and enjoy life involves calling upon and routinely using your most powerful and positive attributes and abilities. This is the path of challenge.

When people apply multiple relevant techniques to achieve a desired personal change, they raise the odds in their favor. The five-one-five plan involves applying five self-management steps to achieve one specific desired result where you go through five stages of change. Here is the general idea: You target an area for change, devise a five-step self-management process to structure the change, then implement the program.

You can apply this five-one-five plan to practically any personal challenge, from reducing extension-of-blame thinking to losing weight. The five self-management steps include:

1. *Assessing your situation:* What change do you believe is in your best interests to undertake?

2. *Defining a direction:* In translating the change into an action plan, consider defining a mission or goal. A mission, for example, can include this general idea: to reduce extension-of-blame thinking in order to achieve a more versatile, positive life. A goal, for example, can include this specific idea: to identify and deal with extension-of-blame thinking when it occurs in my intimate relationship. Goals, however, often serve as a subset of an ongoing general mission.

3. *Planning and organizing resources:* A plan involves the steps you will take to achieve your mission and goal(s). Organization involves deciding then gathering resources and setting time lines for implementing your plan.

4. *Implementing:* This is the action phase where you put your plan to the test. This action-oriented approach allows you to benefit from new insights that may spontaneously occur.

5. *Evaluating:* In this self-development phase, you judge the results of your efforts and, perhaps, adjust your goals and plans based on the information you receive.

The five-step self-management plan blends with the five phases of change in this way: You apply the five-step self-management plan to one target change area where you then go through the five phases of change. For example, by applying the five management steps to the challenge of reducing the impact of extensions of blame in your life, you are likely to experience the benefits of increased awareness, confident ability to initiate positive actions, an accommodation to positive ways of thinking and acting, a growing sense of acceptance without unnecessary acquiescence, and expanded ability to extend your stronger attributes and positive capabilities as alternatives to blame.

Meaningful personal change is more of a process than an event. This process often takes a deliberate amount of time to think through and to engage. But the path is there. The promise is there. You choose the direction. You orchestrate your experiences.

POSTSCRIPT

The ancient Roman poet Ovid saw change thus: "All things change, nothing is extinguished. There is nothing in the whole world which is permanent. Everything flows onward; all things are brought into being with a changing nature; the ages themselves glide by in constant movement."

Change is inevitable. However, we will be at different phases of readiness with many of the personal changes that we can profitably make. That is why it is normally better to deal with your highest-priority challenge first. That will be the more pressing area. You can deal with lesser matters in their time.

We need to be realistic about positive personal change. We live in a culture where we are exposed to quick and often ineffective solutions to complex challenges. Most worthwhile personal changes involve meeting challenges with perseverance and directing effort to priority matters. This process can feel discouraging at times, but by moving forward normally you will get farther faster than do those people who hope for quick, magical, effortless solutions to challenging problems.

Choosing to make important personal changes in areas that involve needless blame sometimes can feel as if we are wading chest high through a mucky swamp of competing ideas. Extensions of blame flood a mental swamp with blocks and barriers to actualization. But when in the muck, why stay stuck? By engaging the process of personal change, you can discover that escaping blame traps is satisfying.

In the following chapter we'll explore perspective as a platform for positive change. In the remaining chapters we'll look at other alternatives to extension-of-blame thinking and to exoneration ploys. These alternatives include building fact-based beliefs, extinguishing anger evoked by extensions of blame, building tolerance, and developing positive self-assertiveness. In the final chapter we'll examine how to avoid blame by staying out of procrastination traps. Through these developmental themes, you'll see different ways how the five-phase process applies to your psychological development and growth.

15

Increasing Perspective

> *We react to stimuli, orchestrate our experiences, and have the power to create our own perspective on reality.*

A person with a clear perspective has the resources to properly assign weight to events that take place in life according to their importance and to his or her ability to manage them. That is why different people can have different perspectives about the same thing. For example, how would you feel about walking between the twin Trade Towers in New York City on a tightrope?

Philippe Petit did so; the thin cable was stretched 1,350 feet above the ground. Most of us would see this act as dangerous, even foolhardy. Yet Petit thought his highwire act was safe. To reduce the risk of a disastrous accident, he spent months planning the feat. Petit said that he thought walking across a Manhattan street was riskier.

Perspective is relative. When you put your thumbnail before your eye, you can cover the moon, a much larger object. It is the proximity of the thumbnail that changes a perspective without changing the actual size of either object. In the same sense, the nearness of a blame experience can prove temporarily captivating. A distant perspective can yield a different understanding about what is going on around and within us.

Developing and maintaining a realistic perspective is one of the greatest gifts that one can give to oneself. Yet we rarely read discussions on perspective. Nevertheless, perspective is pivotal to our emotional well-being. Those with a broad and realistic perspective will have a sounder basis for understanding their options, seeing opportunities, organizing and directing their efforts toward worthy goals, effectively dealing with emerging challenges, and advancing their interests and the collective interests of their group.

Humans can think, predict, anticipate, and apply meaning to events. Although we partially form our judgments from our perception of events, our perspective allows us to put experience into context.

Perception shapes perspective. A fish, for example, would not disturb itself if it were off color compared to other members of its school. It exists without knowing or wondering why. It therefore ascribes no meaning to how it looks. We, on the other hand, can incorporate many views into our outlook. And we interpret what we see through our beliefs. We also have the ability to look beyond the moment to predict the long-term results of our efforts. But there is a downside to this process. We have the ability to draw narrowly into ourselves with preoccupations that our fish friend could not fathom. We fall into a contingency-worth blame trap when we believe we dress less well than a neighbor and blame ourselves for having poor taste. Like a "mental virus," this comparative blame (*comparitivitis*) can quickly spread to weaken judgment.

People with generally realistic perspectives have advantages over those whose perspectives are fogged by blame extensions. In this chapter we'll start with motivations for developing a realistic perspective, then follow up with five phases of change.

MOTIVATIONS FOR DEVELOPING PERSPECTIVE

People with perspective have the capacity to see challenges, opportunities, and ways to time and pace their actions. They are likely to see that the forest is made up not only of trees but many other plants and creatures. They get the "big picture." This form of perspective is an important part of wisdom.

Perspective has other benefits:

➤ You will have a stronger sense of what you can and cannot do in a situation.
➤ What you do may appear risky to others but is relatively safe when your options are measured and clear.
➤ You will have a better understanding of feelings you can trust and of those that can mislead.
➤ Those with a broad perspective are better aware of what is taking place around them and what is in the background of their thoughts.
➤ You can better see how your thoughts, feelings, and actions relate to varying situations that influence you.
➤ A clear perspective portrays valid choices.

PERSPECTIVE AND THE FIVE PHASES OF CHANGE

Because we look at the world from the inside out, our experiences are going to be subjective and our perspective will be colored. Within that electrical pool we call the mind, our thoughts are like dreams until we give them shape, form, scale, and order. That is why an experience is as we think it is until we have a different idea.

A growth perspective involves understanding how we promote change within ourselves and in our surrounding world. Self-development through change is likely to gain momentum when we view our efforts as part of a process that can happen in a twinkle or, more probably, over a deliberate period of time. In developing one's perspective on blame, the five phases of change provide a framework for organizing information, directing efforts, and marking progress.

1. Awareness: Gaining Perspective

In aligning perspective with a fluctuating reality, some ideas will be more helpful than others in broadening a perspective or creating one that was not there before. As our beliefs and intuitions evolve and become factually based, we can better adjust our views to reflect enlightened levels of awareness. The following exercises support that perspective development process whereby our intuitions, feelings, insights, and judgments prove increasingly functional.

Exercises in Awareness

Our perspectives on blame change with new information. The following analogies suggest ways to introduce alternative information into perspective in order to temper blame.

➤ In some situations, we do ourselves more harm than good by blaming. Even if we win, we lose. By analogy, if you had a favored video game as a child, would you break it if you discovered that a child you disliked enjoyed a similar game? Perspective in this case involves recognizing when you are likely to do yourself more harm than good by exercising a choice to blame. When you face a "blame situation," consider alternate actions to take that can support positive relationships.

➤ The analogy of the half-full, half-empty glass suggests how different perspectives occur. The half-empty glass suggests a pessimistic outlook where you focus on what is missing. The perspective changes to optimism when you see a half-full glass and focus on what you have. You also might consider the position of the realist who says, "The glass just is." The just-is view is descriptive. Just-is thinking, for example, portrays blameworthy conditions without extension-of-blame thinking.

2. Action: Creating Word Changes

The Russian linguist Lev S. Vygotsky describes key words as generalizations that reflect reality in a different way from how sensation represents the original event. He describes this as a "dialogue leap" where the meaning of the word goes beyond the information in the physical experience. This dynamic interplay of *meaning* is the point where the emotional and intellectual ways of perceiving unite and where language asserts a directive function on our feelings and actions. The Austrian-born

British philosopher Ludwig Josef Wittgenstein complements this view: "Philosophy is a battle against the bewitchment of our intellect by means of language." Once we are aware of the relationship between language and action, we can subject the way we talk to ourselves to a critical cognitive review.

The relationships among language, thought, emotions, and actions are significant. The words we use to describe reality are more than their dictionary meanings. Seeing the meanings and the directive effects of words on emotions and actions can yield answers to many riddles of the mind.

To understand their meaning, we would best see words in the context of thought and in the situations that we find them. If you doubt this, look up the word "work" in a standard dictionary. Here you will find noun versions, transitive verb versions, intransitive verb versions, and others. Still, the word "work" will go beyond the dictionary definitions.

Our word choices partially define the perspective we experience. Believe something is awful, and you will feel that way. See something as overwhelming and uncontrollable, and your feelings and experiences probably will differ from the person who sees the same thing as disadvantageous.

Exercises in Action
Blame is a cognitive process that we can manage initially through cognitive actions. Here are some cognitive action strategies for putting vague blame words and phrases into perspective to make them accessible to rebuttal or negation.

➤ Make verbal vagaries concrete. The indefinite referent "it" holds center stage. When you tell yourself something like "I can't stand it," what "it" do you blame? Is "it" the tension, situation, difficulty in controlling an outcome, or other? Clarifying indefinite referents such as "it" points where you want to target your change efforts.

➤ Watch for overgeneralized external referents. Here you believe that *nothing* seems to go right. What does "nothing" mean? What are the exceptions to the "nothing" rule? Who is to blame for "nothing"?

➤ Complete incomplete sentences, such as "I hate feeling helpless." Add the word "because" to help flesh out the issue. For example: I feel helpless because _____. You fill in the blank. This approach can help clarify the meaning of the word "helpless" that you've attached to your "self."

➤ Reexamine blanket declarations. For example, if you tell yourself, "I would be destroyed if I failed," what does "failed" mean? What does "destroyed" mean? Who would be at fault? What alternate views are reasonable?

➤ Watch for passive phrases such as "It was decided that . . ." This use of "to be" can obfuscate an issue—perhaps to deflect accountability and blame. For example, who decided what?

Minimizing the negative effects of extremist thinking, however, does not guarantee a positive outlook. A positive outlook is normally the by-product of accommodating to positive actions.

3. Accommodation: Integrating Change

Most people who struggle to understand and change self-defeating habits find themselves in a phase where they watch themselves go through the motions of the old habit pattern. At the same time, they recognize the benefits of changing the pattern. They know what to do differently.

In the initial stages of the accommodation phase of change, we may temporarily break a blame habit. Soon after we draw back to our blame habit where we previously achieved a negative accommodation. It is here where we discover that our self-defeating blame beliefs don't retire easily. That is because these views are practiced and connected to similar ideas.

Knowledge that a habit is self-defeating is an important but not a sufficient condition for change. Repeating positive personal change actions is the more necessary condition for change. Rather than see this phase as dejecting, mark this state as an encouraging sign of progress. Personal change from a blame path to another, healthier path requires a deliberate and progressive shift that we can advance but often cannot rush.

Exercises in Accommodation
Perspective flipping involves turning things about in your mind. This flipping process is a familiar part of a process of accommodation that supports functional ways of viewing and doing. Here are some exercises in accommodation that involve shifting perspectives:

➤ Imagine turning "blame" into charm.
➤ If you feel intimidated by someone who blamed you, consider if that person felt intimidated by you.
➤ Learning arguments from the opposite side of the picture helps build the potential to adjust to alternative points of view while maintaining your viewpoint. This can help you see—but not necessarily agree with—the basis for blame.
➤ Does the absence of a negative emotion call forth a positive emotion? If you rid yourself of fear of blame, are you likely to feel happy? (You may be more disposed to acting socially with others and engaging in pleasurable activities, and, as a by-product, you may feel happy.)
➤ Take extreme positions about extension-of-blame thinking. First list ways to justify blame extensions. Next describe how to create a totally blame-free Utopian world. Next challenge the justifications for the extensions of blame. Then challenge the unrealities of a totally blame-free world. What remains is your accommodation to these extremes.
➤ Understanding the contextual nature of truth is an act of accommodation. To what extent do the views toward blame by a Buddhist differ from those of an atheist, from those of a Calvinist, from those of a satanic cultist? Accommodating to these different views does not require that you believe any.
➤ Within each person exist many values and truths that can contradict each other. Values for expressing oneself openly and honestly may be matched

by values for not needlessly blaming another. When honesty harms, how is this to be resolved? By accepting the inevitable contradictions that lie within us, we can come to appreciate that each contradiction has its role and place. For example, when do you express yourself through simple honesty, and when would you wisely withhold truth?

4. Acceptance: Creating Understanding

When we preoccupy ourselves with blame, might we veer from seeing blame conditions with clarity?

Well-practiced habits of mind stick like glue. Most people don't change their negative patterns of thought by intellectual command. Instead, time and well-directed corrective experiences normally contribute to the formation of functional new perspectives that eventually come to define experience.

Positive changes include the gradual dismantling of ignorance, the development of a fact-based perspective, and the evolution of your cognitive skills. People operating with this mind-set tend to feel self-accepting and tolerant of other people's foibles and faults because they see such as part of a greater picture.

Accepting relapses along with advancements helps promote a positive perspective on the process of change. But change can have some unexpected twists. In a process of getting better by doing better, initially you may have an eye-opening experience where you feel relaxed, in charge, and jubilant. Normally these flights into health are short-lived in the initial stages of change. Such flights frequently fizzle when you think, "Will this experience last?" They also may end abruptly with a crisis, where you believe you need a quick or perfect solution that is not yet available. How you handle such shifts in outlook reflects your resiliency in managing change.

Most people take a few falls into this instant mental health trap before settling down to make the sustained effort necessary to meet basic challenges. Nevertheless, these preview experiences are valuable. They show what life can be like in the absence of a defeatist pattern of negative thinking. However, like most movie previews, these experiences highlight the best of the show. A good movie, like an enjoyable life, may have parts that drag.

Paradoxically, people who don't demand instant mental health often progress with greater surety. They don't paddle against the current by making unrealistic demands about what the pace of change should be. They don't give up on themselves because they are not moving fast enough. In this sense, they are accepting of the trade-offs required for personal development and growth and of the forward movement, plateaus, and dips that inevitably accompany the process.

In developing a broad and realistic perspective, acceptance involves understanding the meaning of change. Sometimes we see this message of acceptance through paradoxes. For example, some people who feel insecure because they are unhappy with themselves wish they were someone else or had different personalities. They focus on becoming what they are not. The introvert wants to be an extrovert. The excitable individual seeks blissful calm. If you count yourself among this group, consider "unbecoming." In unbecoming you quit trying to become someone different. Instead, you seek ways to shed yourself of negative thinking, overly socialized constraints, cliché thinking, extension-of-blame views, and phony exoneration ploys. By shedding such needless restraints, you can open opportunities to understand and accept your "self," build your resources, and find additional ways to enjoy your life.

Exercises in Acceptance

Acceptance is a gift you give to yourself. It often comes about through a perspective where you place a deserved trust in your evaluations. The following ideas about acceptance provide information for these evaluations.

➤ Acceptance of the nature of "self" is like acceptance of the nature of water. Water changes from ice to liquid to vapor. It slips through our fingers but is held in a glass. We cut through it with our hands. Yet in great moving volumes, it wears away rocks and pushes aside all that lies before it. Like water, the "self" is gentle and tough, resilient and yielding, persistent and abandoning, constructive and destructive. If you can accept the nature of water, can you not accept the nature of "self" as changing and moving while exhibiting constancy?

➤ Consider that we are animals living within a complex social network. We have lengthy social training where blame is influential. How does social blame dull your animal nature? How does your animal nature influence your social awareness?

5. Actualization: Extending Your Abilities

Most people do not regret what they have done as much as what they did not do. Distractions, unclear goals, self-imposed miseries, fear of blame, illusions, and other reality-distorting mental processes serve as stumbling blocks that substitute for actualization activities.

The Russian playwright Anton Chekhov, in *A Dreary Story,* tells of an aging professor who led an aimless life and now sees the same potential in his young ward. He feels frustrated because he cannot convey what he has not experienced. If he had experienced a focused and purposeful life, could the aging professor pass on the importance of taking a committed direction? Perhaps he could, in some small measure, by example.

The life you lead depends on many things, including the breadth, scope, and strength of your guiding principles. These operating principles are your standards of conduct based on your sense of ethics, personal dignity, and integrity. They motivate emotionally appropriate decisions that flow with congruity among the principle, feelings, actions, and "self." Extended, they represent a form of actualization. When your actions typically reflect your guiding principles, you can pass on what you believe by illustrating what you do.

Exercises in Actualization

When faced with a "blame" situation, here are some useful awareness-actualization questions:

➤ What is the principle?
➤ How valid is the principle in this situation?
➤ How do you convincingly apply the principle to the situation?

In an actualized state of mind, you 1) hold to strong principles without disparaging those who veer from those principles; 2) feel better positioned to assertively prevent people from treading on your principles; and 3) evaluate through a principle of proportionality, rather than splitting actions between inflexible good/bad dichotomies.

POSTSCRIPT

The British playwright George Bernard Shaw quipped, "Success covers a multitude of blunders." The reverse is also instructive. Success ordinarily includes blunders. I've yet to see anyone change for the better without error and blunder mixed with achievement, development, and success.

A sound self-perspective involves a tolerant understanding of our history, awareness of what is important in the present moment, and a positive and attainable vision for the future. When we know where we are, where we've been, and where we're going, we have a sounder bearing than those normally mired in the past, goalless in the present, and apprehensive about the future.

It helps to keep the perspective that life goes on around you whatever you think and whatever may happen to you. Even when adverse things happen, there are parts of your life that still go well. Under the most difficult of circumstances, you can find ways to contribute to improving your "life" and the lives of others. Needless blame does not have to be part of that process, and that is an important part of perspective.

16

Debunking False Blame Beliefs

> *We are creatures of the mind with the power to use our intellect in many exciting and creative ways.*

We develop and carry our beliefs, abilities, and remembrances with us as we move through time and space. They create a sense of familiarity in a changing world.

Healthy, fact-based beliefs can strongly influence your life in positive ways. Some increase your chances to enjoy your life, such as when you have good reasons to believe that you can meet most of the challenges that you will face. Beliefs also can prove handicapping. When you believe you cannot cope adequately enough, you probably will do one or more of the following: 1) see threats to your self-image everywhere; 2) spend much of your time avoiding make-believe threats; 3) act defensively; 4) play it safe; 5) experience more than your share of anxiety; and 6) blame yourself for not coping adequately enough.

Beliefs range on their own continua. Some are powerful, some are weak, and many are in between. Some beliefs represent strong convictions that lead some people to choose death over life. For example, it is peculiar to think that reasonable people would voluntarily self-immolate or pilot a bomb into a target and blow themselves up along with the target. After all, survival is a prime biological imperative.

Beliefs can override survival instincts. During June 1963 in Saigon, Vietnam, a Buddhist monk, Thich Quang Duc, burned himself alive in a busy intersection to protest the South Vietnamese government of Ngo Dinh Diem. This was the first of eleven self-immolations protesting that government. During April 1997 a Tibetan protester set himself on fire to protest police breaking up a hunger strike. Most people would jump off high buildings rather than burn to death. However, the monks set themselves aflame in the service of furthering their convictions.

The World War II Japanese kamikaze suicide pilots illustrate the extreme power of beliefs. Hundreds of these men flew bomb-laden planes into ships of the

United States naval fleet, sinking thirty-four and damaging many others. The word *kamikaze* described the "divine wind" that destroyed the Mongol leader Kublai Khan's invasion fleets in 1274 and again in 1281. The people believed that the divine wind was heaven's way to protect the Japanese islands. The kamikaze believed in the divinity of the emperor and that they were obeying the command of a god by flying their planes into Japan's enemies.

Powerful beliefs take other forms of myth and magic. These beliefs can remain strong until someone exposes their irrationality. American writer-astrophysicist Carl Sagan, in *Demon Haunted World,* punched holes in many common irrational beliefs, such as alien abductions, faith healing, and other modern fairy tales. Sagan notes that uncritical acceptance of mysticism and superstition defrauds, shames, and even can kill.

Ridding the world of fake spooks that spoof the mind is unlikely. But interested individuals can sharpen their skepticism for peculiar false beliefs and do much to rid themselves of these blights on reason. Thus, if someone offers you utopian hopes and magical solutions to eliminate troublesome life problems, consider the pitch a scam.

The *National Enquirer,* the *Star,* and the *Globe* capitalize on mysticism, superstition, and the implausible. Tabloid fans like to know that Elvis is alive and well in Kansas, 400 pound babies exist, you can tell a werewolf by its purple urine, and the world will end in 1990—woops, 1998—woops, would you believe 2010? And let's not forget "Bigfoot." Has anyone authenticated a Bigfoot skeleton?

The human tendency to think magically makes some people susceptible to pseudosciences that rely on suggestibility, placebo, testimonies, and exceptional examples to support cult beliefs. The American psychic healer Edgar Cayce claimed to cure multiple sclerosis, schizophrenia, Alzheimer's disease, depression, and other physical and mental disorders through "healing" and claimed he could speak to "spirits" through channeling. If Cayce could heal serious illness and mental disorders, why was he not invited to lecture routinely at medical schools? If he could speak to spirits, why did he not talk to Blackbeard the pirate and discover where he hid a treasure?

Science fiction writer L. Ron Hubbard asserted that he could cure mental illness through a device called an E-meter. Allegedly, the E-meter also cured blindness. It would be interesting to discover how the E-meter repaired blindness related to optic nerve damage.

For those who wish to climb higher on the "cure" ladder, Hubbard proclaimed that humans are inhabited by "thetian" spirits sent to Earth 75 million years ago by Xenu, a fiendish galactic leader. By paying a stiff fee, you can be "audited" and then freed of the spirits. We're still waiting for a peer-reviewed journal article to appear in *The American Psychologist* where Hubbard's followers convincingly demonstrate a thetian presence in human emotional disturbance, demonstrate that the E-meter is curative, or show that science-fiction thinking is superior to scientific ways of knowing and doing.

Hope triumphs over reality in other ways. Crystal cures, vampires, zombies, psychic readings, astrology—all testify to the power magical thinking holds over reason. Each myth projects the view that powerful forces control human destiny.

We can use reason and "common sense" to gain freedom from a "demon-

haunted" world. However, our inner worlds normally include false assumptions, illusions, and magical thinking. We have our own demons to exorcise!

MOTIVATIONS FOR CLEAR THINKING

It is doubtful that as a species we will think like the Vulcans in the *Star Trek* television and movie series. These characters used pure logic; there was no room for emotion in their world. Consequently, they were not influenced by feelings.

Most people, from time to time, wish they were not whipsawed by their emotions
and could live without feeling. But our emotions make up our humanness. They represent motivating forces. They warn, teach, and help create bonds between people.
Who'd want to give up levity, humor, joy, love, and the feelings that propel ambition?

What most people mean when they wish they could rise above their emotions is
that they want to eliminate the negative, misleading, and destructively obsessive
emotional states. Working in this direction is legitimate. There are many tested
ways to learn to keep our emotional life relatively uncontaminated by extension-of-
blame thinking, magical beliefs, false assumptions, superstitious thinking, unrealistic expectations, and errors of logic and reasoning. This work is the hallmark of a
sound self-education process. With progressive mastery over our negative thinking
and beliefs that provoke double troubles and misconceptions, we have more space
in our thoughts for positive emotions and constructive actions. For some, this direction is worthy of effort. The following sections describe techniques to support this
positive motivation for change.

BLAME THINKING AND CHANGE

Our blame beliefs powerfully influence our judgments and emotions. These systems
are normally hierarchically ordered, which means that we are likely to feel offended
and blame according to what we consider important and ignore what we don't. This
hierarchy is powerful even when some beliefs are clearly dysfunctional. For example, when perfectionism blame beliefs dominate our perspective, we prime ourselves to filter and organize experience around these beliefs. Then we are likely to
blamefully overreact to practically any deviation from our standards.

Maintaining a clear-thinking perspective involves developing clarity while
peeling away layers of deception that cloud awareness. This perspective development is especially important when our evaluations, judgments, and decisions are influenced by powerful erroneous beliefs.

Self-empowerment often includes fast recognizing and evaluating extension-
of-blame and other forms of erroneous thinking. This identification process sets the
stage for corrective action. Action engages accommodation. Acceptance reflects a
successful accommodation. Actualization represents ownership in the new way of
thinking as an extension of the "self." Let's see how this process unfolds with regard to recognizing and dealing with fictions, fallacies, and blame.

Awareness: Finding Fictions and Fallacies

Psychological illusions, myths, superstitious thinking, suggestibility, magical thinking, misinformation, ignorance, and other perversions of reason can promote unwanted consequences even when blame is absent.

Logical fallacies join with these biasing tendencies to befuddle our enlightened interests. Unless disciplined in the positive use of intellect, we can fall into these reality distortion traps—often without clearly knowing what we are doing.

Exercises in Awareness

Magical thinking is supported by fallacies. Recognizing the fallacies in thinking makes us less susceptible to magical thinking, jumping to erroneous conclusions, and falling into the various blame traps. The first step in breaking from faulty reasoning is to recognize and label the fallacies. The following list describes some common fallacies that can support extension-of-blame and other forms of erroneous thinking.

➤ We fall into the *ad hominem* fallacy trap when we avoid an issue by attacking another's character and motivations. A sheep rancher and a cattle rancher are arguing over who should use the open range for grazing livestock. Instead of solving their problem through negotiation, one turns to the other and says, "You are a dirty, lying polecat." You shift this thinking by seeking alternative ways to negotiate or solve problems.

➤ *"Non sequitur"* means: It does not follow. For example, in an extension-of-blame equation, you tie the observation that a person made a "mistake" to the individual's total personal worth. This is how it works: Joe forgot to bring in a report. Because he forgot, he thinks he's worthless. This trap is made obvious when we see the circularity in the reasoning. You escape the trap by not chaining unrelated ideas together.

➤ *Tautological thinking* involves stringing together redundant statements. This is like throwing mud against the wall in the hopes that some will stick. Here is a "blame" example: "You are a bum with lazy parents whose grandfather was the town loser." You bypass this process by sticking to the specifics.

➤ The *frequency fallacy* involves jumping to conclusions on the basis of limited information. Based on a small sample of observations, one generalizes to the whole. Like the four blind men who touched an elephant and each decided that the beast was something different, people who fall into the frequency trap risk coming to wrong conclusions. A politician hears from four constituents about a local issue and concludes that this is a widespread problem. You escape this frequency fallacy trap by assuming a perspective where you look for disconfirming evidence: Two people tell you "Jane is not to be trusted." You later learn that the pair embezzled Jane's savings.

➤ When you make mountains out of molehills, you magnify or *exaggerate*. In this process you blow an event into a catastrophe. You don't like a phrase someone uses in referring to you. You think that his or her conduct is simply horrible. You personalize and stew about the event. You blame the person for insensitivity and have visions of that person in the middle of January at the North Pole wearing only a swim suit. You escape this exaggeration trap by focusing your attention on what you can control.

➤ In creating *dichotomous divisions* you take an extreme either/or position: "You are taking Joe's side again. You always did favor him. You never gave me a fair shake." Categorical divisions, as in this example, suggest extension-of-blame victim thinking. You break the dichotomus division process by thinking in degrees and by supporting the degrees in which you think. For example, the severity of an infraction exists on a continuum. Even if we were to take a strictly categorical approach to judging the situation, then degrees of fault might best be matched by a penalty proportional to the fault.

➤ *Selective perception* involves semiconsciously excluding information that challenges a pet belief. You feel angered because you received an acceptable performance review but you believe you deserved better. Now as you look at your "evaluator," all you can see are his faults. You amass reasons to question his judgment. As an alternative, accept what you don't like and improve what you can, and refuse to limit yourself to a narrow view.

➤ *Overfocusing* involves fixating on one part of a situation to the exclusion of other relevant views. Piqued by blame, a person focuses and hashes and rehashes a situation, adding and deleting details in a downward spiral of self-righteous justifications to support her rapidly narrowing view. As an alternative; 1) label the process "overfocusing"; 2) observe the process and seek legitimate ways to break from the pattern; and 3) refuse to blame yourself if you don't at first succeed in breaking the cycle.

➤ *Verbal vagaries* practically guarantee that conflicts will continue. Here you express abstract ideas that can lead to *abstract upset*. In a fit of self-blame, you declare yourself worthless because you are not all that you should be. As an alternative, keep to the concrete facts. You can clarify these distortions through honest answers to some basic questions: What should you *be?* What does "worthless" mean? How do the two ideas fit together?

➤ *Reasoning by possibilities* involves asserting that your idea cannot be completely disproved because it is "possible" that you are right. If you assume that "anything is possible," by analogy, you can argue that tiny reindeer live on the planet Mars. Taking the position that these reindeer exist because you have not been proven wrong represents backward reasoning. As an alternative, reason by plausibility and probability: Where is the evidence or proof of a proposition?

Action: The ABCs of Change

We have a long history of knowing that the meaning we ascribe to life's events impacts on how we feel about such events. It is just recently that we systematically put this knowledge to work.

The Babylonian king Hammurabi knew that by controlling people's beliefs, you could control their behavior. Thereafter, Aristotle was among the first to recognize the relationship between ideas and emotions. About 320 B.C. he produced *The Rhetoric*. Within that work he provided a study of speech, described the art of arguing effectively, and showed how to prevail in debate. He outlined his views on how people think themselves into "superiority," anger, and shame.

The Stoic philosopher Epictetus got us on a therapeutic track when he said that it is not so much what happens that causes emotions; rather it is how we think about events. By controlling thinking we can rid ourselves of powerful destructive emotions. In the nineteenth century, Swiss psychiatrist Paul Dubois, the father of American psychology William James, and the French psychologist Jean Payot supported Epictetus' views on the sources of many emotions by pointing to the power of thought in evoking emotions. James went the extra step by saying that by changing our thinking we change our lives.

Throughout the twentieth century, we see this same theme echoed through the writings of Connecticut psychiatrist Thomas Williams, psychologist John Dollard, the general semantist Alfred Korzypski, the constructive psychologist George Kelly, University of Pennsylvania psychiatrist Aaron Beck, cognitive-behavior psychologist Donald Meichenbaum, the founder of multimodal therapy, Arnold A. Lazarus, and my own work on this subject. Currently this cognitive view on emotion has been the dominant force in providing highly efficient strategies for personal change.

The scientific literature now provides impressive scientific data to support the view that we feel as we think. The data point to these conclusions: By reducing dysfunctional thinking habits, we reduce emotional and behavioral disturbances. By supporting rational ways of thinking, we increase opportunities for motivating and energizing positive, purposeful, constructive pursuits.

Perhaps more than any other, psychologist Albert Ellis, who pioneered rational-emotive-behavior therapy (REBT), paved the way for a resurgence of basic ideas for how people think and change.

Ellis inspired the cognitive revolution in psychotherapy and provided a welcome relief from the dark and mysterious "demon-haunted world" of psychoanalytic theory. Ellis and his associates helped wrest counseling and therapy from psychoanalytic and other inefficient methods by pinning the cognitive theory and methods onto scientific foundations. It was Aaron Beck's University of Pennsylvania group, however, that provided the more impressive empirical evidence to support the use of cognitive methods of change.

Exercises in Action
Albert Ellis devised an ABC model to show how to think straight and break free of needless distress. The ABC acronym describes a process for how we react in emotionally evocative situations. In this model, the *A* refers to any *activating event* that is strong enough to evoke emotional consequences. Ellis is concerned with activating events that stir personal distress, such as an unwanted rejection or failure. Evocative events, however, include dreams, physical pain, flashbacks, or real-time situations such as getting splashed by a truck.

The *B* stands for the *beliefs* we have about the activating events in our lives. Our most stressful emotional experiences normally result from cognitive appraisals hot enough to evoke negative emotions such as those generated by erroneous extension-of-blame thinking. The thoughts about these events become targets for change when they meet standards for being irrational and result in needlessly stressful outcomes. If erroneous, fictional, unrealistic, and irrational ideas distort reality, how can you tell an erroneous from a sensible or rational belief? Rational belief systems result from using reason, logic, and scientific ways of knowing and thinking. These beliefs normally will fit with enlightened self-interests, responsibility, good interpersonal relationships, progress, and a rich range of emotions that are congruous with reality.

Harmful irrational belief systems are self-defeating. They often show up through negative stress emotions, such as anxiety and depression, and through self-defeating behaviors, such as bickering, argumentativeness, withdrawal, avoidance, and procrastination. Harmful irrational beliefs impede quality human relationships, promote a diminished sense of control, lead to feeling overwhelmed and seeking fault to explain negative results. These beliefs often interconnect with magnifications, overgeneralizations, extension-of-blame thinking, contingency-worth thinking, performance anxieties, self-doubts, and errors of reasoning such as ad hominem fallacies, reasoning with non sequiturs, and the tautological or "circular" reasoning trap. They often involve condemnation, such as in extension-of-blame thinking.

Irrational beliefs are relatively automatic processes. They "feel" natural. They are normally at the cusp of consciousness for those who seek to understand them. When we don't make the effort either to monitor them or to put them into a context, we repeat them without forethought. Putting irrational thinking that leads to bad feelings into slow motion can help make them transparent. Then we can better see the connection between irrational thinking and its results. Once you recognize harmful irrational thinking, you can question its assumptions profitably.

In the ABC framework, *C* stands for the emotional and behavioral *consequences* of our beliefs. You gamble your life savings because you "feel lucky." When you lose, you feel depressed because you believe that your life is ruined. The *C* represents the ubiquitous excitable feeling of "luck" and ubiquitous negative feeling of depression.

The *C* also represents behavioral consequences. Let's take an extreme example of when you don't censor your response. Assume you believe you must tell your boss off. You feel emotionally charged with anger. So you rush into your boss's office, blurt out your angry thoughts, rail against an "unfairness" here and an "injustice" there. You refuse to back off from your position and get yourself fired.

Once you have worked out the ABCs, you are prepared to go to *D*. The *D* in this change process stands for *dispute*. Disputing includes questioning and challenging irrational belief systems. *D* is more than intellectual play. It involves a fair-minded, sometimes scientific analysis of beliefs that link to needless blame distress. In the *D* stage, we question our assumptions. For example, if you believe that you would be "destroyed" if you made an error speaking before a group, at the *D* stage, you'd ask yourself questions such as: How would I be destroyed? If another made a mistake, how would that destroy him or her?

D also involves applying logic to dispute logical fallacies. In challenging a non sequitur, for example, you expose the circularity. If you think that Joe is blameworthy and worthless for forgetting a report, you separate the blameworthiness from the worth issue. Then you ask yourself: Where is the evidence that forgetting a report renders a complex human worthless? Most reasonable people would recognize the tautology in the worthlessness assertion.

The *D* process has a behavior component. Here is where you put new ideas and ways of acting to the test. These behavioral activities plans can involve rehearsing new ways of thinking, feeling, or behaving, taking reasoned risks, or making other concrete behavior changes. For example, you are afraid to speak up in a group. You join a debating club for practice. You plan to force yourself to speak up in a group and express your opinion at least twice at each meeting. You do this to get practice in developing your confidence in speaking up.

Because of your experiments with new ways of thinking and acting, you produce constructive new *effects* (*E*). These new effects show that you can master challenging personal problems. More important, you show yourself that you have the ability to organize, regulate, and motivate yourself to produce a desirable result. This is the spirit of self-efficacy.

Let's look at how to put this ABC system to work using an everyday example. Since practically everyone has had someone cut in front of them in line, I'll show how to use the ABC process to develop a rational perspective on this issue. I'll use some common examples of irrational thinking to illustrate the point.

A. (List the activating event.)
Stranger stepped in front of me while I waited in line.
B. (Record your thinking about the event.)
Sensible thinking: I don't like people cutting in line. This is inconsiderate and impolite conduct.
Harmful irrational thinking: The idiot should not do this to me. I'll have an ugly confrontation if I say anything. I'm a weak wimp for letting this happen to me.
C. (Describe the emotional and behavioral consequences.)
From a sensible-thinking perspective: Felt frustrated and annoyed with this conduct.
From an irrational perspective: Felt angry. Said nothing. Stewed about the event for the next two hours.
D. (Disputing, reframing, reevaluating, reexamining, questioning, challenging)
Rational response: I don't like people cutting in line. This is impolite and inconsiderate conduct. Disputation: Most reasonable people probably would agree with the conclusion that the individual acted inconsiderately. No dispute is necessary. *Irrational response: The idiot should not do this to me.* Disputation: (1) This pejorative character generalization only serves to justify an animosity that does me more harm than good. I'm still behind in line. Layering a problem onto a problem doesn't change the situation. (2) Following the social convention of waiting one's turn in line is desirable for people. However, where is the universal law that says that people should not violate social conventions that involve me? (Although there is no law, you probably will continue to dislike it when people violate social conventions that directly affect you.) *Irrational response: I'll have an ugly confrontation if I say anything.* Disputation: (1) What is an "ugly confrontation"? This question is designed to clarify an underlying assumption that can link to anxiety. (2) Where is the crystal ball that

precisely foretells that outcome? This question challenges the infallibility of a belief. For example, as an alternative hypothesis, consider the probability that the individual might step back when asked to do so. (Your response might be tempered depending on whether you saw that the person who broke the rules was spoiling for a fight, was joining friends in line, or the line was fragmented and where it ended was unclear.)

Irrational response: I am a weak wimp for letting this happen to me. Disputation: You have no control over the spontaneous actions of others who cut in front of you in line, so you can't be a weak wimp because of that. At the core, how are you a wimp for not acting? How does the blame label "wimp" represent your total essence?

E. (List New effects).

For example, you accept your displeasure. You refuse to condemn yourself or the other person. Because you see the line moving quickly, you take no other action this time.

Take a few practice runs with the ABC system to see how it works for you. Use the following ABC worksheet to describe an activating event that previously evoked a negative emotional response. Work out the problem using this framework.

A. (the activating event)

_____

B. (your thinking about the event)

_____

_____

_____

C. (the emotional and behavioral consequences)

_____

_____

_____

D. (your strategies for disputing irrational belief systems—reframing, reevaluating, reexamining, questioning, challenging actions)

_____

_____

_____

E. (new effects)

_____

_____

_____

Accommodations: Incongruities and Integration

While experimenting with different ways of thinking and acting, you will note some contradictions in your thinking. That which you once believed to be true can come into conflict with reality. For example, you worry about making a mistake because you fear rejection. You make a mistake and no one notices! How is this to be resolved?

You blame yourself for not having the control you believe you require to feel good about yourself. Yet you demand control of yourself in conditions that are outside your influence. How can you feel good about yourself when you insist on control that you cannot acquire? For example, you believe you need to have someone whose views differ from yours to see life your way. But since people invariably see life their way, how is this dilemma to be resolved?

Different ideas will clash with each other because they are paradoxical. In developing accommodation skills, seek resolutions to the contradictions.

Exercises in Accommodation

Playing opposites, you intentionally look for contradictions in your thinking and then seek ways to resolve the contradictions. The resolution leads to accommodation.

➤ If you believe that you deserve to roast for past mistakes, then should all persons who erred deserve eternal damnation? If not, why not?

➤ If you believe a friend is fair-minded, tolerant, and wise, the opposites would include biased, intolerant, and foolish. Predictably, you can find evidence for the opposite. Which view is true?

➤ People who feel emotionally vulnerable are prone to view challenges as a threat and thus avoid them to maintain a shaky sense of stability. In playing with paradoxes of opposites, look for the "opportunity" in the "threat." Look for the challenge in the opportunity. (People with a challenge outlook normally experience a greater sense of inner control than those with a threat mentality who prioritize escape and avoidance over accomplishment.)

Acceptance: Fluctuations and Variabilities

We are responsible for how we view reality, but blaming ourselves for creating negative patterns of thought is self-limiting. We have the power to think about our thinking and to change beliefs that lead to undesirable results. That is a realistically optimistic view.

The spirit of acceptance includes the idea that sometimes we will feel prepared to think rationally and respond reasonably and sometimes not. For example, in the heat of an emotional conflict, you may figure out how to productively avoid casting dispersions and blame. But what about those situations where you seem locked into a position in which you suspect you could do yourself more harm than good by speaking your mind?

Exercises in Acceptance

Accepting that you don't have to have an immediate answer or solution can help defuse any urgency you may feel to bring a quick and probably unfavorable resolution to a conflict. This acceptance provides opportunity to reformulate your thinking and to guide your actions so as to increase your chances for a beneficial outcome. In this time interlude, you return to the ABC process to gain an objective perspective.

> ➤ Take a break and come back to the problem in, say, half an hour. You don't have to finish what you feel compelled to start on the spot, and a "time-out" may help you to refocus.
> ➤ During this time, use the ABCDE framework to work out the problem.
> ➤ Reexamine your original description of the situation for accuracy and match your recorded thinking against the criteria for rational and irrational thinking.
> ➤ Define and accept your rational thinking.
> ➤ Note the irrational, implausible, or disputable ideas.
> ➤ Dispute, question, or challenge these irrational elements of thought under "D."
> ➤ Test the approach.
> ➤ Record the new effects ("E").

Albert Ellis suggests that people give themselves unconditional self-acceptance (USA). Our foibles, faults, mistaken impressions, erroneous views, illusions, myths, magical thinking, suggestibility, oversensitivity, anxiety-producing thoughts, extensions of blame, and other limitations on our thinking will not disappear totally. Blame won't take them away. However, a USA view, combined with a problem-solving approach, suggests a tolerant, accommodating approach to life that frees our thoughts and energies for constructive pursuits.

Actualization: Initiatives in Clear Thinking

Most reasonable people agree that it is wiser to exercise beliefs that lead to benefit and to expunge those that lead to harmful results. Nevertheless, cultivating beneficial belief systems often proves challenging, because multiple views normally exist within the mind. It takes a deliberate effort to separate beneficial from harmful blame beliefs and to make beneficial beliefs extend into how we feel and what we do. Expanding the positive over the negative through a focused ABC analysis is an act of actualization.

Exercises in Actualization

The following offers a list of contrasting blame and actualization beliefs.

➤ *Blame belief:* Sharply condemning people for undesired conduct will cause them to stop the behavior.

Actualized belief: Undesirable behavior normally doesn't go away on demand. You can increase your chances for making your point by finding ways to get your views across without using blame and evoking defensiveness.

➤ *Blame belief:* By repeatedly blaming and criticizing others, you can come to control what they do.

Actualized belief: Blunting blame through finding common ground and common interests increases the odds that friendship will be freely given and changes freely made.

➤ *Blame belief:* If you don't criticize every infraction, people will think they can get away with whatever they choose to do.

Actualized belief: Many of the faults we ascribe to people are preferential, subjective, and discretionary. Nitpicking and nagging normally causes people to turn a deaf ear. Paradoxically, this solution invites the behavior that the "blamer" wishes to discourage.

➤ *Blame belief:* People who violate customs, traditions, and conventional rules justly deserve the worst they can get.

Actualized belief: People occasionally will find some customs, rules, or traditions unnecessary or inconsistent with other customs, rules, and traditions that they prefer to follow. Understanding the basis for a variation in customs or rules creates opportunities to discriminate fairly between what is functional and what is not and the degrees of difference that exist between. The result is extending customs through behavior that has the greatest benefit.

POSTSCRIPT

Shakespeare said, "Nothing is good or bad but thinking makes it so." The Bard of Avon understood the power of thought in emotional experiences.

Monitoring our thought processes to see how hot blame thoughts can spike our emotions sets the stage for clear thinking about our thinking. It also shows that thinking makes it so.

17

Busting the Blame–Anger Connection

> *Few people wish to lead a life of anger. Most prefer to live and let live. Paradoxically, "live and let live" frequently involves dealing with anger.*

You are a weary warrior returning home from battle. Your armor weighs heavily. You think of casting your shield to the side of the road to ease the burden. But soon your thoughts drift to feelings of thankfulness that you survived five years of clashing swords and of moaning men dying. Finally the foe fragmented into small bands and retreated. The war is over.

You touch the hilt on the sword by your side and dream of plowing and planting the earth to again make golden fields of wheat glimmer in the sun. As you walk the long cobblestone road to your home, you think of your wife and now-grown sons and daughter. You feel a sense of pride that you did your duty to keep the hordes of Vandal invaders from your family's door. You imagine the many nights of fantastic adventures you can tell your future grandchildren. But now you are most interested in learning of the lives of your sons, daughter, and wife: What happened in your absence? What are your children doing with their lives?

You round a bend in the road and feel shocked to see Vandals putting a family to the sword. You see the back of a farmer on his knees with both hands holding a wooden staff against a Vandal sword. He is no match for the bearded warrior. You hear a woman scream and watch as she throws her body over that of her child. A Vandal raises a spear to plunge it into the woman. You see two more by the roadside laughing and shouting "Kill, kill!" All this happens together in a flash.

In an instant, you feel a rage inside. You shout *EEEEE!* as you unsheath your sword and swing your shield before you. You see the Vandals' attention shift from the family to you. You charge. Two meet your forward flight. In a moment, after the

153

clashing of steel, the two lie wounded. But the others rush forth to carry on the fight. Now driven to one knee, you shield the blows from one while parrying the sword of the other. The surge of strength you first felt wanes in this struggle. Your final prayer is that the family took flight.

You see the sword of your enemy poised to strike the fatal blow. You hear a *whoosh, crack,* and that Vandal falls. As the other turns, you hear *whoosh, crack,* and the second falls. Through eyes blinded by sweat, you see the hazy image of a young man with a staff. Then you hear, "Father?" The family you saved was that of your eldest son.

The warrior's protective anger was appropriate. It's short-lived, directed, and dissipates after the crisis passes. However, anger takes other forms, including irrational patterns, that erupt for foolish reasons and linger. In this chapter we'll focus primarily on how to recognize and manage the thoughts behind these unproductive angers.

THE FACES OF ANGER

Anger can arise from our perceptions and from our beliefs. It occurs on a continuum from irritation to rage. It can be a legitimate signal for action or represent a harmful, narrow, distorted perspective. In this section we'll look first at functional, perceptual, and cognitive forms of anger. They we'll examine irrational angers that grow from extension-of-blame thinking.

Functional Angers

Perceptual anger is a hardwired, adrenaline-charged survival mechanism. Like fear and love, it is a primary emotion that is wired in from birth. This emotional driving force erupts when we perceive a danger requiring a powerful focused action. Then our reaction is near instant. Anger gives direction to our thoughts and actions when we first perceive that fight is better than flight. Because of its primitive brain origins, perceptual anger bypasses logical circuits, but thoughts are not far behind. Perceptual anger can arise in response to a drive to protect others.

The neural mechanisms for anger branch to and from our higher mental processes. Through secondary conditioning, these pathways attach to social threats and acquired motivations, such as preserving one's image, maintaining control, enforcing standards for conduct, and other core beliefs that relate to "self" and "territory." That's what makes them cognitive angers; they are stirred by what we think.

Although we might feel anger toward inanimate objects (you stub your toe on a rock), cognitive anger normally is directed toward ourselves or other people. Self-anger can involve reprimanding oneself for poor behavior. We see angry discharges among those whose income is threatened, in protecting property, and in defending one's reputation.

Both perceptual and cognitive anger can be based on misperception or misunderstanding. You see an ominous shadow and feel a surge of anger as you prepare to hold your ground. You discover that the shadow was that of a cat. An acquaintance doesn't meet you for lunch as promised. You feel angered. Then you recheck your calendar to find you have the wrong date. By getting valid new information, we can change our views and thus our feelings—even in situations that can stimulate powerful forms of anger.

Irrational Anger

Irrational anger (i-anger) is a form of cognitive anger that reflects irrational demands, intolerance for tension, and extension-of-blame thinking. In an externalizing mind-set, the irrationally angry person blames others for his or her problems. In an internalizing mind-set the person denounces, demeans, and faults him-/herself for sometimes minor matters.

Irrational anger and aggression normally are frowned upon socially. In response to this social awareness, some persistently i-angered individuals bend over to put on an image of social cordiality and may conceal these feelings through pasting a smile on their face. In the service of avoiding public censure, some deny their problem to justify their anger: "People start up with me, that's why I'm angry." "I'm a victim and can get no justice. I have a right to feel anger." "People deserve what they get." "We live in an unfair world." Each of these thoughts includes the belief that other people are to blame.

Rage and hate are among the more dangerous forms of i-anger. People in fits of rage color their minds with irrational thoughts. In piqued states of emotional arousal, they lose perspective by a preoccupation with blame and vengeance that feeds upon itself. Primed to explode violently, they frequently don't see alternatives other than hostile, vengeful solutions.

Querulous Demands

The German-born American psychiatrist Karen Horney thought that some people had a basic tendency toward hostility. She correctly noted that "hostile" individuals are primed to make irrational demands. Their lexicon froths with tyrannical *should, ought, must* thinking. Living in an inner house of misery, these blame-prone individuals obsess over events, dwell on lacks, and smart over what they claim are their unfulfilled needs. They lead lives of double troubles. They have normal problems of living to contend with plus their blame-proneness.

Refusing to let go of grievances, some hostile people carry grudges for decades. Having secret rules for what others owe and should grant them, they routinely hold inner court where they are the judge and jury and where they list one-sided, negative evidence to support extension-of-blame conclusions. In some instances the affected people have trouble stopping this process even when they know that what they are thinking and doing is irrational.

Truly, i-anger is an anguished state of mind. Even if you show few signs of this blame process, it is wise to recognize what people are putting themselves through when this dysfunctional form of anger clouds their reason. For example, when dealing with pervasively angry people, it often helps to remind oneself that their hostility is *their* problem.

MOTIVATIONS FOR DEFUSING ANGER

Perceptual and productive cognitive forms of anger won't disappear because these feelings are normally healthy and motivational. I-anger is the problem. Fortunately, since extension-of-blame thinking is learned, people can find ways to drop blame extensions from their mental equations, and usually they can experience less stress and more pleasure in their daily lives.

Thinking clearly with perspective has obvious advantages. But this is not the only reason to act to rid yourself of i-anger. This form of anger elevates your risk for health consequences. Recent research in the stress connection in the acquisition of coronary heart disease points to anger-related stress as a prime heart attack risk factor. There is a higher death rate among persistently angry people.

Hostile time-urgent people put themselves at significant risk of coronary heart disease compared with their even-tempered comrades. "Hot reactors" to everyday stresses place themselves at greater health risks. Those who regularly "blow off steam" are twice as likely to suffer from stroke. Defensively hostile people suffer more frequent and severe ischemia episodes (a decrease in blood supply to organs due to blood vessel constriction) than those who actively cope with hostility. Indeed, the work of University of Buffalo psychologist Jim Blascoviche and his colleague on the physiological effects of threat demonstrates that people with a threat mentality (prone to blame and anger) exhibit constrictions in their peripheral vascular system, thus reducing cardiac efficiency. Blaskoviche's research on threat also shows that people who adopt a challenge mentality show improved cardiac efficiency.

An alternative to the i-anger choice is to learn to deal effectively with its extension-of-blame component. For example, taking extension-of-blame thinking out of anger would eliminate a significant proportion of the destructive forms of i-anger.

Health reasons justify efforts to shrink the frequency and internal effects of i-anger. However, there are other personal and social benefits to overcoming i-anger:

➤ *A sense of inner control!* People who genuinely command themselves are normally better able to get their views over to others, negotiate, and assert their preferences effectively.

➤ *A broader, more realistic sense of perspective!* A realistic perspective increases the probability that people will recognize opportunities within the range that exists between negative and positive conditions.

➤ *Increased resource availability!* Once they free themselves of i-anger, people have more available time and intellectual resources available to engage in constructive, purposeful pursuits.

➤ *Reduced levels of emotional distress!* A deeper sense of personal acceptance and acceptance of others correlates with clearer thinking, viewing alternatives, and selecting and meeting worthwhile challenges.

➤ *Improved interpersonal relationships!* People who feel accepted rather than blamed are more likely to reciprocate with positive behavior.

➤ *Increased persuasive ability!* There is a greater likelihood of logically persuading others to your view if you have a compelling argument and don't present yourself as a person wrangled by intense, angry, urgent, condemning motivations.

FIVE PHASES FOR DEFUSING IRRATIONAL ANGER

Anger management involves forcefully confronting extension-of-blame thinking and other forms of irrationality that contribute to acting emotionally against the self and others. You can defuse i-anger by following the five phases of change.

1. Awareness: Defining the Idea

Perceptual, cognitive, and irrational anger represent hot emotions. Perceptual anger is easy enough to understand as it is a short burst in response to a physical threat. Cognitive anger directs our energies toward a productive result. Irrational anger includes demanding, self-righteous, blaming, intolerant states of mind. This often feels qualitatively different from perceptual and cognitive forms of anger. I-anger signs include rehashing grievances, smoldering, inflexibility, and sometimes verbal and physical abuse. Although you can use the emotional and behavioral signs to name the feeling, defining the ideas behind the anger is a premier step to change.

Exercises in Awareness
Here are some awareness-raising thoughts and exercises for understanding anger.

➤ Aristotle advises that to understand anger involves understanding the angry person's state of mind, the people whom the individual normally feels anger toward, and the grounds for the anger. This information provides a perspective for avoiding unnecessary conflict.

➤ Use anger as a signal, and learn to look at its meaning. Is the cause legitimate? What parts of your view are appropriate? Do extension-of-blame components appear in your thinking? If so, what do you tell yourself to extend blame?

➤ Separate functional cognitive anger from i-anger. Cognitive anger can involve blame but is free from extension-of-blame thinking. I-anger has a cognitive signature that typically includes rigid demands (should, ought, must, requirements, insistence), extensions of blame, intolerance, damning, condemning, and thoughts and actions associated with vengeful punishment. By separating cognitive anger from i-anger, you open opportunities for making enlightened choices.

➤ What "general" situations are likely to evoke i-anger in you? What specific thoughts and images are you likely to have about such situations? What adaptive alternatives are available? Now, imagine yourself going through the paces applying adaptive cognitive anger or productive blame responses.

➤ If you experience a smoldering anger that is ever ready to erupt, what extension-of-blame ideas are you holding in? What are your legitimate gripes? Whom are they directed toward? What beliefs are keeping you from expressing legitimate grievances that are without extension-of-blame complications? What appropriate channels are available for anger expression?

➤ Most of our daily threats are "ego threats" to our self-image, expectations, rules, roles, responsibilities, values, and identity. Separate physical threats from ego threats, from economic threats, from relationship threats, and so forth. Which threat do you find most troublesome? What are your best options in overcoming the threat?

2. Action: Attacking Angry Thinking

Cathartic activities such as hitting a pillow, kicking the door, throwing objects, or screaming to vent anger seem intuitively correct. After all, isn't it better to express than suppress anger? Although some psychotherapy schools actively build screaming and hitting into their procedures, the results are less than impressive. Psychologist Arthur Janov's primal scream therapy and psychiatrist Daniel Casrael's work on catharsis through screaming and hitting pillows may help some overly inhibited people, but often such approaches enforce a negative pattern in those people who would better learn to deal with the extensions of blame nested in their angry outbursts.

While anger expressions such as throwing objects at walls are "cute" in the movies, this response pattern doesn't ordinarily prove to be a helpful form of anger resolution. Indeed, people who scream and yell and appear to lose control often get more practice throwing temper tantrums. Given the choice between squelching and stewing or volatile expression, kicking doors is possibly less health damaging, but it still is health damaging! It is also better to kick a door than a person. However, why not learn to effectively deal with i-anger patterns? By doing so you'll have fewer i-anger relapses and you'll decrease a health-dangerous activity that can artificially limit your quality human relationships.

Anger management involves learning to deal effectively with anger-provoking problems, to get nonproductive extension-of-blame thinking out of the picture, and to reduce the frequency of other i-anger reactions. Saying how you feel, asserting your interests, and taking protective actions are normally more elegant alternatives than hitting pillows. Some communication methods, such as active listening and paraphrasing, reduce the risk of misunderstanding and convey an empathic and acceptant attitude. Empathic responses take the "i" out of i-anger.

Exercises in Action
The illusions of insight and judgment are major cognitive distortions. Here you convince yourself that your judgments and intuitions are correct. You have no need to question your beliefs—even those that repeatedly lead to undesirable outcomes. When these illusions incorporate i-anger thinking, this blame state of mind can alienate those who view this illusion as arrogance. You take an important step to break from illusion-of-insight and judgment traps when you tie the illusion to its results.

You take another important step when you make conscious efforts to qualify your judgments to yourself. Preceding judgment statements by "I assume," "I perceive," or "I believe" moves us from the realm of rigid absolutes to that of flexible probabilities.

The following exercises can be used to deal with extension-of-blame thinking:

➤ You can cognitively override extension-of-blame thinking by refusing to accept the extensions.

➤ Substitute consequential thinking for extension-of-blame thinking. Here you predict the probable outcome of extending blame and of actively coping by drawing the other into joint problem solving. Now you have a plan to test rather than an impulse to express.

➤ In conditions where you are primed for a tirade, it is normally best to put distance between yourself and the event. Go for a walk. Take a break. Drink a cold glass of water. The idea is to buy time to gain a constructive perspective.

➤ Rather than counting to ten, do a cost-benefits analysis. What are the short- and long-term benefits and disadvantages of i-anger processes? The short-term benefit of i-anger expression may include feeling relief from bottled-up tension. The long-term benefits are likely to be few, and disadvantages can include a list of potential health and relationship problems. The short- and long-term analysis sets the stage for looking beyond the moment. Once you begin to make choices about how to respond, you already have put reason between an angry impulse and your reaction.

➤ Create an anger thermometer by making a wallet-size circle. Put a movable dial in the center. Divide the circle equally into green, yellow, and red sections. Green means a functional cognitive anger. Yellow means a mixed functional and extension-of-blame condition. Red signals a primary extension-of-blame anger reaction. When you feel angered, pull out the card and use it to alert yourself to the signs of escalating anger. When you are feeling i-anger, put the dial on the red. Work to get the dial into the yellow or, better yet, green zone.

➤ The expression of an angered intent can evoke change in others providing one keeps to the issue and avoids adding needless forms of blame.

➤ Someone shows anger toward you. In perception checking, ask for clarification. Seek understanding rather than confrontation.

➤ Consider that most daily events are rarely as catastrophic as they seem in the heat of the moment. For example, how many times have you gotten yourself distressed only to find no basis for the strain you visited upon yourself? On the other hand, if you have a serious challenge to face, normally it is better to face the situation with tolerance and perspective.

➤ Write out a role-reversal sequence. If you believe your anger is justified, how would you prefer to be treated if the roles were reversed? By looking at what you've written, you can better position yourself to edit out responses that you would find ineffective if directed toward you.

The following REBT problem-solving framework provides a direct approach to defeat self-injurious i-anger thinking. We'll use a common experience, waiting for help in a store, and assume a mild level of i-anger when this help is not forthcoming.

Activating Event	Blame Belief	Consequence	Dispute
Clerks not available when you want them.	Can't depend on lazy jerk clerks to do their jobs.	Frustration; anger; pacing and fuming.	Where is it written that people need to be available exactly at the time you want them? If a clerk is not available, might he/she be busy with people who attracted his/her attention first? Where is the evidence that all clerks in the store are lazy and jerks? If someone is not available to serve you, how does that justify their termination?

While waiting can evoke frustration, this "impediment" can turn to anger when we add surplus meaning to the situation.

Although the language in this REBT change example is not so dramatic as it might be if I used demand terms like "should" and "must," and although I've used no expletives, as might commonly result from i-anger, the model does include a subtle demand, blame, extension-of-blame thinking, intolerance, and punishment.

3. Accommodation: Integrating the Change

Accommodation involves recognizing the presence of multiple forms of anger and adjusting one's thinking to keep them in perspective. For instance, in a situation in which you might ordinarily get immersed in extension-of-blame thinking, but don't allow yourself to fall into this trap, you're accommodated to a broader understanding.

We have the ability to reason. That ability can provide a reconciliation between the normal human emotion of anger and the meanings we ascribe to social and personal situations that evoke i-anger.

Exercises in Accommodation
Most people think that the situation causes the emotional flurry. The following exercises show the power of the mind to adjust to cognitive i-anger conditions.

➤ Invent a situation where you might feel i-angered. See if you can't produce anger by artificially causing yourself to think following the i-anger process of demand, blame, extension of blame, intolerance, and punishment. Next, imagine yourself thinking about the situation and feeling calm. When you experience "calm," it is useful to see what is missing from your thoughts.

➤ If you anger yourself by waiting "too long" in line, consider how you would feel if you got paid $100 for every minute you spent in line. If your anger would dissipate and you would feel pleased, what would have changed? If you now view the situation as desirable, then your next step is to determine how you accommodate both angry stewing and delight about waiting.

➤ We don't typically respond with the same degree of anger to all people. Often we judge based on perspective. This perspective involves what we think is their ability to assert power, how friendly we normally feel toward them, and so forth. You might verbally lambaste your mate for displeasing you; would you use the same words and tone with an armed terrorist who was in a notably foul mood?

4. Acceptance: Facing Reality

The dangers of anger were known to the ancient Chinese, who emphasized developing a Buddha-like calm and serenity to prevent anger. However, even Buddha presumably evolved through many lives before reaching calm wisdom.

The ancient Stoics believed that any strong emotion was dangerous, so they sought ways to calm the mind to quell emotions and did a reasonably good job at working out ways to maintain perspective. However, the elimination of the emotion of anger is a pipe dream. It is in human nature for people to experience anger. The spirit of acceptance involves recognizing the improbability that we can control all anger for all times.

Exercises in Acceptance

Aristotle notes that calmness is the opposite of anger. To achieve calmness over anger, we consider what frames of mind are calm, when we feel calm, and what the means of promoting calm are.

➤ Acceptance can turn a stress emotion into a more manageable, and perhaps calmer, emotion. If you feel angry, you might as well accept the feeling. To do otherwise invites double trouble. Accepting anger has the benefit of shifting attention to the conditions that gave rise to the affect.

➤ You can practice "acceptance of the feeling" by recognizing that a hardwired primary emotion is here to stay. What you can change are the ideas behind acquired social forms of anger.

➤ Although you can accept the feeling, you don't have to accept the premises behind the feeling if they prove irrational.

➤ In the heat of the moment, a strategic retreat may be desirable so that you can sort out your thoughts. This retreat is not cowardice but sometimes a smart move. If strategic retreat is not feasible, then focus beyond the moment on the sort of resolution you think is both reasonable and realistic. Take the steps to bring about the desired resolution.

➤ People anger themselves over what they think they need that they believe others are withholding. However, what is reasonable from one person's perspective may be unrealistic from another's. Keeping this perspective can help you accept that when people have a conflict of interest, neither may find a satisfactory resolution.

5. Actualization: Extending the Positive

You are acting in a heathy way when your feelings are congruent with your rational thoughts and actions. You are acting in an actualized manner when you see stress conditions as challenges that provide the opportunity to extend your principles and views effectively.

Exercises in Actualization

➤ The martial artist practices blocks, strikes, and movements under many different conditions. If faced with an unexpected crisis requiring defense, the person is prepared to deal with the threat. Managing anger involves a sort of mental karate that also takes practice—often lots of it. Mental karate is the idea that when we feel in command of ourselves, we are better able to assert control over the events that take place around us. Such self-command is actualization.

➤ Part of actualized anger management involves learning and practicing "rational thinking." Practice can provide an edge when you face spontaneously arising conditions where thoughts pass in microseconds and a quick and honest response is needed.

➤ With a prepared mind, you are better able to parry word blows, fallacies, deceptions, and illusion. Questions, for example, sometimes have greater impact than declarative assertions. People practiced in the art of question asking often can find answers that help them understand what is happening.

➤ In an actualized state of mind, you are largely free from extension-of-blame thinking and have positioned yourself to see and solve problems.

➤ Freedom from extension-of-blame thinking invites others to seek resolution: Most people who don't feel threatened and judged are responsive to reconciling differences.

POSTSCRIPT

The American scientist and diplomat Benjamin Franklin writes, "Anger is never without a reason, but seldom a good one." By implication, Franklin taught that we often create our own demons. He took this idea to heart by practicing diplomatic skills in order to avoid needlessly evoking hostility in others.

Anger is here to stay. The question is, how do we most effectively respond to our anger and the anger of others? When you feel confident and in charge of your "self," you'll have fewer threats to deal with because you won't be as inventive in seeing crises where they don't objectively exist. You'll view more daily matters as challenges. You can say what is on your mind without demeaning others and accept that others can have alternative views without feeling pressured to force them to change. Anger, then, becomes a constructive expression.

18

Frustration Tolerance Training

Low frustration tolerance imperceptibly blends with
misconceptions to form needless human misery.

In Jonathan Swift's *Gulliver's Travels,* Gulliver awoke one morning to find himself
tied to the ground with thousands of small threads that were attached the night before by tiny people called Lilliputians. He was immobilized.

The story of Gulliver's encounter with the Lilliputians points to a universal human experience. Many of us at times feel like Gulliver, bound by restraints. When
bound or blocked from doing what we want, most people would feel frustrated.

While no one small thread of frustration can tie us down, a continuing pattern
of frustrations, such as getting caught in traffic when you are in a rush, collectively
can take a toll on your emotional well-being and physical health when you give
yourself double troubles over them. Major frustrations are like stresses that linger.
A divorce, loss of a job, or loss of economic security can heighten our frustrations
and stay with us longer than we might prefer.

When we feel frustrated, we may blame the obstacles that stand in our way.
How we manage this secondary blame process can determine whether we will fall
into a pattern of double troubles or act to solve the problems that the feelings of
frustration represent. As we routinely deal effectively with the inevitable barriers
and problems in life, our tolerance for frustration grows.

Is frustration tolerance worth developing? In my thirty-five years as a psychologist and psychotherapist, I have yet to meet a person with high frustration tolerance who felt emotionally stressed for very long, engaged in abusive practices,
routinely overreacted to inconvenience, or blamed to excess. Most people I know
with high frustration tolerance have a healthy self-concept and accomplish more
with less stress and strain.

Frustration is a complex process that we can better understand by examining its different forms: normal frustration, low frustration tolerance, and frustration disturbances. Let's start this process with normal frustration.

NORMAL FRUSTRATION

Frustration is natural. It occurs before we have language, as those who observe young infants are quick to see. After that, frustration also can result from attitudes of the mind, such as when we believe we could have done better.

We generally feel frustrated when our wants, wishes, and desires are blocked, interrupted, hindered, or thwarted. When we cannot complete what we set out to do, or cannot complete our work in the way we planned, we can frustrate ourselves over the outcome. Frustration also can impel quick action where necessary. You face a frustrating setback and instantly rebound to meet the challenge.

Frustration can come about for different reasons: You believe that a desired goal is unattainable. You have more to do than you have time available. You misplace your car keys and arrive late for an important meeting. Your mate interrupts you when you are in the middle of a sentence, and you forget what you thought was a brilliant idea. You cannot locate an address you wrote down the other day.

Few people can avoid the feelings of frustration about events such as running out of gasoline or misplacing an important document. You may feel frustrated when your favorite team loses, when your job application is turned down, or when a person you want to date has eyes for someone else. You are taking an important test and come upon a question where you know you knew the answer the night before but now can't recall it. The list of potential frustrations goes on.

Frustration occurs on a continuum and the intensity influences how you might respond. When you have a problem to solve and experience a barely perceptible twinge of frustration, you may not feel motivated to act. At moderate levels, frustration motivates our problem-solving efforts. If sufficiently intense, frustration can disrupt short-term memory. At high levels, frustration can disorganize our complex-thinking ability.

What can you do about frustrations? Accept them as inevitable.

LOW FRUSTRATION TOLERANCE

When you fear frustration, have a low tolerance for delay, or believe you must have what you want right away, you are adding a double-trouble component to your frustration. People with low frustration tolerance have a "short fuse" for discomfort.

As a practical matter, low frustration tolerance comes with computerlike speed. It is the impulsive, urgent intensity of this perceived need for immediate gratification or relief that partially distinguishes low frustration tolerance from normal frustration.

What do people actually do when they react with low frustration tolerance?

Low frustration tolerance, a strong, compelling urge to throw off discomfort, occurs when we do not pay much attention to the ideas that come immediately before the frustrated feeling or to the consequences that may follow. Low frustration tolerance frequently involves the following *signature* process:

1. You view a situation as a hindrance when you cannot get or do what you want.
2. In an instant, you magnify the tension by focusing on it, and this dramatizes the feeling.
3. You experience your feelings of frustration as a sense of urgency to react.
4. Depending on how you view a frustrating situation, you might stew, act overcontrolled, or let off steam. You also might attempt to dodge the discomfort through some diversionary ploy, such as blaming someone else for your tensions.

People prone to low frustration tolerance often blame the barrier, inconvenience, or hassle for their distress. Some use the feeling as a signal to blame themselves and add a layer of complications that typically evokes more needless agitation. Some of this agitation includes *cognitive signatures* of a nonproductive urgency such as: 1) I can't stand not having what I want right now. 2) I should not be thwarted. 3) It's awful and terrible for me to have to suffer in any way.

Low frustration tolerance seems puzzling because it occurs in different disguises. However, the pattern becomes clear when you know the classic examples. People who restlessly tap their fingers demonstrate impatience. Those who quickly quit when challenged show instability of purpose. Some use frustration tension as a signal to procrastinate. We see pressured people who repeatedly display a sense of obsessive urgency. Others automatically blame their problems on others, on themselves, or on fate. The person who brusquely overrides others shows low frustration tolerance. Some impatiently complete people's sentences or start their mouths in motion before others finish talking. We see people impulsively yell, scream, hit, or throw objects when thwarted. The low frustration tolerance process is visible in people who magnify trivial inconveniences, then anger themselves as they would about a major threat. At the extreme, we see Rumpelstiltskin-type fits where the person rants and stomps when thwarted.

The enigmatic low frustration tolerance process has other characteristics. Some people act like "comfort junkies," with a desperate need to feel good, to suffer no inconvenience, and to have a hassle-free life. Members of this group act as if they believe discomfort is intolerable. Low frustration tolerance is at the core of habits of consumption, such as substance abuse. For example, smokers continue to light up partially to avoid their recurring feelings of withdrawal. Many people abuse alcohol to snuff out feelings of tension. People who are overweight because of compulsive eating habits often don't recognize or adequately address low frustration tolerance issues. Most procrastinators put things off to avoid discomfort. Predictably, people with low frustration tolerance are prone to blame because they will have more complaints.

FRUSTRATION DISTURBANCES

In the 1950s psychiatrist Abraham Low told us about the growing *cult of comfort.* He said that people's fear of tension contributes to their mental health problems. In the past forty years, psychologist Albert Ellis pointed to low frustration tolerance as a mechanism for human disturbance. In 1983 I wrote *How to Conquer Your Frustrations,* where I identified and defined frustration disturbances. I identified this process as a thread that weaves through practically all forms of unnecessary distress and emotional disturbance. Indeed, frustration disturbance cuts across distressful states such as anxiety, hostility, and depression. The low frustration tolerance process is a nemesis to millions. Treatment professionals often ignore frustration disturbances entirely, to the detriment of their clients. Nevertheless, low frustration tolerance and frustration disturbances are striking, negative symptoms of many acute, pervasive, but changeable forms of needless emotional distress.

Low frustration tolerance is a trigger for frustration disturbances. But what distinguishes the latter from the former? The difference is in the quality and duration of the distress. Frustration disturbances tend to be pervasive; the person seems vulnerable to stress and has a shaky sense of stability. On the other hand, low frustration tolerance seems acute, episodic, and event-related.

We suffer from frustration disturbances when our forbearance for the unpleasant is brief and the duration of our suffering is long. In this charged state of mind, you feel primed to respond to frustrating events: You magnify your tensions and tend to feel overwhelmed, distressed, confused, and disorganized. You are prone to blame your life situation for your frustrations, your past, your uncertain future, your current inability to "feel good," and the "self." Indeed, in your desperation to relieve tension, you are likely to heighten your frustrations: You *demand* that you feel calm. You additionally frustrate yourself because your tension increases following this double-trouble insistence.

A frustration disturbance normally includes three or more of the following:

1. A hair-trigger circular reaction characterized by sensation sensitivity to the feelings of frustration, rapid processing of information about the onerousness of the sensation, overfocusing on tension sensations, magnification of the tension, intolerance for the magnified tension, and heightened sensation sensitivity
2. An unrealistic fear of the feeling of frustration that propels discomfort dodging and shortsighted avoidance or escapist activities
3. Going for short-term relief rather than long-term gain
4. Ruminations of helplessness and powerlessness that keep the emotional juices swirling
5. A distorted, magnified sense of self-loathing where one views one's ability to face stress and challenges as inadequate
6. Compensatory perfectionism striving

7. Negative states such as anxiety, depression, hostility, resentment, staleness, lethargy, restlessness, uneasiness, and fatigue

8. Blaming what you believe is the source of your tensions and extending that blame in a way that exacerbates your plight by evoking a secondary i-anger

Within this frustration disturbance process, people sensitized to frustration prime themselves to fear being overwhelmed by tension. In this sorry state people add to their worries and woes through what-if questions: "What would happen if something transpired that I could not handle?" They keep *emotional thermometers* where they watch how they feel: "Do I feel comfortable enough?" "Will feeling good last?"

MOTIVATION FOR BUILDING FRUSTRATION TOLERANCE

Perhaps the most compelling argument for directly addressing low frustration tolerance and frustration disturbances is the relief that comes from living without these forms of strain. With less strain, you'd be less prone to blame.

With increasing tolerance for frustration, predictably, your relationships with people will improve. That is because high frustration tolerance correlates with less complaining or extending blame. People who feel less compelled to complain and extend blame engage in congenial relationships, mutual problem solving, and "fair" negotiations. With a grounding in tolerance, you are more likely to express your feelings constructively without extending nonproductive blame into your communications.

Frustration disturbances weave through the major forms of emotional distress (depression, anxiety, and hostility) and common psychosomatic health problems (stress-induced hypertension, gastrointestinal disorders, and headache). Feeling physically well correlates with frustration tolerance. The more persistently effective you are in maintaining a positive perspective and problem-solving style, the more likely you are to experience the important reward of "wellness."

People with short fuses, intolerance for tension, and demands for immediate gratification are hardly likely to shift immediately and radically to a new way of thinking and operating. But one can begin anywhere to start making positive changes.

FRUSTRATION TOLERANCE TRAINING

At this point, you may have recognized some low frustration tolerance symptoms in yourself and have decided that you'd rather manage the normal frustrations in your life than pay the more onerous price of potentially "graduating" to frustration disturbances. You may have already concluded that you had better start to work on developing tolerance.

When you decide to improve your ability to cope with frustrating circumstances, *frustration tolerance training* can help. In a nutshell, frustration tolerance training is a process where you teach yourself to clearly define your frustration zones, set a course to manage them, and stay the course. It includes frustration management techniques such as:

➤ *Building your body* through exercise so as to fortify yourself against stress
➤ Developing a realistic *perspective*
➤ *Liberating the mind* so as to better recognize opportunities and to figure out how to take advantage of them
➤ *Changing the patterns* associated with low frustration tolerance and frustration disturbances
➤ Maintaining disciplined problem-solving *efforts*
➤ Fostering a realistic *patience*
➤ Using objective *feedback* to improve coping skills

Some frustration patterns are more amenable to change than are others. Thus, you may find yourself at different levels of change in different frustration problem zones. However, by engaging the following five-stage change process, you can systematically develop your constructive capabilities for managing frustration and feel like a "self" that you can greatly appreciate. Through this process you may experience the truth in the observation by the nineteenth-century French psychologist Jean Payot: Once you choose a constructive direction, you will find yourself drawing nourishment from everywhere to feed your goals.

Awareness: Getting the Picture about Frustration

To help you to sharpen your frustration awareness, we'll start with awareness exercises.

Exercises in Awareness

In the process of developing frustration management and mastery skills, start with this premise: Acting to shut off normal frustrations is a futile, ill-advised effort. Our ability to feel frustrated is hardwired in to our nervous systems. It is an important cue. How you interpret that signal, however, will determine whether you will overreact, start blaming, strategically retreat, act to solve a problem, or accept a stalemate.

➤ You need not feel frustrated about feeling uncomfortable. Feeling uncomfortable is natural. If someone asks you to do something that runs counter to your interests and values, you'll likely feel uncomfortable. This is a helpful emotional signal.

➤ Discomfort does not necessarily lead to emotional distress. An uncomfortable idea may involve the view that you may someday grow old. If you momentarily feel uncomfortable about this prospect, this may be a reasonable response.

➤ Not all lingering frustrations result from low frustration tolerance, nor are they self-defeating. Some ongoing frustrations reflect maturity. Thus, we may temporarily continue with a frustrating and unsatisfying job because we have children in college and the job pays well enough to cover the tuition and our own living expenses. Other lingering frustrations may represent long-term efforts to solve a complex problem.

➤ It is important to distinguish between low frustration tolerance and a reasoned, quick, spontaneous, and forceful judgment with an emotional emphasis. For example, you act quickly and decisively to stop a child who is starting to run out into the street between two parked automobiles. You are unwilling to accept a colleague's flippant excuse so you assert your displeasure.

➤ People who define frustrations in terms of constructive challenges are likely to enjoy their lives more than those who see frustrations as threats to their sense of stability.

➤ We all have frustrated aspirations and feel disappointed when we fall short of our most cherished ambitions and goals. However, when these aspirations start as lofty but unattainable expectations, this frustrated state of mind normally leads to the sort of exasperation that contributes to frustration tolerance disturbances. Here you work to change your mind about meeting impossible expectations.

➤ Frustration fears or intolerance frequently lead to self-defeating discomfort-dodging efforts. Facing the frustration squarely promises a better result.

➤ Frustration disturbances blend time, event, and "self" to distort perspective and jumble priorities. However, people who know they will find a way to deal with their frustrations eventually are less likely to experience magnified tension.

➤ For people with high frustration tolerance, time provides the leeway to find ways to solve problems to manage or overcome their frustrations and add to their sense of self-confidence. Thus, time takes on added value when it is part of a challenging process of self-discovery and change.

Action: Building Frustration Tolerance

We'll begin the action phase of frustration tolerance training by looking at frustration tolerance action exercises.

Exercises in Action
➤ In developing the body to withstand stress, physical exercise is among the more useful actions that you can take. Scientific evidence suggests that three half-hours of active exercise each week has a positive effect and that you may notice results within the first six weeks. Check with your physician if you haven't exercised lately or need a medical checkup, and to get some advice on how to begin and how to pace yourself.

➤ There is a difference between knowing and doing. Thus, your frustration management program won't go beyond the joys of self-revelation unless you put knowledge into practice. For example, if you studied the writings of Ernest Hemingway, you may not be able to duplicate his imagination. However, you still can learn from his work while developing your own style.

➤ When a valued goal appears unattainable, wait for a better opportunity, try a different plan, or reset your sights.

➤ *Stress inoculation* is a process of intentionally subjecting yourself to small doses of frustration in order to build an immunity to larger doses of frustration. For example, start a frustrating project every day that normally you might delay.

➤ Walk yourself through the thought processes you follow when you experience low frustration tolerance. This exercise brings the *cognitive signatures* of low frustration tolerance into a sharper focus. Then show yourself the absurdity of some of the assumptions that contribute to the process.

➤ There is some tentative evidence that thinking in the *transitive* verb correlates with positive mental health. "*Do* the best you can within the time you have available" is an example of the use of the transitive verb "to do." By practicing the transitive, your outlook may come to consistently reflect an action style of thinking. For example, the more you think in a can-do way and follow through with action, the more likely it is that you will have a growing base of experiences to illustrate that your actions make a positive difference.

➤ When unpleasant occasions arise, allow yourself to feel the sadness, frustrations, or disappointments that are there to feel. Your most natural feelings are not fearsome, unless you make them so.

Disputing Frustration Disturbance Self-Talk

The thoughts of people who experience low frustration tolerance and frustration disturbances are quite similar. Predictable cognitive signatures accompany this process. Although people do show context and cognitive variations in reaction to frustration-triggering events, knowing the general form these signatures take increases your chances for identifying and dealing with them effectively.

Here are some common cognitive signatures of low frustration tolerance self-talk:

➤ *Distress phrases* reflect beliefs such as "I don't feel right"; "I'm having a nervous breakdown"; "I'm falling apart"; "I can't cope." The distress message is one of anxiety or panic. At the extreme of this "catastrophic thinking" continuum, people experience an irrational but groundless fear of going crazy.

➤ *Woe phrases* reflect beliefs such as "I can't do anything right"; "I'm a real loser." These ideas reflect a poor-me outlook that both excuses one's behavior and signals others not to expect too much.

➤ *Urgency phrases* reflect beliefs such as "I can't stand waiting"; "I must have what I want right now." They convey a sense of immediacy, haste, and a hurried, insistent drive to relieve tension.

➤ *Shock phrases* reflect beliefs such as "It's awful, horrible, and terrible." Psychologist Albert Ellis calls this process *awfulizing*. The awfulizing code words overdramatize the person's sense of threat. When related to unfortunate personal experiences, such as being ignored, this form of irrational thinking may turn into whining and complaining. What comes closer to the meaning of the word "terrible" is the death of a close friend.

➤ *Resignation phrases* reflect beliefs such as "I'm helpless"; "I'm powerless"; "It's hopeless"; "I'm never going to get anywhere"; "This is too much for me." These phrases represent a defeatist, depressive coping style.

➤ *Intolerance phrases* are characterized by absolutes and imperatives such as *got to*, *should*, *must*, and *ought*. These demands reflect perfectionist striving.

Recognizing the cognitive signatures of frustration disturbance is an important step. If you observe yourself using some of these phrases, what can you do to challenge and disable this self-defeating self-talk?

To boost your awareness and action capabilities, let's take on the low frustration tolerance disturbance phrases. We'll look at their underlying fallacies and support their rational counterparts. By practicing the rational alternatives until they become second nature, you reduce low frustration tolerance strains as you boost your tolerance.

➤ *Distress phrases* such as "I can't cope" are overgeneralized, anxiety-evoking beliefs that often extend into self-blame for not coping. You can take this in small doses. In greater degree, this process can turn your life into a tornado of distress. To reduce the persistence of such anxiety-provoking ideas: 1) Identify and examine the pros and cons of possible actions. Do this and you have signaled your interest in following a pathway that is radically different from a can't-cope way of thinking and being. 2) If you don't come up with any good ideas at first, consider this aphorism from the ancient Chinese *Book of Change:* "In your darkest moments, wait. Change is near at hand." 3) Stubbornly refuse to engage in self-blame for not coping. This form of blame detracts from problem solving.

➤ *Woe phrases* such as "I can't do anything right" suggest that you are completely inept. Come on! Do you really believe that? For example, if you put on your shoes correctly that day, spoke on the phone, or solved a problem, you did do something right! Fortunately, woe phrases are vulnerable to reason. To change: 1) List the actions you have taken where the results were positive. 2) Look again. If you are totally inept, how do you explain the exceptions?

➤ *Urgency phrases* such as "I cannot stand inconvenience" are misleading. To challenge this process, think about this: 1) What do you tell yourself that stops you from resolutely bearing up to the unpleasant? What are the flaws in that *intolerance logic*? 2) What resources you can bring to bear on your current problem? 3) Test these resources.

➤ *Shock phrases* such as "It is awful," when applied to practically any inconvenience or hassle, normally escalate the distress. To change this pattern: 1) Instead of shock description, consider relabeling unwanted experiences as unpleasant, unfortunate, or undesirable. 2) Identify three forceful arguments that you can use to convince yourself that hassles are not horrible. ("Horrible" technically means very inconvenient, but most people use the term to express incomprehensible shock.) You can save the word "horrible" for war, genocide, serial killings, or other extraordinary disasters.

➤ *Resignation phrases* such as "I'm helpless" often occur in the context of self-blame. (1) The helplessness self-blame paradox invites this question: If you are helpless, how are you blameworthy? (2) If you think you are helpless, consider all that you can do that a two-month-old infant can't do. Now, how helpless are you?

➤ *Intolerance phrases* such as "You should do as I expect" is authoritarian in both tone and direction. (1) The language suggests that you demand total obedience from those over whom you probably do not have absolute control. If someone doesn't comply with your demand, are they blameworthy? (2) Instead of repeating this inflexible non-sequitur fallacy, try thinking in terms of desires and preferences and see how you feel. For example, when you can convincingly substitute "I prefer" for "I expect," you are thinking in softer but more realistic terms.

Accommodation: Levels of Representation

Metaphorically, we can say that we organize information, experience, and action around schemas. These are like databases, mental representations, or templates of organized information within our minds. Some are innate, such as our primary reflexes and action patterns. We acquire other schemas. A Vietnam veteran hears a helicopter, feels enveloped by fear, and ducks into an alley. He associates the sound of the chopper with explosions, the death of his comrades, and a near-fatal wound he received after his squad jumped from a copter and got hit with mortar and small-arms fire. Call this schema posttraumatic stress. While it is extremely resistive to change, it can be changed.

Our schemas form networks. Extension-of-blame thinking can network with perfectionism, i-anger, depressive thinking, and other negative states.

Accommodation involves the development of and competition between functional frustration tolerance schemas and dysfunctional ones. It normally takes time to build these high frustration tolerance schema networks. That is why change is more of a process than an event.

Exercises in Accommodation

The schema metaphor describes interconnected networks of mental representations and action patterns that strengthen when repeated. Schemas can radiate to other schemas. A schema for blame can interconnect with cognitive signatures associated with low frustration tolerance and frustration disturbances. Theoretically we also have schemas that represent core concepts for depression, anxiety, and other powerful emotional states with links to a blame schema.

It bears repeating that networks of interlaced memories, ideas, beliefs, emotions, and action patterns require time to unravel and replace with stable, functional views. This accommodative process doesn't just happen. The changes that occur result from creating contrasts, testing alternative behaviors, and comparing the results with one's low frustration tolerance type prejudgments. For example, through testing this book's techniques for extracting blame extensions, you act to strengthen the connection between problem-solving schemas as you develop mastery over your frustrations.

Progressively mastering frustration involves practicing frustration tolerance and problem-solving methods until they are dominant schemas. As a start:

➤ Use frustration as a signal for positive action. Direct your efforts toward constructively accepting or resolving the frustration.

➤ When blame schemas link to low frustration tolerance schemas, identify the network of ideas associated with them. To bring the schemas into focus, ask what you are telling yourself about your ability to withstand frustration. What functional parts of your self-view can you prioritize to shift from low frustration tolerance talk to self-efficacy talk?

➤ When in a low frustration tolerance state of mind, examine the sensitized feelings, frustration magnification, intolerance, and avoidance aspects of this process. Then interrupt the low frustration tolerance discomfort-dodging schema at its different links: sensitization, magnification, intolerance, and avoidance.

➤ Focusing on your feeling of frustration amplifies the experience. Instead of preoccupying yourself with frustration, look for ways to deal with the problem represented by the frustration.

Acceptance: Living with the Inevitable Frustrations of Life

The idea of acceptance involves an enlightened sense of self-understanding and tolerance for the unpleasant. Here you realize that any person, in the process of developing, cannot be perfect. Otherwise, what's the purpose of developing? This idea opens the opportunity for a richer range of pleasant experiences and joy.

Exercises in Acceptance
Consider the following acceptance ideas:

➤ Your willingness to live with tension and frustration without blaming shows that you recognize that tensions and strain are part of the human condition. This ability to "accept" barriers and blocks yields a sense of inner control even when you do not feel calm.

➤ Acceptance does not negate the idea of accountability and responsibility. You are responsible for your thinking and actions. Still, it is possible to accept yourself and still accept that, at times, you are going to behave on the basis of false beliefs. Within this accepting state of mind, you normally will have more control over what you think, feel, and do. You will be more open to reality checks. You will have fewer reality distortions and, therefore, less to be defensive, frustrated, or blameful about.

➤ Liberation from frustration-related blame involves exercising an assertive tolerance. In assertive tolerance, we make a radical shift in perspective by:

1. Distinguishing between legitimate fault and manufactured conditions for blame
2. Accepting responsibility for our feelings and actions
3. Giving ourselves and others the benefit of the doubt when warranted
4. Asserting our enlightened self-interests

Actualization: Getting Beyond the Moments of Frustration

Although actualization is a *demand-free* state of mind, the experience may involve frustration. But this is the kind of frustration that is natural, motivational, and understandable. When you view yourself as capably living through and beyond your current frustrations, you've made this important belief an extension of yourself.

Exercises in Actualization

➤ Find a way, every day, to turn a frustration into a challenge. You actualize target abilities when you concentrate on actions that make your dreams and wants attainable. In a self-renewing process, you become absorbed in developing your resources.

➤ Some people find it difficult to tolerate being alone. You can gain practice in frustration tolerance by remaining alone and undistracted for five hours. Don't have a clock available. Do have an alarm in another room to signal when the five-hour time limit is up. Now, do nothing. After a while, inaction may seem frustrating, then the frustration may pass. Tolerating the experience of a passing frustration can feel actualizing.

POSTSCRIPT

> *The torment of human frustration, whatever its immediate cause, is the knowledge that the self is in a prison, its vital force and mangled mind leaking away in wasteful self-conflict.*
> —Elizabeth Drew, Anglo-American author and critic

False memories, incomplete information, and a smattering of images can evolve into a frustration problem that exists nowhere but within. In these ways, Elizabeth Drew's view is useful when it comes to understanding frustrating inner conflicts that recur without meaningful purpose or resolution. Usually, however, we can learn what we need to know and do to conquer our frustrations. Even people with frustration disturbances have many opportunities to get beyond their frustrations.

Although building frustration tolerance is a significant challenge, it promises to be a rewarding experience. This chapter brought to light a number of possibilities that can contribute to experiencing such rewards. The following chapter on self-assertion provides an active way to use frustration as a catalyst for effective self-expression.

19

Overcoming Blame through Assertiveness

> *Courage is an act that often follows discomfort or fear.*

In William Shakespeare's play *Hamlet,* the lord chamberlain Polonius gave this advice to his son, Laertes: "This above all: to thine own self be true and it must follow, as the night the day, thou canst not then be false to any man." With the spirit of this advice we begin our journey into the art of assertive expression.

How often have you wanted to say something and you kept your mouth shut but, on reflection, wished you had spoken up? When was the last time you slipped into a pretense of politeness and subjugated your desires to appear nonoffensive? Have you said yes when you meant no, or no when you meant yes? Have you too often overreacted by blaming and then regretted the action? If you place yourself in any of these categories, perhaps you'd prefer to feel more confident in your ability to speak up assertively in a manner that is true to your enlightened "self."

Assertiveness training has gained popularity among those who suspect they may act too passively, spend too much time doubting themselves, and stymie themselves fearing possible disapproval. That is because assertive skills counter artificial inhibitions and help decrease anxiety.

Psychologists Robert Alberti and Michael Emmons describe assertiveness as a form of self-expression directed toward equalizing interactions with other people in order to better get along with them. Such cross-talk provides opportunities for you and another to discover your similar views and hash out different interests.

People who speak up for themselves have less need to extend blame. They have the confidence to take a stand without having to put the other person down. But assertiveness has its downside. For example, in the 1960s after the beginning of the assertiveness training movement, a television situational comedy satirized the process. The show was *The Smothers Brothers Comedy Hour.* One of the brothers, Dick, attended an assertiveness training workshop. Thereafter, he confronted a bully who cut in front of him in line. The remainder of the show centered on comedic episodes in which the bully followed Dick to get revenge. The message: "Discretion is the better part of valor."

ASSERTION AND BLAME

Along with conditioned reflex therapist Andrew Salter and behavior therapist Joseph Wolpe, multimodal therapist Arnold A. Lazarus is frequently credited with pioneering assertiveness training. Lazarus succinctly supports a nonblame assertiveness position: "Assertive people do not heap blame on others. They address their feelings about the issues. They do not say, 'It's your fault that we were late for the movie because you did not check the starting time carefully.' They might say, 'Next time we must be sure to check the starting time carefully.' Because they typically give 'I-feel messages' (I feel upset that you insulted my mother) and not 'You-are' messages (You are a louse for insulting my mother), they keep blame out of the interaction." Assertive people take responsibility for saying what they mean, meaning what they say, asking for what they want, and expressing dislike or disapproval without blaming the other.

Lazarus's authentic, nonblaming, expressive style has numerous positive applications. Rather than stewing about slow service at a restaurant, you speak up and insist on efficient service. When you fearlessly and affirmatively express warm feelings for another, you are more likely to establish a positive relationship than someone who holds back expressing such feelings out of rejection fears. You are more likely to command respect when you respect the rights of others. Moreover, when you accept responsibility and choose to make yourself accountable, you act ethically in concert with your personal dignity. In this spirit, "I" messages invite others to present their views in the same way.

INDIVIDUAL DIFFERENCES IN ASSERTIVE STYLES

The same assertive approach is not going to work for everyone. We vary in temperament, histories, and prejudgments. Some of us are private; others are like open books. We'll have moods where we feel invincible or moods where we are defeated before we begin. We bring these and other learned and inherited variable tendencies into our communications.

Most people would agree that humans show a wide range of traits, qualities, and characteristics and that their attributes will impact differently on different people. Some people will have combinations of qualities that will please us and others that we will dislike. Those who ignore other people's personalities and feelings are frequently astounded when their "logic" fails to persuade: Getting one's point across often goes with establishing rapport and making a positive emotional connection.

When you take an assertive view, it also helps to take individual differences and preferences into account. However, even when we attempt to simplify what we know about people's personality styles, there are still going to be complications. For example, psychologists Gordon Allport and Henry Odbert found 4,500 trait words in a standard English dictionary and suggested that they may collapse into a handful of distinct "trait" or personality categories. Psychologists Ernest Tupes and Raymond Christal factored these traits down into a Five-Factor Model (the "Big Five") of extroversion-introversion, agreeableness, neuroticism, conscientiousness, and openness. Each category is significantly independent of the others, and each represents a dimension where people fall along a range between high, medium, and low.

Predictably, people with divergent Five-Factor profiles will find it more challenging to communicate with each other. People assert their positions in congruence with their temperaments and beliefs. Warm, introverted people likely will deliver their assertions in a different manner from "tough-minded" extroverted individuals. However, there is a certain consistency in the assertiveness process that goes beyond individual temperament and style. In an assertiveness zone, you:

1. Bypass extension-of-blame thinking
2. Focus on constructive initiations for going after what you want
3. Unambiguously state opinions
4. Refuse to capitulate to unreasonable demands
5. Stick up for personal rights and freedom
6. Express feelings distinctly
7. Stay on the right side of a principle
8. Commend others
9. Ask for assistance when necessary
10. Express a willingness to cooperate when warranted
11. Project empathy when appropriate
12. Register agreement in a manner that is "true to yourself"

ASSERTIVE BODY LANGUAGE

We convey assertive messages through our body language. Ideally, one's assertive words fit with one's tone, which fits with one's body language. Timid-acting individuals and aggressive people will display an expressive style that is consistent with their attitudes but generally is different from that of an assertive individual. The following is a sampling of body language cues for each of these three styles.

People whose lack of assertiveness is due to a timid, passive, insecure, and self-protective style will display this style in one or more of the following ways:

➤ Looking down at the ground
➤ Hunched shoulders
➤ Twitching when they make important points
➤ Apologizing for their opinions

➤ Speaking softly so as to be virtually inaudible
➤ Diluting an assertive message with many qualifications
➤ Presenting a stiff, intense, inhibited demeanor
➤ Throat clearing and coughing
➤ Flush marks on throat, chest, or cheeks

Aggressive styles have their own distinguishing features:

➤ Talking with unnatural sternness
➤ Finger wagging or pointing
➤ Arms defiantly crossed over chest or on one's hips
➤ Standing over someone who is seated
➤ Using the pronoun "you" to preface an accusation
➤ A loud and abrasive tone
➤ Immature expression in the form of muttering, eye rolling, and sneering

An assertive style is radically different from both timid and aggressive styles. When you assertively express yourself, your body language is congruent with your affirmative thoughts and feelings. Assertive body language can include:

➤ An open, declarative expression
➤ Maintaining good eye contact without staring or glaring
➤ A spontaneous and natural tone
➤ A projection of clearness of purpose
➤ Facial expression consistent with the feeling or sentiment expressed (you don't show a sheepish smile when making an appropriately angry assertion)

The three samples can help you decide if you are sending the signals you want to make through your body language. The remainder of the chapter describes how to build assertive expression skills.

MOTIVATION FOR BECOMING MORE ASSERTIVE

By building on your assertive skills, you position yourself confidently to get more out of life. You probably will experience less anxiety, loneliness, social anxiety, shyness, hostility, and low frustration tolerance. Instead, you are more likely to feel in charge of yourself, spontaneous, and able to meet interesting developmental challenges without hesitating and second-guessing yourself.

Here are some thoughts about a positive perspective on assertiveness that can support motivation for self-improvement by strengthening your assertive self-expression:

➤ You are likely to experience decreased anxiety when you know you can express your position clearly.

➤ You are not likely to have others talk you into activities that you don't find relevant, meaningful, or necessary.

➤ You can initiate activities to promote self-advantages without needlessly disadvantaging others.

➤ You can build self-efficacy by making assertions to bring about helpful changes in your life.

➤ You can better understand both your rights and your limitations in your negotiations with others.

➤ You reduce the frequency of inhibitory feelings.

➤ You'll be less likely to feel shortchanged.

➤ You view yourself as a person who can take a meaningful stand, and this confidence is its own reward.

➤ You'll have less reason to be evasive or indirect, or to send double messages, so people will better understand where you stand.

➤ You are less likely to stew over what you could have said because you are more likely to have said what you believed was important.

➤ You are less likely to fall into a hostility trap when you keep your communications positive.

➤ You are likely to think better of yourself by speaking better for yourself.

➤ You find that although you don't have to be fully knowledgeable about all issues, you can negotiate gray areas to gain clarity.

➤ You come increasingly closer to being true to yourself.

ASSERTIVE SKILLS DEVELOPMENT

We'll begin with awareness exercises for assertive skill-building.

Awareness: Choosing Challenges

Action without direction is aimless. By completing the following assertiveness inventory, you can help yourself to identify where you can improve and where you have assertive skills that already serve you well. From there, you can identify your assertiveness goals and plan for boosting your ability to express yourself effectively.

Exercises in Awareness
The following inventory samples common assertiveness situations. You can use it to help identify trouble spots that you can address through action. (The inventory is not a standardized measure; I designed it to help you survey some general assertiveness issues to use in defining your assertiveness goals.) Read each statement; circle "Y" if the statement ordinarily describes what you do in that circumstance and "N" if the statement does not normally characterize your actions. Thereafter, I'll provide ideas about interpreting the material and an assertiveness goal-setting framework.

ASSERTIVENESS INVENTORY

1. Do you ordinarily stand up for your rights when someone acts unfairly toward you?　　　　　　　　　　　　　　　　**Y　N**

2. Do you squarely face difficult interpersonal conflicts before they escalate?　　　　　　　　　　　　　　　　　　**Y　N**

3. If someone kicks the back of your chair when you are in a theater or movie, do you ask that person to stop?　　　　**Y　N**

4. Your neighbor borrows and then fails to return several important possessions. Do you retrieve them and then set future limits on what you will lend?　　　　　　　　**Y　N**

5. If a vendor fails to deliver on a commitment, do you normally require that person to live up to the contract before making additional payments?　　　　　　　　**Y　N**

6. Do you quickly end a conversation with a pushy salesperson who is trying to promote something you don't want?　**Y　N**

7. Do you take direct responsibility for your feelings and actions?　**Y　N**

8. When people who are vulnerable cannot speak for themselves, do you speak up for them?　　　　　　　**Y　N**

9. Do you confidently speak up in a meeting or group?　　**Y　N**

10. Do you act decisively when faced with a conflict that requires a quick resolution?　　　　　　　　　　　**Y　N**

11. Do you set limits that make clear what you will or will not do?　**Y　N**

12. Do you view yourself as a "pushover" who permits others to infringe upon your time and rights?　　　　　　　**Y　N**

13. Do you look away when you see someone that you know approaching, in order to avoid initiating a greeting?　**Y　N**

14. When you don't care about an issue, do you express that sentiment?　　　　　　　　　　　　　　　　　**Y　N**

15. Are you normally direct and factual in your expressions?　**Y　N**

16. Do you speak to the issues without getting sidetracked?　**Y　N**

17. Are your assertions and expressions normally specific to the individual and situation?　　　　　　　　　　**Y　N**

18. Is what you say an honest expression of yourself and not what you think other people want you to say?　　　**Y　N**

19. Are your expressions socially responsible?　　　　　**Y　N**

ASSERTIVENESS INVENTORY (*Continued*)

20. Do you typically speak up in a way that affirms your rights and interests without denying others their rights and interests?   Y   N

21. Do you ask people for favors or advice when this is in your best interest?   Y   N

22. Do you normally listen attentively to other people's positions before expressing your own?   Y   N

23. Do you feel a sense of inner control that translates into an ability to command attention through what you say?   Y   N

24. When treated unfairly, do you normally stick to the important issues and avoid personality issues?   Y   N

25. Do you compliment people for their good efforts and deeds?   Y   N

26. When faced with a potentially negative encounter, do you manage the situation at the earliest possible opportunity?   Y   N

27. When you see someone attractive that you want to meet, do you typically introduce yourself?   Y   N

28. Do you say "I don't know" when you don't have an answer?   Y   N

29. Do you forthrightly ask for help when you lack information, knowledge, or ability?   Y   N

30. Do you maintain openness in the presence of someone you dislike who asserts a position that normally displeases you?   Y   N

If you answered no to questions 12 and 13 and yes to the others, you are an assertiveness superstar. However, most people will find at least one, and probably more, areas where they can improve their assertiveness skills.

Setting Goals.   The inventory items can stimulate thinking about areas where you can profit from developing your assertiveness skills.

Make your goal specific (e.g., to speak effectively before a group; to be clear with my mother-in-law that "I do not want her criticizing my housekeeping, cooking, or child rearing").

Assertiveness Goal: _____

Goals remain in the realm of Never-Never Land with Tinker Bell, the magical fairy, unless given a form and design. The plan may involve identifying the problem for your mother-in-law, saying how you feel, and seeking a solution you both can live with.

Assertiveness Plan: _____

_____

_____

_____

   Unless you list specific measures to take, you are not going to have a sound foundation for judging the quality of your assertiveness plan. The measures can include assertive body language, a positive and firm tone, and a clear, declarative definition of what you desire.

Assertive Measures _____

_____

_____

_____

Action: Taking a Stand

The following assertiveness exercises support achieving your assertiveness goals. They include: 1) Sighting beyond the moment; 2) sticking with the issues; 3) speaking from concepts; 4) using affirmative words; 5) avoiding approval by omission; 6) expressing assertions objectively; 7) employing warmth and humor; and 8) applying escalation methods when required.

Exercises in Assertive Actions
Sight beyond the Moment.   In most day-to-day encounters, sighting beyond momentary issues can help maintain perspective. The following questions can help you sight beyond the moment: What do you want to accomplish? What types of relationships would you prefer to forge through an assertive process? How would you like to feel about yourself through this process? What image do you want to project? Such questions can help you keep personality, emotions, and expression proportionate to the situation.

Stick with the Issues.   You probably cannot control what someone else may say or think. Nevertheless, you can control what you say and do because that is a behavioral choice! One prime choice is to stick with the basic issue.

Speak from the Concept.   People who try to think out every word before they speak often can defeat their own purpose. Thinking out each word is feasible in written assertions but has limitations when you spontaneously carry on a dialogue with someone. What if you forget a word? What if you sound *too* scripted?

When you *speak from the concept,* the idea is more important than the specific words you use. The concept is the idea behind your words. When you have confidence in the idea, you'll tend to be clear in your expression and responses.

Positive Word Choice. Use positive words that clearly support your thoughts. This helps you avoid distracting your audience with negatives, and your respondents are more likely to hear what you say.

Speaking to the issue and honestly substituting positive words for harsher ones can improve the impact of your assertion. There are exceptions to this guideline. In some circumstances, your most rational response is a forceful, unequivocal, strongly worded declaration of "truth."

Avoiding Approval by Omission. Omissions can cloud issues. People will commit errors of omission when they fear the truth or fear offending someone, or fear disadvantaging themselves, or feel threatened. What you don't say can cause a problem when your omission leads to misinterpretations of your position.

Objective Assertions. You express yourself objectively when you use the best information available. You state what you have confidence in saying, label what you believe are impressions, and allow your respondent to correct any misunderstandings that you might have expressed.

Warmth and Humor. People who express themselves in a "natural," nonhostile, open, warm, agreeable manner are more likely to get their point across. They don't confound their messages with tones of anger; thereby they tend to avoid needless conflicts that anger might help create.

A sense of humor during an uncomfortable conflict is a valuable attitude to develop. If you take conflict too seriously, humor is normally absent from the picture. When you take a matter seriously but not personally, you are in a better position to reduce tension with humor. Your thought processes are likely to move with fluidity, and you may be quicker to see and enjoy the incongruities that occur.

Escalation Methods. Asserting your interests does not have to be an all-or-nothing affair. Arnold A. Lazarus notes that an escalation approach is sometimes useful in getting your point across. Following this model, you convincingly apply the minimal assertion that you believe can help you to achieve the result you seek. You increase the intensity of your assertions when your respondent doesn't accept the message.

In considering an escalation method, it helps to balance others' feelings and probable interpretations against the final result. The woman who has no future intention of dating an admirer turns down a date by saying "Call me at another time." She does not follow this principle of escalating assertions because the message is ambiguous. To spare someone's feelings, she may cause both herself and the other person a needless future hassle. A minimal assertion in such cases might include this idea: "Thank you for your kind offer, but I'm not interested." In the unlikely event that she needs to make a second assertion, an escalated assertion might include: "I don't want to date you and I have no intention of changing my mind." At a third level, "You are harassing me and I want you to stop."

Additional Assertion Techniques. The following exercises suggest ways to practice improving your personal impact:

➤ Have a talk with yourself about the merits and disadvantages of saying what you mean and meaning what you say. Tape-record this conversation. Play it back. Note what you consider to be constructive. Carry out one of these constructive assertions each day.

➤ If you think the word "no" is naughty, get some practice saying the word. Go to a store with pushy sales personnel. Resist their sales pitches by using the word "no." Examine what is wrong with saying no or maybe. Consider what you gain by saying yes when you mean no.

➤ If you act like a clown to grab attention to make your point, reverse your typical modus operandus. Put others at the focal point and in a positive light for their valid positions.

➤ Formulate an opinion about a controversial news topic and present it to friends or colleagues for their reactions. If a debate results, stick to your point. Try to repeat this exercise at least once a week.

➤ If you feel you get pushed around too much, practice standing up for your rights with friends who will help you role-play new forms of self-expression. Next, test these expressions in real-life situations. Remember, others are not going to remain passive as you develop assertiveness skills. But facing tough issues and practicing your assertiveness skills strengthens those skills.

➤ By joining a recognized advocacy group where you work with others to protect the interests of more vulnerable people, you can get valuable practice sticking up for others' rights. Then you can apply this know-how in sticking up for your enlightened interests.

➤ If you feel dissatisfied with someone's behavior, consider whether pointing this out would be helpful. If so, put on your diplomat's hat and try.

➤ Where there are points of agreement and disagreement, often you can gain by identifying the common ground. This simple act can help defuse tensions, refocus the issues, and make clear where you will take a stand and will not back down.

Accommodation: A Theory of Assertive Change

When we go from a passive to assertive style, we've made strong cognitive, behavioral, and emotional changes. Changes in thinking from negative, ruminative, blaming and complaining to a positive, affirmative, assertive style is the outcome of a strong accommodation process.

Moving from blaming complaining to an affirmative, assertive style requires many accommodations. For example, an anxious and depressed person anticipates the worst and says he is powerless to cope. He backs off from conflict and feels like a wimp. Through talking out the problem, he discovers that his thinking includes a double-trouble self-blame process where he magnifies his sense of powerlessness and minimizes his abilities to assertively manage his daily affairs. By restructuring his thinking and testing functional new behaviors, he learns that he can do more than he originally thought. He feels relief. What changed? He got his mind off his insecurities and on to solving his problems. His views shifted to reflect a change from a threat to a challenge outlook. He experienced recalibrations of thought and feelings from pessimism to realistic optimism, and he accommodated to this encouragingly optimistic way of thinking and acting.

Changes in what we think, feel, and do can reflect changes in our brain functioning. Boosts in the brain chemicals serotonin and dopamine presumably accompany these accommodation recalibrations. According to National Institute of Mental Health–sponsored studies, positive emission tomography (a brain scan) shows depressed patients who were successfully treated with cognitive therapy have increased prefrontal cortex activity associated with feelings of well-being.

Exercises in Accommodation

Looking at contrasts and opposites to assertiveness can help put blame or passivity into perspective. Here are some contrasts to provide accommodation opportunities.

➤ Some effective assertions partially involve adjusting one's thinking and actions to take other people's personalities and interests into account. A contrast is that of a self-absorbed victim thinking approach, where we blame others without seeing them clearly and knowing our flexibility.

➤ Knowing what you want to accomplish simplifies making adjustments in your assertions to achieve the results you seek. The contrast is vagueness about your interests and self-blame due to a lack of direction.

➤ Whenever there is an assertive action, there is a reaction. The opposite of this progressive order is withdrawal.

➤ The philosophy of dialectical materialism creates black-and-white extremes and synthesis of these opposites. The contrasting view is that one sometimes will need to stand firmly for one's rights and principles. No synthesis or compromise makes sense.

➤ With contrary situations, there can be assertions and hope for growth or progression. The contrast is neutrality and stagnation.

➤ A pattern of protecting oneself by withdrawing from the natural conflicts, challenges, and contentions of everyday life can provide immediate relief. At the same time, the avoidance pattern raises one's risk to experiencing stress-related physical and psychological problems. In contrast, patterns of assertively facing conflicts and problems can feel uncomfortable in the short term yet promote long-term health.

Acceptance

You don't have to feel comfortable as a precondition for assertively expressing your feelings or beliefs. Feeling uncomfortable in contentious circumstances is normal. The assertive individual accepts this discomfort and moves forward to speak up.

Exercises in Acceptance

Assertiveness will typically get you further than passivity. However, accepting that assertiveness has limitations and boundaries affords one greater flexibility.

➤ You will have legitimate conflicts of interest where there is incentive for others also to assert their self-interests. Negotiations and compromise are sometimes necessary.

➤ Typically most people improve their chances for cooperation with others by keeping their assertions positive. However, even when you are correct and speak up in positive and convincing ways, you still may get nowhere with those who have a fixed agenda.

➤ You are likely to have limited change opportunities when you encounter people whose beliefs clash with your beliefs and whose sense of worth and identity tie in to their belief system.

➤ Voluntary conflict resolution is rarely possible with people who operate out of logic-tight compartments and can see only one way.

➤ Competitive people who intend to have the final word can turn communications into win-lose contests that they have every intention of winning.

➤ People with Sophist interests can make a silk purse out of a sow's ear. Your argument may be valid, yet you may hear your words twisted to your disadvantage.

➤ Practiced debaters sometimes can turn a losing position into a win through humor, satire, or sarcasm. However, when the facts are squarely on your side, repeating them in different ways can help win the point.

➤ Some people won't get the point you want to make because they don't want to get it.

➤ People's illusions and myths cloud their perspective, making it difficult for them to see what you want them to understand.

➤ Some people may not be ready to understand or accept your point of view.

➤ Some people are practiced bullies who follow rules that are outside normal social conventions.

➤ In some cases, a strong assertion, no matter how confidently, positively, and constructively delivered, can provoke a defensive reaction.

➤ Assertiveness has its downside when an important relationship is dissolved because of unalterable differences on critical issues.

Actualization: Saying What You Mean

The medical maxim "Do no harm" applies to actualization through assertiveness. Here we change the maxim to "Take no steps to cause unnecessary harm."

Exercises in Actualization

Actualization often implies that we operate according to higher principles. In this spirit, consider the following assertion-actualization guidelines where you strive to:

➤ Express facts or make high probability statements

➤ Avoid needlessly putting someone else down

➤ Act out constructive and positive principles

➤ Avoid criticizing and demeaning another's position

➤ Apply only enough pressure to establish your position

➤ Escalate the intensity and forcefulness of your position when others choose not to listen

➤ Apply common sense to each situation—in some instances, discretion is the better part of valor

➤ Initiate or accept legitimate areas of compromise in those many gray areas of life

➤ Stick to your points in a constructive manner

POSTSCRIPT

Therapist Andrew Salter noted, "It is possible to be both inhibitory and successful but at the price of happiness." He further noted that *emotional freedom* involves the ability to act assertively or what he called to act with excitation. Assuming that happiness is a by-product of trusting your feelings and striving for excellence, then happiness also can be a by-product of asserting preferences, interests, and desires.

Perhaps the most common reasons for self-assertion include: taking initiative to go after what you want and responding to situations that threaten your rights and interests. People who act assertively within these two parameters display self-confidence by expressing their positions effectively. They typically have fewer inner conflicts because they deal with matters as they arise. They prevent problems by anticipating them before they occur.

Although an assertive approach loads the odds in your favor, you have no guarantee that by standing up for your rights, or by clearly expressing your impressions and desires, you'll achieve what you wish. However, consider the alternative: What can you gain by repeatedly waffling and backing away from what is important?

20

Procrastination, Blame, and Change

> *People who feel in control of their lives organize their time, thoughts, and actions without sacrificing their spontaneity and creativity.*

"Procrastinate, procrastinate, it's so much fun to do it late. Oh hesitate, oh hesitate, you don't have to make that date." That said, you've entered the wily world of procrastination where you will surely find little mirth.*

People have procrastinated throughout the ages. Procrastination probably originated about 2.5 million years ago, when our ancestors first grouped into small clans and someone decided to put off doing something, such as gathering firewood for the night fire. As civilizations grew, social demands increased and our opportunities for procrastination mushroomed. The ancient Babylonian leader Hammurabi, recognizing the disadvantages caused by needless delays, penalized procrastination through one of his 282 codes. De Paul University psychologist Joe Ferrari noted that procrastination appeared in ancient Egypt.

The Romans provided the roots for the word "procrastination": *pro* means "forward" and *crustinus* means "of tomorrow." The first-century A.D. Roman emperor Marcus Aurelius cautioned against unnecessary delays. The thirteenth-century invention of the clock created opportunities for us to measure performance economically against time. Psychologist Tim Pychyl discovered a 1682 printed sermon equating procrastination with sin. The eighteenth-century North American scientist and diplomat Benjamin Franklin described the personal virtues he worked to actualize and how others could do the same. Franklin included among his thirteen virtues:

---

*D. David Bourland (1968), writing on the use of non-Aristotelian language, cites benefits for eliminating the verb "to be." Eliminating the verb reduces inaccuracies due to overgeneralizations. Except when used in quotes, I wrote this chapter without the verb.

"Resolve to perform what you ought. Perform without fail what you resolve." Now, in an electronic age, the computer, the greatest of all efficiency tools, serves as a two-edged sword when used by some for gain and by others to dally and procrastinate.

Procrastination gained heightened visibility in Western society with the industrial revolution. With the 1651 publication of *Leviathan,* the English philosopher Thomas Hobbes defined human worth as a function of what the person contributed to society and, by inference, how time applied to serve the public good. Thus he defined social and personal worth. This seventeenth-century definition continues to influence Western thought. However, connecting the use of time, human worth, and social value requires an intellectual leap where we disregard the significance of thousands of traits, characteristics, emotions, talents, and deeds that more truly characterize each person's humanity. That contigency-worth definition is best left in the seventeenth century.

If intrinsic personal worth does not depend on using time effectively, then why make any effort to act effectively? Procrastination can and often does have social and personal consequences. The effective use of time can boost performances, social advantage, level of income, career advancement, and status. People who routinely do things late risk being the subjects of extensions of blame and positioning themselves to make up excuses and waste time and energy covering themselves with other exoneration ploys. Those who get reasonable things done in a reasonable time typically gain deserved advantages.

THE PROCESS OF PROCRASTINATION

How do we go about procrastinating? We procrastinate when we needlessly postpone, delay, or put off a relevant and priority activity until another day or time. People who procrastinate choose to delay needlessly. Often this decision to delay continues despite numerous opportunities to change the pattern. And despite optimistic hopes for the future, people who procrastinate yet still believe they will have adequate time to finish sooner or later face Murphy's law: Something that can go wrong eventually will go wrong.

Knowing the process you follow when you procrastinate can give you an edge over those who glide through the procrastination paces without much forethought. This "silent" procrastination process can include:

1. Recognizing an activity as difficult, undesirable, boring, unchallenging, or unpleasant
2. Experiencing a strong emotional and visceral resistance to the activity
3. Telling yourself you don't want to do it, at least not right now
4. Making a decision to delay
5. Promising yourself you'll get to it later
6. Engaging in substitute activities
7. Engaging in eleventh-hour activities

8. Seeking ways to buy additional time
9. Periodically giving up on finishing
10. Recalling and fretting over the incomplete task
11. Excusing your procrastination to sanitize the delay to gain exoneration from blame
12. Promising yourself you won't put yourself through the same process again
13. Accepting a promissory note to yourself about a proposed change without seriously planning how to change the pattern
14. Repeating the same or another variation of the procrastination process at a different time and place

Not all procrastination precisely involves this process. Some people tell themselves, "I don't want to," and that is sufficient for promoting delay. Of course, not all delays involve procrastination. Strategic delays before deciding a course of action can prove advantageous. Other things make little sense to prioritize or to do. We also find a certain relativism about procrastination. The procrastinator in a highly efficient organization may act like an efficiency superstar in another.

Do we consider the German writer Johann Goethe a procrastinator? Goethe developed his book, *Faust,* throughout his working life. Between the ages of twenty and fifty-one, he first contemplated then later wrote the first part of this now-classic work. At eighty-three, he finished part two.

Although many members of society fulfill their obligations with regularity, have perfect attendance, eat on schedule, and pay their taxes before April 15, this punctuality does not assure greatness. The greatness of people like Goethe follows their unique contributions. However, if lightning had fatally struck Goethe before he penned his first draft, his concept of Faust would have vanished.

Few people can assert confidently that they can develop and progress by waiting to achieve vague goals and by functioning in a disorganized and undisciplined manner. On the other hand, tightly regulated, overly controlled people lead oppressive lives. Neither extreme proves healthy. The middle ground may seem appealing, but the lesser of two extremes rarely does more than create a whipsaw pattern. We have, however, a *do-it-now* alternative. In this chapter we'll look at how to develop *progressive mastery* over this habit of delay by steadily decreasing procrastination through gradually increasing a do-it-now approach. The do-it-now approach involves doing reasonable things in a reasonable way within a reasonable time in order to increase personal efficiency, effectiveness, and satisfaction with living.

PROCRASTINATION CAUSES

What fuels procrastination? Most commonly, procrastinating individuals delay because of one or more of the following where they:

1. Don't want to do something
2. Feel uncomfortable or uncertain

3. Have a low tolerance for frustration
4. Define the activity as onerous and unpleasant
5. Engage in self-doubts leading to hesitation
6. Hew to impossible perfectionist ideals
7. Rebel against social time restraints, schedules, obligations, and duties
8. Feel depressed and helpless
9. Experience a very stressful emotional resistance that they relieve through avoidance
10. Habitually follow automatic thought and emotional avoidance patterns

PROCRASTINATION ZONES

Let's look at where and why procrastination occurs. We'll start with basic categories of social and personal procrastination. Then we'll probe mild procrastination, the fallback pattern, and other common procrastination styles. Then we'll look at common procrastination-causing motivations. The more you know about procrastination patterns and styles, the quicker you can recognize and change them.

Social Procrastination

Neanderthals lived in small tribal communities, organized hunts around chasing animals with spears in hand, maintained few records, and paid little attention to evolving and transmitting culture. Although they hunted together and showed they cared for each other as evidenced by the flowers they placed over their deceased, that was not enough to assure their survival.

Cro-Magnons developed orderly societies, passed on tradition, and evolved their cultures. The more disciplined, organized, and plan-oriented Cro-Magnon groups flourished. Has anyone seen a real Neanderthal lately?

You can't have an orderly society without reasonable regulations, schedules, and deadlines. What normally works best for both individuals and society involves organizing systems that support meaningful objectives and plans. For example, successful corporations have proprietary control systems that enable them to transact their business efficiently and effectively. The systems provide structures and controls to support the corporate mission. A bank whose management procrastinated in paying employees or let you decide when you would pay back your debt would not long exist.

When you delay social responsibilities, you fall into the *social procrastination* trap. You show up late for meetings. You return library books late. Your employer asks you to complete a report and you delay starting. You promise to help a friend with a project, then find reasons to put it off. You're routinely late on your taxes. You academically procrastinate when you put off completing your share of a class project or turn a term paper in late then pressure the professor to change your incomplete grade. At least some of this procrastination would not exist if rules, regulations, schedules, and deadlines did not exist. However, rules do exist. Without organization, society would go the way of the Neanderthals.

Social procrastination applies to delaying socially prescribed, fixed-schedule responsibilities. As a worker, your employers expect you to show up for work on time and produce results. The state government expects that you will have your motor vehicle inspected annually. Parents expect their children to complete their household chores. Delays in these areas typically put people at risk of censure and blame.

Socially procrastinating individuals often have different agendas from the authorities who set the rules. These agendas include: to avoid task discomfort; to do something more pleasant; to oppose the system (oppositional procrastination). Some people take the position that if they don't feel like doing it, they should not have to make the effort.

People who socially procrastinate risk blame by those who are affected by their behavior. Good organizing systems support personal and community effectiveness and reduce the risk of blame.

Personal Procrastination

Overdue taxes, showing up late for appointments, or delaying the completion of assignments characterizes what most people commonly think of as procrastination. The needless-delay definition covers a broader range of postponed activities that include putting off developmental challenges such as exercising and losing weight or standing up for your rights.

You personally procrastinate when you put off the developmental challenges that can give you long-term advantages. You want to lose weight, then you eat an extra piece of cake. You dream about developing your musical talents, then call a friend to talk about the weather. You panic at the thought of going outside alone (agoraphobia), and put off dealing with the fear. You have a moribund relationship, and tell yourself that someday you will work to make it better. Your talent and abilities lie dormant because you prefer to avoid the feelings of awkwardness that sometimes comes at the initial stages of learning and development.

We find a most serious version of procrastination among those people who make active efforts to stabilize their lives by avoiding change. However, since one can't freeze time and stop change, such status quo efforts normally fail. Yet change procrastination persists even when a person clearly goes against a strong current of reality.

Social and personal groupings overlap. When we routinely don't meet deadlines for submitting an application for desired jobs, we limit our career opportunities and shortchange our families by producing less income. A problem drinker procrastinates on overcoming the problem habit. Doing this can lead to legal, economic, and personal health problems and contributes to family discord and social health costs. Rather than feel like a terrible person for socially procrastinating, one would wisely face the problem and resolve it.

Procrastination Divisions

Like looking through a crystal, we can view procrastination from different but often related angles. These angles include procrastination as a problem habit, a defense, a symptom, a skill deficiency, or a reciprocal loop.

The procrastination time-thief pattern sometimes falls squarely into the problem habit category. Here your procrastination thoughts, behavior, muscle tension, emotions, and chemistry interlace. You get better at connecting these elements of a procrastination habit through practice. Such complex problem habits normally require a sustained effort to break.

Procrastination can symbolize a defense against, say, fear of failure. Here you can say that if you tried, you could have succeeded. Getting beyond defensive barriers normally requires recognizing the defense, determining its purpose, and acting to change the underlying dynamic.

As a symptom, procrastination represents low frustration tolerance and discomfort dodging, self-doubts, hostility, escapist impulses, and rebellious ideas. By tracing your procrastination process to its psychological source, you can bolster your understanding about how your thinking directs it.

Procrastination can represent difficulties in executing executive functions such as organizing and follow-through. Memory lapses, inattentiveness, low frustration tolerance, and distractibility can contribute to an organizational deficit. Members of this group have organizing challenges when it comes to dealing with detail. They put it off, then often frustrate themselves looking for misplaced materials, or repeating preliminary work, or "forgetting" to bring things with them that they will need, or duplicating their efforts.

Executive function procrastination can prove significantly self-handicapping, but you can reverse it. Rather than focus on the onerousness of detail, challenge yourself by combining activities. For example, while on the phone, file materials and tidy up. This combining technique can help support organization skill development and lead to procrastination reduction.

Time-thief practices can exist on a reciprocal loop of insecurity and discomfort dodging. A subpopulation of procrastinators compound their distress by acting as if they told themselves they can't cope because the stresses of doing will feel terrible and overwhelming. They prime themselves to experience anxiety about the discomfort they anticipate. They set themselves up to feel a lack of control, vulnerability, and more anxiety by procrastinating to avoid the discomfort.

The reciprocal loop often includes double-trouble thinking. You blame yourself for not controlling the procrastination process. You procrastinate because this stress-related extension-of-blame thinking takes time and energy. Challenging this powerlessness double-trouble reciprocal loop helps weaken this repetitive procrastination cycle.

Procrastination Styles

Persistent procrastinators follow different delaying styles. Some of the more common include decisional procrastination, mild-impact procrastination, behavioral procrastination, the fallback pattern, and lateness procrastination. Overcoming these styles helps eliminate significant reasons for blame.

By deciding to delay, one sometimes can avoid the sort of blame that one believes results from imperfect performances. However, *decisional procrastination* involves a different type of decision. The person refuses to decide among alternatives. This indecision often follows the sort of perfectionism thinking that practically guarantees frustration and procrastination. A solution to this classic hesitation dance involves following the 49 and 51 percent rule. Whatever choice carried slightly greater value gets the nod. If each has equal value, flip a coin.

Mild-impact procrastination involves delaying small details, often because the person doesn't want to waste the time doing it. However, a collection of small-matter delays can combine with the more dramatic forms of delays to the point where the person feels overwhelmed, out of control, and blameful of self and circumstances. A solution involves refusing to engage in extensions of blame and excuse making and pressing onself to dispense with the details so that they do not grow to the level of the proverbial straw that broke the camel's back.

Behavioral procrastinators typically do well in getting themselves set to execute a plan. They have a vision and action design, and can organize their resources to fulfill the plan. But like the long-distance runner who quits before reaching the finish line, behavioral procrastinators retreat in sight of victory. A solution involves establishing a new pattern where you focus beyond the immediate goal on to the next in order to provide a follow-through momentum and learning to get comfortable with success by repeatedly experiencing the sort of success that comes from completion.

In the fallback pattern, the person plans, organizes, and executes, then retreats from the do-it-now process and backslides. When this pattern recurs with sufficient frequency, it becomes distinctive and destructive.

The fallback pattern can occur for different reasons, including a mild cyclical depression, a fear of success, or an unrealistic view that one magnificent effort will forever change the pattern. A solution involves recognizing the fallback motivations underlying the pattern and overcoming them. We can help ourselves diminish a fear of success, for instance, by focusing on the advantages of success and refusing to capitulate to old, defeatist, self-sabotaging thinking and behaving. This effort requires accepting that you have as much right to succeed as does anyone and that you can effectively resist succumbing to familiar feelings of inadequacy, undeservedness, and defeat.

People engaged in *lateness procrastination* processes typically fiddle and twiddle with many nonconsequential things in lieu of preparing to leave or to get something done. As a result they show up late for appointments. They breathlessly finish their assignments at the eleventh hour or later.

People who typically show up late often dress and groom at the last minute, make phone calls that they could do later, or fuss with dusting and cleaning—practically anything to slow themselves. Often conflict arises with their mates over their lateness. Some people embarrass themselves by the excuses they make to explain their lateness. A solution to lateness procrastination involves this *progressive mastery* approach: identifying habit activities that result in delays, and systematically eliminating them one at a time, one each week, until they no longer impede progress. You might also pay people you delay ten dollars for each minute you are late. You can, of course, avoid the penalty by showing up early.

PROCRASTINATION SIGNATURES

Scratch the surface of procrastination and you will find strong emotional resistance to put off an activity. These feelings accompany thinking such as "Not now, later."

If procrastinators did not experience a significant emotional resistance when faced with an unwanted activity and did not verbally direct themselves to avoid the task to avoid this unpleasant feeling, procrastination would greatly diminish. Because task resistance can feel so uncomfortable and stressful, often people will automatically duck work at the first sign of feeling uncomfortable. Many justify the delay by telling themselves "Not now, later."

People fool themselves into delaying what needs to be done by giving themselves false justifications and by substituting lower-priority activities for the higher ones. These activities fall under mental, emotional, and action diversions.

Mental diversions include the mañana ploy, where we tell ourselves we'll do better later; the contingency mañana ploy, where we tell ourselves that we must do something else first; or catch 22, where we tell ourselves that we can't succeed, then blame ourselves for not trying.

We can describe the classic mental procrastination diversionary ploys as wheedler activities. Historically, the wheedler plays the role of the conniver, con artist, Siren, or flim-flam specialist who takes advantage of human vulnerability and suggestibility. President Lincoln's wife, Mary Todd Lincoln, understood this riddle of procrastination. She wrote, "My evil genius Procrastination has whispered me to tarry 'til a more convenient season."

The wheedler voice has a simple message: Later, not now. You can help yourself beat this wheedler by asking your wheedler voice this question: "What makes the future a *more convenient season* for action?" Sensible answers to this question can throw chaos into the wheedler plot.

Emotional diversions include preoccupations with negative feelings, such as tension, that detract from purposeful actions. Emotional diversions complement the contingency mañana ploy when you wait to feel inspired before acting to do something that normally won't inspire you. But how many people feel inspired and motivated to perform the same mundane activities?

The wheedler promotes feel-right thinking. "Wait," it tells us, "until you feel ready and won't waste time." The logic has an appealing but highly flawed quality. Some activities will prove boring, distasteful, uncomfortable, inconvenient, or stressful. However, waiting until later rarely changes the conditions. The wheedler prevails when you convince yourself that delay is best. It dominates when left unchallenged.

Action diversions involve substituting a low-priority action for a relevant one, such as going to the movies rather than writing a pressing report, smoking to avoid facing a problem, reading, napping—practically any activity that substitutes for a priority activity. They are *always* involved with procrastinating. I call these diversions *addictivities* because they often rise to the level of a thoughtless substitution habit. The humorist Robert Benchley recognized these action diversions when he said, "Anyone can do any amount of work, provided it isn't the work he is supposed to be doing."

PROCRASTINATION AND EXONERATION

The dictionary burgeons with pejorative terms, clichés, and phrases to describe procrastination: lazy, self-indulgent, carelessness, dawdling, shilly-shally, cunctative, negligent, laggard, tardy, malinger, slipshod artist, sluggish, laissez-faire, lax, slack, slovenly, not trying, remiss, superficial, complacent, dragging one's feet, late, drifter, let the grass grow under one's feet, or fall asleep at the wheel. Clearly, these extension-of-blame words and phrases reflect a disdainful view of procrastination that most reasonable people would not want applied to themselves.

In a blame culture, how does one justify engaging in irrational procrastination behavior and at the same time avoid blame and maintain a positive public image? Most people give themselves the benefit of the doubt. Individuals look for loopholes to buy extra time or to justify evading responsibility, take advantage of deadline extensions, or concoct fraudulent excuses to exonerate themselves in order to maintain a positive public image while avoiding punishment for their delays. Indeed, the excuses people give themselves for procrastinating rival the excuses most politicians give for promises they did not keep. (Excuses differ from valid explanations, where we describe or clarify without exaggeration or deception.)

Procrastinators risk falling into the duplicity exoneration trap. What we say to ourselves to justify procrastination and what we say to others to explain the delays have different distinctive features. You tell yourself that you feel bored at the thought of writing a college term paper. You tell yourself that you'll get to it tomorrow when, say, you feel energized. Since you don't feel energized when tomorrow comes, you put it off again. When you run out of time, you excuse your procrastination by telling the professor that your dog ate your term paper. While many members of this diversionary group believe they can avoid blame through excuse making, a persistent procrastination pattern often proves transparent.

People in the duplicity trap rarely think to question the difference between the reasons they give to themselves to justify procrastinating and the excuses they give to others after they have procrastinated. Imagine if you told your professor, "Gee, I was waiting to feel energized before I started, and I never felt energized"!

MOTIVATION FOR CHANGE

Extensions of blame, shame, guilt, self-consciousness, self-recrimination, excuse making, or attempts to discredit the "victims" of procrastination normally will not reverse an entrenched procrastination pattern. Keeping extension-of-blame thinking out of the picture, challenging exoneration ploys, and attacking the procrastination process at its various links are ways that offer promise for positive change. The following describes internal and external incentives to support your counterprocrastination efforts. By working to overcome procrastination, you will predictably:

➤ Experience fewer occasions where you get blamed or blame yourself for delays
➤ Improve your credibility because you don't have to make up flimsy excuses
➤ Put time and energy into productive pursuits rather than procrastination ploys
➤ Have a broader range of choices
➤ Develop the sort of frustration tolerance that comes about as a result of tackling unpleasant activities as they arise
➤ Take a directed and assertive approach to life
➤ Experience a growing sense of self-efficacy
➤ Show improved ability to contribute and gain from your timely, purposeful, organized, and creative efforts

CONFRONTING PROCRASTINATION PATTERNS

Life would feel like the dreary "Volga Boatman" song if it primarily involved completing one onerous task after another and fending off blame for delays. Yet assuming that it makes good sense to operate responsibly and effectively, and effective and efficient actions increase one's opportunities to obtain advantage, approval, and self-confidence, then how does one significantly increase such opportunities? Part of the answer involves initiating change methods designed to deal with the often-diverse and complex mechanisms fueling procrastination while you move toward achieving your life missions.

The following five-step change process involves flowing together awareness, action, accommodation, acceptance, and actualization to provide a useful and flexible do-it-now framework.

Awareness: Getting in Touch with Procrastination Processes

Although we rarely pay major penalties for isolated, situational procrastination acts, generally we pay a stiff price for *persistent procrastination*. This entrenched, habitual procrastination style significantly impedes the quality of the procrastinator's life in one or more significant zones, such as social and personal directions. A lawyer who doesn't meet court deadlines can seriously degrade her law practice and subject herself to legal action by frustrated clients. The process of change involves recognizing and decreasing procrastination process ideas, feelings, and activities and substituting follow-through actions.

Exercises in Awareness
The following strategies provide awareness perspectives on procrastination:

➤ Procrastination inevitably involves doing something other than the priority activity. This active phase of procrastination can include napping, making telephone calls, watching television, lamenting—practically anything except for starting and progressing with the priority activity. This active process in procrastination buys time, but for what? List the activities you substitute for priority activities. Ask yourself about the purpose these sidestepping activities serve and how you can refuse to indulge them.

➤ Procrastination frequently includes a passive intellectual excuse-making process of substituting rationalizations for action. In addition to doing something active to avoid a priority, you make up excuses to justify your procrastination or to explain it away. You may tell yourself "tomorrow is better" or "maybe" you'll get to it soon. An important first step in this passive process involves the recognition of the *cognitive signatures* or procrastination-evoking and -sustaining ideas that accompany the procrastination process. For purposes of this exercise, list the excuses you give yourself for procrastinating and the excuses you give others to explain your procrastination. This exercise exposes exoneration ploys used to justify an irrational procrastination process.

➤ Think about standing at point A and wanting to get to point C. Between point A and C you will find B, the procrastination barriers to change. Enter the gap between A and C, then label the barriers such as mañana ploy, extension-of-blame thinking, emotional resistance, and so forth. Now get beyond these barriers to get to point C. Use whatever you learned in this book and elsewhere to bring about this result.

➤ Procrastination patterns, like a revolving filmstrip, reappear within the mind. This film has many scripted frames. We produce and direct the negative frames that lead to procrastination. What do the frames look like? How does the script read? What can you rewrite? This awareness exercise can help put procrastination-inducing ideas and images into slow motion and make them accessible to reflection, challenge, and change.

Action: Learning How to Overcome Procrastination

People stop procrastinating by taking the necessary *behavioral* steps to finish relevant activities within a reasonable time.

Exercises in Action
The action phase of change involves taking steps to overcome procrastination by applying practical solutions, empirical analysis, and core problem solving. At the *practical solution* level, we include a do-it-now plan. That plan includes implementing practical techniques such as the following:

➤ Use organizing systems, such as a cross-out sheet where you daily identify, list, and order your priorities. Cross activities off the list as completed. This action can produce a sense of satisfaction as well as a record of accomplishments.

➤ Employ start-up strategies, such as the *five-minute method*. Here you commit to beginning and continuing for five minutes. At the end of that time, you decide to quit or continue for another five minutes, and so on. This practical technique helps start the ball rolling.

➤ Follow a *bits-and-pieces approach*. Even the most complex undertaking has a simple place to start. Start there and work by bits and pieces until done.

The *empirical analysis* approach provides a deeper level of intervention to change procrastination process thinking. It applies scientific ways of knowing to personal problem solving. At the level of empirical analysis, you predict the potential outcome of several courses of action, then follow the pathway that appears to have the more productive outcome. The following describes an empirical analysis approach for overcoming procrastination.

➤ Procrastination always involves substituting a lower-priority activity for the higher-priority one. Instead of finishing a report, you go to the beach or fall asleep. By refusing to substitute lower priorities for the higher ones, we can measure the results of this shift in increases in personal efficiency.

➤ Empirical analysis includes questioning irrational procrastination process logic. Here the procrastinating person's major premise can include the view that the task will prove threatening, unpleasant, tedious, boring, or inconveniencing. The secondary premise normally involves the magical belief that "later will lead to action." This conclusion follows: to delay until another day or time. Even assuming that the major premise proves correct, the second premise and conclusion can prove irrational. For example, people who follow a procrastination pattern rarely operate efficiently or effectively by waiting until later.

➤ The empirical analysis emphasizes using self-statements as hypotheses. You hypothesize that the mañana view, later will lead to timely action, will regularly produce positive levels of personal efficiency and effectiveness. As a scientist you review the assumptions and logic underlying the belief that doing it later leads to timely action. If the assumptions and logic behind the hypothesis don't hold up under scrutiny, discard it for another. You also can logically assess an alternative hypothesis: "Do it now" leads to timely task completion. If the assumptions and logic behind the do-it-now hypothesis do not hold up, discard it for another. Repeat the do-it-now hypothesis test, when it proves valid.

At the core problem-solving level you meet personal procrastination challenges by directly acting to: 1) arrest the procrastination problem habit; 2) stop using procrastination as a defense against, say, fear of failure; 3) undermine core procrastination concepts that represent self-doubts and the processes of low frustration tolerance and discomfort dodging; 4) build efficient organizing skills; or 5) break the procrastination reciprocal cycle. The following supports this core change process:

➤ Separate rational from irrational thinking for each target procrastination zone. Apply the ABC strategy for change described in chapter 15. Include psychological homework assignments where you confront irrational belief systems by both disputing them and taking productive do-it-now actions.

➤ Outline a cognitive-emotive-behavioral process that includes: 1) the task; 2) how you feel before you decide to procrastinate; 3) the basis for the procrastination decision; 4) mental diversion that accompanies the decision (i.e., the mañana ploy); 5) emotional or action diversion; 6) exoneration ploy used to impress others about the necessity of the delay. Devise a strategy to disrupt procrastination at each of the six points.

Accommodation: Adjusting to a Do-It-Now Pattern

By testing new counterprocrastination ideas and behaviors, you challenge yourself to face normal and extraordinary resistance to change. In this process you challenge the view that you cannot, say, stop procrastinating by starting now to kick the procrastination habit.

Exercises in Accommodation

➤ Visualize, then act upon, a healthier self-view where you organize and regulate constructive actions to achieve worthwhile objectives. Evaluate the differences between productive actions and procrastination avoidance.

➤ Low frustration tolerance followed by discomfort dodging forms a common platform for procrastination. You decide to clean your basement then hear your wheedler voice saying "You don't want to do that. You feel too tired." You feel a swelling of tension. Normally you take the tension as an avoidance signal. After all, doesn't that fit with wheedler logic? However, this time you switch voices. You instruct yourself to clean the basement. You talk yourself through the paces and clean the cellar. As part of this accommodation process, you contrast the wheedler activity with the do-it-now action. You compare the results of wheedler instructions against the results of do-it-now instructions.

➤ The spirit of accommodation involves acknowledging that procrastination habits and personal worth reside on different planes within the mind.

➤ Some procrastinators tend to think poorly of themselves, procrastinate because they fear failure, and still prefer to project a favorable public impression to avoid blame. How does one reconcile the two concepts? Making the contrast helps sharpen the issues in this accommodation process.

Acceptance: Tolerating Imperfections

In this phase, people come to accept that their worthwhile qualities don't disappear even if they procrastinate. However, they can use do-it-now abilities to finish priority activities on time.

Exercises in Acceptance
Three thoughts help create an inner view of self-acceptance.

➤ Acceptance includes acknowledging that the potential for procrastination exists in everybody. This idea makes it easier to judge procrastination as negative without judging people the same way.

➤ The *double-trouble* phase of procrastination and blame for procrastination typically sap time and energy from more productive pursuits. In the spirit of acceptance, you acknowledge the strains of layering a problem onto a problem while stubbornly refusing to put yourself down for procrastinating.

➤ People who procrastinate paradoxically tend to think harsh thoughts about other procrastinators. This projection of anger and recrimination frequently represents a core *cognitive signature* process of self-blame and condemnation. To reverse this anti-acceptance form of thought involves developing tolerance for one's procrastination and tolerance for fellow procrastinators. However, one can feel tolerant of people and still refuse to put up with their procrastination.

Actualization: Maintaining and Generalizing Gains

Actualization involves prioritizing do-it-now over needless delay. The process involves an integration of 1) problem understanding; 2) action planning; 3) implementing the action plan; 4) accommodation to new self-understanding accompanying or following effective actions; 5) acceptance of personal variations in efficiency and effectiveness and foibles and faults accompanied by measurable efforts to improve; and 6) generalizing the do-it-now approach to alternative situations, where applicable.

Because you make a habit of following through with your most important and constructive desires, predictably you'll have fewer would-have, could-have, and should-have regrets.

Exercises in Actualization
In the actualization phase, procrastinating individuals make do-it-now a relatively consistent extension of themselves. They establish, generalize, and modify their abilities to support, strengthen, and maintain this positive orientation.

➤ Maintaining your do-it-now philosophy involves vigilance. Occasionally you will experience wheedler activity. You will hear your inner procrastination voice invite you to tarry. To maintain your gains, beat the wheedler by refusing to go along with the program.

➤ Extend the do-it-now view into areas where you normally would procrastinate. In doing so, you will crowd out the procrastination process and its complications.

By generalizing *do-it-now* processes into ways to both save time and to advance your personal interests, you will likely find that you have less time for dallying.

This strategy can help you reduce the risk of lapses and relapses to procrastination patterns.

The actions you take to generalize do-it-now initiatives, helps you strengthen a pattern that counters procrastination. These actions also extend your abilities in an actualizing sort of way. You can use the following chart to structure this actualization plan.

Generalization and Expanding Your Gains

Expansion Goal	Plan	Potential Results
1. Combine routine activities.	A. Use time on phone to save time.	A. Increased time for meeting challenging, personal development activities.
	B. Use shopping trips to do multiple routine activities.	B. Increased time for developmental activities.
2. Expand growth activities.	A. Find relevant multiple applications for work products.	A. Created broader range of opportunities.

By stretching personal resources into challenging new areas, we can learn more about what we can accomplish as well as about our limitations. In this spirit of expansion, or generalization of learning, every day pick something new to do that can cause you to stretch. Plan ahead for this purpose, then follow the plan. Create a chart like the one above to map out and assess your expansion program.

POSTSCRIPT

The Spanish writer Miguel de Cervantes observed, "Delay always breeds danger; and to protect a great design is often to ruin it." In a related sense, people who postpone their desires have much to regret both during and at the end of their lives.

Procrastinators can, to one extent or other, learn to act more productively, experience greater accomplishments, and feel happier with their ability to direct and control their actions. Now even acclaimed procrastinators can increase their opportunities to profit from their successes, learn from their mistakes, reduce procrastination, and avoid blame for procrastinating.

Joseph Ferrari, Corey Hammer, and I found that people who persistently procrastinate tend to over-emphasize the use of the passive voice in describing their procrastination. This chapter emphasized the opposite. Try thinking using the active voice tense and see if your procrastination lessens.

Endnote

The poet Robert Frost left us with an important message: "The woods are lovely, dark and deep / But I have promises to keep, and miles to go before I sleep."

Pretend for a moment that you freed your mind of all extensions of blame. Can you feel your mind expand as your thoughts and visions break free from the restraints of blame? Now close your eyes. In your mind's eye, look forward into the future. Look to your visions of what your life can be. Can you develop your positive values, gain direction, and predict consistency in what you can do? Now do you not see a life path filled with possibilities? Can you not feel a sense of freedom to make your vision a reality? Within this vision, can you make yourself a promise that is worth keeping before you sleep?

PROMISES AND REALITIES

This book has dealt with our very human tendency to find fault and to cast blame. It also has dealt with ways to overcome the unnecessary negatives of blame.

Extension-of-blame thinking is an emotionally jarring prelude to tarnished relationships and, less frequently, to emotionally evoked violence. These blame extensions, fault finding, finger pointing, false accusations, criticism, whining, victim thinking, and false exonerations represent a darker side to human relationships. It is a foolish optimism to believe that the human race will lay these tools of destruction aside permanently. An individual, however, can progressively move toward this goal.

One of the more subtle and pervasive lessons of history is that it is easier to blame than to understand and correct. We can't change history, but any motivated and reflective person can learn to turn away from extensions of blame and false exonerations to accept consistently an empirical view whereby one sees actions in terms of their consequences and acts in ways to secure positive consequences.

Your intellect is your tool for anticipating then discriminating between effective and self-destructive actions and for figuring out a reasonable direction to take. This effort predictably increases the probability that you can take actions that lead to enjoying a broader range of positive emotions and to a richer and more spontaneous, creative, and challenging life.

You have many alternatives to blame and its extensions. And while you can't control what others think and do, you can establish the inner control that translates into command over the direction of your life and the quality of your experiences. You can take charge of forging that direction now.

Index